THE LAWS OF
DEUTERONOMY

THE LAWS OF
DEUTERONOMY

Calum M. Carmichael

CORNELL UNIVERSITY PRESS
ITHACA AND LONDON

This book has been published with the aid of a grant from the Hull Memorial Publication Fund of Cornell University.

First published 1974 by Cornell University Press.
Published in the United Kingdom by Cornell University Press Ltd., 2-4 Brook Street, London W1Y 1AA.

International Standard Book Number 0-8014-0824-5
Library of Congress Catalog Card Number 73-19206

Printed in the United States of America by Vail-Ballou Press, Inc.

To Norma, Lachie,
Roderick, and John Allan

Preface

This study in biblical law attempts to solve the long-standing problem of the arrangement of the laws in Deuteronomy. No problem in biblical studies has proved more perplexing; as Robert H. Pfeiffer says in his *Introduction to the Old Testament* (p. 232), "The disorder is so extreme that one would almost call it deliberate." It will be argued here, however, that there is a method to the arrangement of the laws, one that is comprehensive in scope, covers the entire code of laws, and clarifies the unique character of the Deuteronomic legal material. This material, it should be noted, is legal only in a broad sense. By incorporating allusions to narrative traditions and proverbial sayings it combines legal and nonlegal elements in a most consistent and interesting way. To understand the arrangement of the Deuteronomic laws is to realize the extent to which the laws are related to such traditions as those, for example, in the book of Genesis. This mixture of law, wisdom, and tradition, often found in a single law, is the novel feature of the Deuteronomic code and presents the student of antiquity with an unusual type of ancient document.

Samuel Johnson, trying to curb Boswell's enthusiasm for his projected history of Corsica, said, "I wish there were some cure, like the lover's leap, for all heads of which some single idea has obtained an unreasonable and irregular possession." I am conscious of the dangers involved in presenting a thesis in which a single idea (as to the method used in arranging

a law code) is doubtless irregularly possessed. Having subjected it to my own scepticism and to scholarly criticism over
the past few years, however, I hope the thesis is not without
reason but rather illuminates a problem in biblical research.

I should like to express my gratitude for the generous en-
couragement given to me by Norman W. Porteous of Edinburgh University, W. D. Davies of Duke University, and the
late Austin Farrer when he was Warden of Keble College,
Oxford. I am especially grateful to Reuven Yaron of the
Hebrew University, Jerusalem, for his helpful criticism when
I spent a year in Jerusalem under the auspices of the Friends
of the Hebrew University, Great Britain. I am indebted to
David Patterson of St. Cross College, Oxford, and Nancy
Basham, Secretary of the Department of Semitic Languages
and Literatures at Cornell, for their invaluable aid in the
preparation of my typescript.

I owe most to David Daube, emeritus Regius Professor of
Civil Law at the University of Oxford and currently Director
of the Robbins Hebraic and Roman Law Library Collections
at the University of California, Berkeley. To study under
him was a privilege and a pleasure. His scholarly production,
with its subtle observations, deep insights, and immense
learning, has provided an unfailing source of inspiration.

The Scripture quotations in this publication are from the
Revised Standard Version Bible, copyrighted 1946, 1952 and
© 1971 by the Division of Christian Education of the National Council of the Churches of Christ in the U.S.A., and
used by permission.

The study is based on the Hebrew text (*Biblia Hebraica,*
ed. R. Kittel, 3d ed., Stuttgart, 1945), and the translation
of the Revised Standard Version is sometimes modified in
order, for example, to distinguish between the use of the
second person singular and the second person plural, or to
give a more literal rendering of the Hebrew original for the
purposes of analysis. The numbering of the Hebrew Bible is

consistently used, and where the numbering of the Revised Standard Version differs it is given in italics, for example, Deut. xxiii. 8, 9 (*7, 8*).

CALUM M. CARMICHAEL

Cornell University

Contents

Abbreviations

ANET	*Ancient Near Eastern Texts Relating to the Old Testament,* ed. J. B. Pritchard (3d ed., Princeton, 1969)
AO	*Archiv Orientálni*
BDB	F. Brown, S. R. Driver, and C. A. Briggs, *A Hebrew and English Lexicon of the Old Testament* (Oxford, 1906)
BZ	*Biblische Zeitschrift*
CBQ	*Catholic Biblical Quarterly*
D	The book of Deuteronomy or the author of the book of Deuteronomy
HUCA	*Hebrew Union College Annual*
ICC	International Critical Commentary
JAOS	*Journal of American Oriental Society*
JBL	*Journal of Biblical Literature*
JBR	*Journal of Bible and Religion*
JCS	*Journal of Cuneiform Studies*
JE	The Y(J)ahwistic and Elohistic literary strand in the Pentateuch
JJS	*Journal of Jewish Studies*
JNES	*Journal of Near Eastern Studies*
JR	*Juridical Review*
JSS	*Journal of Semitic Studies*
JTS	*Journal of Theological Studies*
LXX	The Septuagint
M	The Mishpatim (Ex. xxi. 2–xxiii. 19)
MT	The Masoretic Text
P	The Priestly literary strand in the Pentateuch
RB	*Revue Biblique*
RIDA	*Revue internationale des droits de l'Antiquité*

RSV   Revised Standard Version
SVT   *Supplement to Vetus Testamentum*
VT   *Vetus Testamentum*
ZAW   *Zeitschrift für die alttestamentliche Wissenschaft*

THE LAWS OF DEUTERONOMY

1. The Setting of Deuteronomy

The formal setting of Deuteronomy (D) is a speech by Moses to the people of Israel (i. 1). G. von Rad points out that this setting is different from that of the other law books of the Old Testament, which present an address by God to Moses.[1] The speech is in fact a valediction. Because of God's anger toward the people, Moses is forbidden to enter the land (i. 37, iii. 26). Later, Moses, still speaking to all Israel, says, "I am a hundred and twenty years old this day; I am no longer able to go out and come in. The Lord has said to me, 'Thou shalt not go over this Jordan'" (xxxi. 2). His death is imminent, and just as the patriarchs Isaac and Jacob before their deaths blessed their sons (Gen. xxvii, xlix) so Moses blesses the sons of Israel (xxxiii).

The picture of the honored man of ripe old age gathering his sons or disciples around him, passing on his counsel, foretelling the future, and giving his blessing of life and prosperity is a feature of wisdom literature (especially extrabiblical, ancient Near Eastern material), and the D setting is fashioned along similar lines. The laws are for the future, when Israel shall have inherited the land; the blessing of life and prosperity will depend upon obedience to these laws.[2]

Mosaic instruction is the main element in D's setting (i. 5).

[1] *Studies in Deuteronomy* (Eng. ed., London, 1953), p. 11.
[2] M. Weinfeld, "The Book of Deuteronomy in Its Relation to Wisdom" (in Hebrew), *Jubilee Volume for Y. Kaufmann* (Jerusalem, 1960), pp. 104ff., examines the idea of reward in D. The promise of life, well-being, longevity, abundance of children, health, plenty, joy, and in-

Moses begins to make plain (באר), to explain the law. The term "torah" in i. 5 should itself be understood as instruction.[3] The Egyptian Ptah-hotep's instruction has a somewhat similar setting to D's: an old counselor instructs his son, his designated successor, in the conduct befitting a wise state official.[4] In addition to the general similarity of setting there is also the particular parallel with the direction of the leader, Moses, to his successor, Joshua (i. 38, xxxi. 7).

Recent research has indicated the affinities between D and the wisdom literature.[5] The recurrent use in D of "hear"

---

heritance of the land is reminiscent of the idea of reward in the wisdom literature.

[3] Weinfeld (*ibid.*, p. 104) argues that "torah" in i. 5 means didactic-historical instruction. The term does not refer to the actual commands of the torah in Deut. xii. 1ff. Rather it refers to the moral lessons to be derived from past history and is similar to the "torah" in the didactic Psalm lxxviii. 1, "Give ear, O my people, to my teaching [torah]." *Cf.* B. Lindars, "Torah in Deuteronomy," P. R. Ackroyd and B. Lindars, eds., *Words and Meanings* (Cambridge, Eng., 1968), pp. 129ff.

[4] *ANET*, p. 412.

[5] J. Malfroy, "Sagesse et loi dans le Deutéronome," *VT*, 15 (1965), 49–65; M. Weinfeld, "The Book of Deuteronomy" and "The Origin of the Humanism in Deuteronomy," *JBL*, 80 (1961), 241–47; D. J. McCarthy, *Treaty and Covenant*, Analecta Biblica 21 (Rome, 1963), pp. 114, 119, 135.
The wisdom literature is primarily that genre of literature from the Near Eastern world of the second and first millennia that is noted for its didactic aim. In this kind of writing, the wise man or sage imparts preceptive counsel to his pupils, whom he refers to as his sons. The book of Proverbs offers a familiar example of the genre. But the wisdom literature also includes works of greater scope than Proverbs. While instruction in sayings that can act as a guide to a successful life constitute "wisdom," the presuppositions and ideas that underlie such sayings are given expression in more sophisticated compositions. Job and Ecclesiastes are examples. Wisdom beliefs and interests appear also in works not included in the wisdom literature, for example in the story of the Creation and the Fall, the Joseph story, and the book of Esther. See, respectively, A. M. Dubarle, *Les Sages d'Israël* (Paris, 1946), pp. 7–24; G. von Rad, "Josephgeschichte und ältere Chokma," *SVT*, 1 (1953), 120–27; S. Talmon, " 'Wisdom' in the book of Esther," *VT*, 13 (1963), 419ff.

compares with the common "hear my son(s)" of Proverbs.
In Proverbs the command "hear" often occurs in the context
of a student's instruction in wisdom by his teacher, or a son's
by his father. That D's instructional setting is similar is suggested by the description of the relationship between Yahweh
and Israel as one of father and son; Yahweh is disciplining
Israel as a father does his son (viii. 5; *cf.* Prov. iii. 11, 12).
D's concern with the instruction of the young is clear in iv. 9,
vi. 7, xi. 19, where there are explicit commands to educate
them.

Other words used in D echo wisdom settings. The noun
"discipline" and the verb "to discipline" are examples. A
son, questioning his father about the commandments, is referred to Yahweh's mysterious activity, his signs and wonders,
in Egypt (vi. 20ff.). These signs and wonders constitute
Yahweh's discipline (xi. 2ff.; *cf.* Job v. 17).[6] In iv. 34, vii. 19,
xxix. 2 the word "testings" precedes the signs and wonders;
use of this word recalls the pedagogical theory that God tests
a man's heart to prove the rightness of his ways.[7]

In Prov. xxiii. 19, Job xxiii. 11, right conduct is synonymous with the "way." In D, Israel is to walk in a certain way
(v. 33), and this means keeping the commandments. The
humbling and testing in the wilderness are construed as a
"way" (viii. 2). "On the way" a man is to talk of the commandments (vi. 7); or, confronted there with a certain situation, he is required to practise right conduct by protecting
a straying animal (xxii. 4) or respecting a mother bird (xxii.

---

[6] In this reference to the signs and wonders there is possibly an
echo of the concept of wisdom as an understanding of mysteries. The
wise man is the initiate who sees an intelligible pattern behind
the mysteries. In the schools of Mesopotamia, the privileged pupils were
those who were permitted to be noviates for the high office of seer as
well as consulters of the divine oracles. See C. J. Gadd, *Teachers and
Students in the Oldest Schools* (Inaugural Lecture, School of Oriental
and African Studies, University of London, 1956), p. 22.

[7] *Cf.* Deut. xiii. 4, *3;* see also, Dubarle, p. 215.

6).[8] In Eccles. x. 3 the fool "on the way" makes clear to every-
one that he is a fool. The sense of location in the idea of
right conduct as a "way" is noteworthy. Since this manner of
speaking and thinking implies confinement and limits, it
is surely significant that D uses this language and also shows
a major concern with idolatry. In D, idolatry "makes thee
leave the way in which the Lord thy God commanded thee to
walk" (xiii. 6, 5). Idolatry is wrong practice and wrong teaching—one does not learn to act in accord with the foreign nations' abominations (xviii. 9). The idolater oversteps the
boundaries of correct knowledge laid down by D and flouts
the latter's (Mosaic) authority. A public example is therefore
to be made of him (xiii. 12, *11*), a command that recalls the
warning in Proverbs to heed the authority of Wisdom as she
calls aloud in public places, for instance "beside the way"
(Prov. viii. 1, 2).

The word "eyes" in D has a parallel use in the wisdom
literature. In D, the eyes of God are always upon the land
(xi. 12); in Prov. xv. 3 the eyes of the Lord are in every place.
The human eye is powerful and requires control: "I have
made a covenant with my eyes; how then could I look upon a
virgin?" (Job xxxi. 1). Evil may result from letting the heart
follow the eyes (Job xxxi. 7). D expresses a similar thought
in iv. 19, which mentions the vacillating weakness of the eyes:
"Lest thou lift up thine eyes to heaven, and when thou seest
the sun and the moon . . . thou be drawn away." A man
must not do what he thinks right in his own eyes (xii. 8) but
rather adhere, the law implies, to a norm of conduct. A bribe
blinds the eyes of the wise (xvi. 19). The eyes should be fixed
on the right things and should look directly forward (Prov.
iv. 25). In D, the words of the law are to be frontlets between
the eyes (vi. 8, xi. 18),[9] and the things seen with the eyes

[8] This respect for a parent bird suggests a wisdom concern. The
law is a peculiar one (see Chapter 8).

[9] Malfroy, "Sagesse et loi," p. 59, notes how in D the words of the

(Yahweh's testings and signs) must never leave the heart (iv. 9; *cf.* Prov. iii. 1). Wisdom counsel warns about the miserly, grudging eye (Prov. xxiii. 6, xxviii. 22) and urges that the eyes should not be hidden from the poor (Prov. xxviii. 27). Likewise in D, a lender's eye is not to be grudging toward someone in need (xv. 9).

The frequent use of the word "eyes" in both D and the wisdom rules reflects a common concern with how things look and with appearances, correct or shaming as the case may be. The young student of wisdom, bent on success in life, is trained to observe keenly the consequences of his conduct so that it will always be publicly acceptable. In D, many statutes show a concern that God shall find the behavior of Israel acceptable, and not so disgusting that he must look away (as could happen, for example, when he walks in the camp, xxiii. 15, *14*).[10]

Many other words and phrases in D are paralleled in wisdom usage.[11] Indeed Malfroy argues that most of the words that are typical of the vocabulary of Israelite wisdom are used in D,[12] a view that supports the suggestion that there is a close parallel between the D setting and the preceptive settings in the wisdom literature. It is also worth noting that the authoritative fashion in which Mosaic instruction is imparted in D shows an affinity with the wisdom scribes' awareness of their public responsibility to preach about the call or claim

---

law are to be upon the hand, the eyes, and the heart, while in Proverbs (iii. 3, iv. 21, vii. 3) loyalty and faithfulness are to be around the neck, the words of the sage within the heart, and his teaching on the fingers and on the tablet of the heart.

[10] This shame–cultural concern in D has been observed by David Daube. See pp. 181ff. for further discussion and references.

[11] On the word "abomination" in D and Proverbs, see J. L'Hour, "Les Interdits To'eba dans le Deutéronome," *RB*, 71 (1964), 481–503. On Egyptian material (Teaching of Amenemope), D, and Proverbs, see M. Weinfeld, *Deuteronomy and the Deuteronomic School* (Oxford, 1972), pp. 267–69.

[12] "Sagesse et loi," p. 59.

of Wisdom (Prov. i. 20ff., viii). The Torah, or Law of Moses, has a public claim like that of Wisdom. The book of Proverbs is a later compilation than D, and it is quite possible that the thinking in Proverbs about Wisdom as an institution, as a special discipline exerting a claim, and as a public guide may be later too. Still, the affinities exist, and a chronological placing of ideas is a risky undertaking.

Inevitably the question arises as to how closely D is related to the wisdom literature. Weinfeld argues for a close connection between D and the wisdom literature of the ancient Near East in general and the book of Proverbs in particular.[13] He associates the composition of D with the scribal activity in the reigns of Hezekiah and Josiah. Whether or not his view is correct, it is certain that D shows many wisdom characteristics. D should not be categorized as wisdom literature, only as associated with it.[14] T. Muraoka, drawing on Weinfeld's comparisons, points out that even where close parallels can be found between statements in D and in Proverbs a linguistic difference is to be noted.[15] Statements in D are negated by לא, while similar ones in Proverbs are negated by אל. Muraoka comments that, "אל is often used as a negative expression of the more direct, imminent and specific will of the speaker, whereas לא is used to indicate a negative expression of the speaker's will of more indirect and general

[13] See, in addition to "The Book of Deuteronomy" and "The Origin of the Humanism," his "Deuteronomy—The Present State of Inquiry," *JBL*, 86 (1967), 249–62.

[14] J. L. Crenshaw, "Method in Determining Wisdom Influence upon 'Historical' Literature," *JBL*, 88 (1969), 129–42, criticizes attempts to explain aspects of nonwisdom literary works in terms of direct wisdom influence. The many interests of the wisdom literature are, understandably, reflected in other literature, but these reflections do not imply direct connections between them. While this argument is correct, and while such words as "know," "hear," etc. in D would be part of a common cultural stock, as Crenshaw claims (pp. 132, 133), use of these words in D does echo rather closely their use in, for example, Proverbs, and this fact is worthy of attention.

[15] "Notes on the Syntax of Biblical Aramaic," *JSS*, 11 (1966), 162.

nature." Such a linguistic distinction denotes two different settings in life. In Proverbs, the written compilation of wise sayings is drawn directly from the real-life situation of a son's instruction by his father or a pupil's by his teacher. D is at least one literary stage removed from this. Moses' address to the children of Israel represents a conscious imitation of features found in a wisdom teacher-pupil setting.

Our discussion of the instructional aspect of D began with the consideration that D is a farewell speech by Moses to the children (sons) of Israel and contains his counsel. The model for this formal feature may be that of the wise old counselor surrounded by his sons or pupils. Such models exist in the ancient Near Eastern wisdom literature, and some similarities between D and wisdom have been observed. There exists, however, a biblical model that influences D directly. The biblical authors must have associated Jacob, who is Israel, the ancestor of the nation, and Moses, who leads the nation out of Egypt. The model for D's farewell speech by Moses to the children of Israel is the farewell speech by Jacob (Israel) to his sons in Gen. xlix.

There is a clear formal similarity between the two. Isaac also speaks formally in his farewell blessing to Jacob and Esau, but his testament is part of the story about the tension between his two sons. Jacob's, on the other hand, is a self-contained composition. It seems feasible, therefore, that D, who was composing a major work and who may have been imitating an existing farewell testament, would have turned to Jacob's. The case is strengthened if the obvious and exact parallel between Jacob's testament to his sons and that of Moses to the sons of Israel (Jacob) in xxxiii is noted. The latter has a literary structure precisely analogous to Gen. xlix. Moreover it contains a reference to the law as a possession for the assembly (קהל) of Jacob (xxxiii. 4), which appears to be an acknowledgement of Jacob's assembly in Gen. xlix. The question, however, is whether the Jacob model has a wider effect on D beyond this exact imitation. Does it inspire D's setting of a farewell speech by Moses to the children of Israel?

The best evidence that the Jacob model does have a wider effect is in D's laws on the assembly of Yahweh (xxiii. 2–9, *1–8*). This assembly—idealized—is another name for Israel's assembly in Gen. xlix. Jacob gathers his sons together and, on the basis of their past conduct, makes predictions about them.[16] Simeon and Levi's behavior has so antagonized Jacob that he calls for his own spirit to be excluded from their assembly (קהל). Moreover he foresees that their conduct, which affected both the Hivites and the Israelites adversely (Gen. xxxiv), will redound to their own future misfortune. Reuben's action in lying with his father's concubine is condemned; this fault, Jacob predicts, will result in the loss of Reuben's pre-eminence.

The key to the composition of D is that its author, said to be Moses, looks back on the conduct of Israel both before the exodus (in considering Jacob or members of his family) and after the exodus (in considering the conduct of the nation, Israel) and forms judgments, laws, and statutes based on what he observes. In some matters Moses' judgment differs from Jacob's; some new standards prevail; and Israel's assembly is now the assembly (קהל) of Yahweh. The conduct of Simeon and Levi, for example, is seen in a different light, as is suggested by Levi's high standing in Moses' testament in xxxiii. Reuben's action, however, is still abhorred—the only law in the D code concerning forbidden degrees of affinity (that preceding the list of laws about the assembly) has Reuben in mind. The phrase "the first-fruits of a father's strength" (the first-born son) occurs only in a D law (xxi. 17) and Gen. xlix. 3. This is no accident; the substance of the Jacob testament influences the author of D. Jacob gives special attention to Reuben because he is his first-born son, "the first-fruits of his

---

[16] See C. M. Carmichael, "Some Sayings in Genesis 49," *JBL*, 88 (1969), 435–44.

strength." D considers the case of a man who has two wives, one loved and the other unloved, and whose first son is born of the unloved wife. The model in mind is Reuben, who is Jacob's first son by the unloved wife, Leah. The D law allocates to this first-born son a double share of his father's inheritance because he is the "first-fruits of his strength." D excludes a eunuch from the assembly of Yahweh because a eunuch can have no first-fruits, no strength of this kind—a serious departure from D's ideal, which is that an Israelite should perpetuate his name in the land through offspring.

The connection between the farewell speeches of Jacob and Moses is not just formal, and certainly is not coincidental. The same process motivates each speech: reflections on the past lead to predictions and directions for the future. Sometimes it is even the same past that is under consideration. The result is important: D works with an existing literary model and is inspired by it.

D's Literary Relationship to Earlier Traditions

Critical scholarship, while acknowledging that Moses was not the author of D, has not seriously investigated the question of the book's fictional authorship. An unstated assumption prevails that a literary work would have been attributed to an ancient authority, in this case Moses, as a matter of course, and that such an attribution would not be likely to be questioned by those to whom it was addressed. Yet a fictional work raises important questions. For example, if its ancient readers accepted the work as Mosaic, how has the author achieved this? The Mosaic stamp in D is strong. It is not something that has been attached to the work as an afterthought. How has the seventh century author (I follow the scholarly consensus concerning the date of composition) gone about creating such a fiction? An interesting aspect of this question is the way in which an author views and treats the past. In D the use of traditional material is obvious.

Von Rad challenges the accepted view that D's relationship

to the earlier JE traditions is one of literary dependence.[17] While not dismissing such a view entirely, he is nonetheless inclined to think that D is dependent on a briefer source no longer extant. His criticism is directed at the complex nature of D's apparent dependence on JE. In many cases, a D story displays a coincidence of language and content with two different accounts of a story in JE. Von Rad asks whether D could have first cut up the stories and then combined them. His view is that the homogeneity of D's narrative argues against this, although he admits that the striking correspondence with the earlier stories remains a tantalizing feature still to be accounted for.

S. R. Driver accepts the theory of D's literary dependence on JE but is nonetheless aware of the complex nature of the dependence. He draws attention to the fact that a JE phrase originally used in the description of one incident is employed by D in the description of another. For example, phrases in the message of Moses to Sihon (ii. 27b, 28b) are borrowed from Num. xx. 17, 19b, the message of Moses to Edom. A further, more detailed example from Driver's survey concerns the appointment of men to assist Moses in judging the people (i. 9–18).[18] There are parallels between the language used here and both Ex. xviii, which contains Jethro's counsel to Moses on how to administer justice, and Num. xi, where Moses complains about the burden of administering justice and elders and officers are appointed to aid him. Driver regards Ex. xviii as the primary influence, and its subject as the occasion that D is in fact describing. D and Num. xi may be compared first:

Deut. i. 9b = Num. xi. 14: "I am not able alone to bear you [D], all this people [Num.]."

---

[17] *Deuteronomy* (Eng. ed., London, 1966), pp. 38ff.
[18] *Deuteronomy*, ICC (3d ed., Edinburgh, 1902), pp. xivff, xviii, 10, 14, 15.

Deut. i. 12: "How can I bear alone the weight and burden of you and your strife?"—*cf*. Num. xi. 11: "Wherefore . . . that thou dost lay the burden of all this people upon me?" Also *cf*. Num. xi. 17b: "And they shall bear the burden of the people with thee that thou mayest not bear it thyself alone."

D describes a situation of expansion and progress. The people are to choose their leaders. The dialogue is between Moses and the people with references to God in the third person. The book of Numbers has the dialogue between Moses and God amidst a situation of misfortune and misery. Moses is to gather seventy men who are already elders and officers. The dialogue between God and Moses is reported to the people.

Second, the coincidences between D and Ex. xviii are to be noted:

Deut. i. 13a: "Choose wise, understanding, and experienced men"—*cf*. Ex. xviii. 21a: "Choose able men from all the people, such as fear God, men who are trustworthy and who hate a bribe."

Deut. i. 15: "So I took the heads of your tribes, wise and experienced men, and set them as heads over you, commanders of thousands, commanders of hundreds"—*cf*. Ex. xviii. 25: "And he set them over the people, commanders of thousands, commanders of hundreds."

Deut. i. 17b: "And the case that is too hard for you, you shall bring to me"—*cf*. Ex. xviii. 26: "Hard cases they brought to Moses."

In D, Moses and the people agree with the idea of the appointments, and Moses explains how he addressed "your" judges at that time. In Exodus, Jethro instructs Moses and directs him about the judges' function.

D and JE: Observations on Their Different Settings

In JE, the setting is usually one in which God addresses Moses who then addresses the people (in Ex. xviii Jethro addresses Moses, who then carries his counsel into effect). In D, the setting is more compressed: Moses addresses the people. Interesting consequences follow from this difference—a factor not sufficiently considered by von Rad in his examination of D's relationship to JE. Much background knowledge in D is simply implied. This observation partly explains why the JE material in D is often greatly pruned and also counters von Rad's view that D is dependent upon an account of considerably shorter compass than JE. For example, Jethro's counsel to Moses (Ex. xviii) and Caleb's words about the conquest of the land (Num. xiii. 30) are excluded from D. But in D, Moses has appropriated his father-in-law's counsel and passes it on. In fact, the history recounted by Moses in D assumes an awareness of the JE traditions. In terms of the D setting, this awareness means that Moses, whose main function is to impart instruction, has appropriated much knowledge and reflected on it and now transmits it to the children of Israel. Such a setting is echoed in Prov. iv. 3, 4. The sage says, "When I was a son with my father . . . he taught and said to me, 'Let thine heart hold fast my words; keep my commandments, and live.'" The sage transmits the knowledge he has received from his father; similarly, Moses passes on what he has learnt from his father-in-law, more often from God, and also from his own experience as it is known from the JE traditions.

Whereas in the JE narrative God plays a central role, it is often the case in the corresponding D version that God is excluded altogether. There is the matter of aid for Moses in judging the people's disputes. In D, Moses raises the problem directly with the people themselves, while in Numbers he raises it with God. There is also the question of the spies. In

i. 22, the people initiate a request for spies to explore the land; in Num. xiii. 1, 2 God does the prompting. It is unlikely that D would not acknowledge the hand of providence in these matters. The divine role is assumed, perhaps to permit concentration on the role of human responsibility.[19]

Driver's view of the relationship between D and JE is that D's references to JE have a didactic aim:

Accordingly, while numerous passages, longer or shorter, as the case may be, are incorporated *verbatim,* as a rule the substance of the earlier narratives is reproduced freely, with amplificatory additions calculated (in most cases) to suggest to the reader the lessons which the author desired it to teach.[20]

Von Rad's reservations are nonetheless important. He cites the homogeneity of the D narratives as evidence against a selective borrowing from different strands in the JE traditions. However this homogeneity requires closer attention. D achieves homogeneity at one level only—in its gripping, picturesque presentation of the history.[21] Details and events not relevant to a didactic purpose are excluded. The addressee is made part of the recorded history. Tension is built up. The rebellious refusal to conquer the land comes as a surprise after the preceding expansive theme of the promised land and the enthusiasm of "It is a good land which the Lord our God gives us" (i. 25). There is an element of suspense in the words "Whither are we going up?" (i. 28) and in the dramatic description of the enemy which follows them.

In other respects, however, D combines the different strands of the JE traditions in a manner that produces a less

---

[19] Von Rad claims for wisdom and allied literature a sparing attitude to direct statements about God's activity, and this may also be characteristic of D's description of incidents; see "Josephgeschichte und ältere Chokma." B. S. Childs, "The Birth of Moses," *JBL,* 84 (1965), 120, makes the same observation in relation to the pericope in Ex. ii, on the birth of Moses, which he claims shows wisdom affinities.

[20] Driver, p. xvii.

[21] *Cf.* Driver, p. xviii.

than homogeneous narrative. Parts of JE that are not wholly
suitable to D's viewpoint are incorporated. The words "How
can I bear alone the weight and burden of you and your
strife" (i. 12) reflect the despairing context of Num. xi. 14,
15, where Moses complains bitterly about the burden of gov-
erning the people. In D's expansive context, i. 12 is out of
place because it contrasts sharply with the explanation of the
equivalent words in i. 9, "I am not able alone to bear you,"
namely, because God has blessed the people, multiplied them
greatly, and is being asked to multiply them a thousand times
more (i. 10, 11). JE's unequal influence on D is also seen in
the latter's use of "you" and "thou." The "you" form of
address usual in JE is carried over into some sections of D
where, in the intimate setting of D, "thou" is the appropriate,
and eventually the predominant, form. It is in the historical
retrospect (dependent upon JE) that D has the greatest concentration of the "you" form. In Deut. i the usage is "you"
in vss. 6–20, "thou" in vs. 21, "you" in vss. 22ff., "thou" and
"you" in vs. 31, and "you" in vss. 32–46.[22]

[22] The influence of the JE "you" material is overlooked in G. Minette
de Tillesse's discussion of the problem of the changing address, "Sections 'tu' et sections 'vous' dans le Deutéronome," *VT*, 12 (1962), 29–
87. Tillesse's thesis is that the "you" sections are additions to the original "thou" work of D by the Deuteronomistic historian (Dt). Tillesse's methodology raises doubts. She finds that the "you" language in
D has literary parallels in the work of Dt. But so too has the "thou"
language. There may be some significance in the fact that certain vocabulary in the "you" sections does not occur in the "thou" sections
and is paralleled in Dt, but one must be cautious. מרה, Tillesse points
out (p. 56), in the sense of rebelling against God, only occurs in "you"'
sections (in Deut. i, ix). It recurs, however, in xxi. 18, 20, as Tillesse
notes, in a "thou" section, in the sense of rebelling against parents,
which is not such a different kind of rebellion as Tillesse suggests.
    Tillesse's observations are made in support of M. Noth's thesis that
the historical sections of D serve as an introduction not to the D code
but to the historical work, Joshua–II Kings; see *Überlieferungsgeschicht-
liche Studien* I (2d ed., Tübingen, 1957). There is, in fact, a close
relationship between the introductory historical sections in Deut. i–iv
and the D code, as I shall indicate. This relationship means that the

In analyzing D's use of traditional material, von Rad rightly presses the question of how far D depends on and how far it diverges from the different strands in the JE traditions. He suggests that to argue for a literary dependence upon the existing JE material involves a complicated hypothesis and advances the alternative theory that D is modeled on another, briefer, unpreserved prototype. The older hypothesis is certainly complex; but so too would von Rad's new one be, especially in accounting for the striking correspondence between the D and JE materials. Its complexity, however, is no argument against an explanation's validity; indeed, the complex explanation may do more justice to the facts than a simpler one.

It is clear that D's relationship to earlier material poses a problem. But the problem is connected with D's creativity in producing a convincing fiction. The laws also exhibit, in a way not hitherto realized, a similar pattern of contact with, and divergence from, earlier legal and narrative material. To account for this pattern it will be argued that D combines different strands of tradition and works out his own distinct creation. This picture of the JE legal and narrative traditions lying before D, who freely works over them, is not an unreasonable one. Such eclecticism could be accounted for by the preservation of old traditions and the construction of an ideological reform program which is put forward as possessing the authority of venerable tradition. By the time of

---

"you" sections are not later additions to an original D work. In any case the theory that a later Dt redactor inserted the "you" sections here and there throughout D is unconvincing. The suggestion that these insertions were motivated by theological considerations begs the question. Tillesse states (p. 40, n. 3) that some "you" insertions are without great theological significance. But they still require explanation, especially if it is believed that a redactor went to such care to insert "you" sections at special points throughout D. Moreover, in view of the overall homogeneity of D it is unconvincing to claim that the theology of the "you" sections is special and distinctive.

D's composition in the seventh century, JE traditions were centuries old, so an impetus toward preserving them in a new way may have developed. The archaic character of D can be explained as an attempt to present the author's own material along with, or rather as part of, old tradition, an attempt that involves a deliberate exploitation of the past. This preservation and creative use of as much of the past as possible, collected and combined from many different sources, helps to explain why so many different solutions to the puzzle of the origin, provenance, and authorship of D have been proposed. D's diversified nature is best explained in terms of a complex attempt to produce something new which, to all appearances, partakes of the letter and spirit of many earlier traditions.

More light is shed on D's archaic character if we note how in ancient didactic literature there is an orientation toward the models of the past. Wisdom is sought in ages long past, and conformity to the precepts of the past is valued highly. A writer's desire to affect the milieu of an earlier time issues from the belief that wisdom belongs with the ancients. The Egyptian instruction of Ptah-hotep is composed in the spirit of the old kingdom, whereas the instruction of the minor official Amen-em-Opet is in the spirit of the centuries following Egypt's great power. J. A. Wilson explains that between five hundred and two thousand years separate them.[23] Yet there are passages in the later work that are almost identical to passages in the earlier. The first impression that the similarity gives is that practical wisdom and the application of the Egyptian ethos to everyday life were unchanging and un-

[23] *The Culture of Ancient Egypt* (Chicago, 1956), pp. 91ff. A strange, more modern example of a writer affecting an earlier milieu is that of the Bristol boy-poet, Thomas Chatterton, who died, aged 17, in 1752. Keats, Shelley, Blake, and Wordsworth were among the Romantic poets who were influenced by him. Chatterton created a fiction by attributing his own works to a 15th-century source and using medieval language and spelling.

changeable. Wilson shows how radically different the works in fact are, each reflecting the circumstances of its time. Likewise D, a composition of the seventh century, is set in the much earlier Mosaic period, with much of its material being drawn from and modeled on the earlier JE traditions.

Summary

Two literary features of D have been stressed: the formal shape of the work as a farewell address, and the fictional Mosaic authorship. The significance of the former is that the author puts himself in the position of looking back on the past, which then provides a perspective for him to make judgments about the future. The significance of the latter is that the authority and wisdom of the past are sought. These two features are not haphazard aspects of D. They reveal much about the book's author—for example, his considerable preoccupation with literary traditions. In particular, D has studied and been influenced by the literary model of Jacob's last testament. Working along the lines suggested by this model, he has ranged widely and reflectively over many early (JE) traditions. In the process, he reveals his contact with a cultural world of ideas governed by the concept of wisdom. This is his social setting. Indeed if a guess were to be hazarded about the real-life situation of the author of D, it would be that he was closely acquainted with the teacher-pupil setting of the wisdom schools of the time. In his work, however, his status transcends that of a teacher. He casts himself in a national role and assumes the responsibility of instructing the whole nation about its destiny.

2. The Peculiar Nature of the Deuteronomic Laws

D's distinctive language and style are observable through-out his composition. One therefore finds that the language and style used in the historical narratives and the hortatory sections are also used in the laws. Critics are aware of the hortatory or parenetic clauses attached to the laws; but the assumption is always made that the two elements are to be separated, that the laws are only presented in this way for the instruction of the people.[1] Yet it is questionable whether such a process of separation is necessary, for, although elements of tradition stand behind the laws, D does not simply add to them his parenetic comments. The distinctiveness of D is that the author makes the laws and these traditional elements serve his constructive purposes. The laws themselves, not merely their parenetic presentation, are permeated by a style and intention that are peculiarly Deuteronomic.

Language

The individualistic language of the D law code produces some remarkable statements of "law." One of the most note-worthy is the recurring command in the sacrificial and feast laws, "And thou shalt rejoice" (xii. 7, 12, 18, xiv. 26, etc.). Nothing could be further from a formal legal rule embody-ing a penalty for failure to observe it. Expansive language is

[1] See G. von Rad, *Studies in Deuteronomy* (Eng. ed., London, 1953), pp. 14ff.

used throughout the code. There is the largesse of: "The rest and inheritance which the Lord thy God gives" (xii. 9); "In order that it may go well with thee" (xii. 25, 28); "But there will be no poor" (xv. 4); "Thou shalt lend to many nations . . . shalt rule over many nations" (xv. 6); "Thou shalt furnish him liberally" (xv.14). There is the amplitude of: "Thou mayest eat as much flesh as thou desirest" (xii. 15, 20); "And spend the money for whatever thou desirest, oxen or sheep or wine or strong drink, whatever thine appetite craves" (xiv. 26); "He [the runaway slave] shall dwell with thee, in thy midst, in the place which he shall choose within one of thy towns, where it pleases him best" (xxiii. 17, *16*). There is the unusual statement (unusual in the use of such an adjective in a legal formulation), "And thou seest among the captives a beautiful woman" (xxi. 11).

This use of expansive language in the laws reflects a concern with religion, morality, and wisdom as well as law. It also indicates the doctrinaire aspect of the laws and suggests that one purpose of the code is the presentation of an ideal moral, social, and religious program. The laws are to take effect on entering the new land; they imply a beginning and a need for renewal and reform. The eloquence of the language also suggests an affinity with practice in the educated circles of the wisdom schools. Wisdom's emphasis on eloquence of language is illustrated in the account of Ptah-hotep's asking the pharaoh for permission to instruct his son. The king tells him to teach the boy rhetoric first.[2] The largesse and amplitude of D's language also echo the offer of life held out by wisdom, which, as Weinfeld indicates,[3] has close ties with the D promises of material blessings and the full life represented by fertility in man and beast, peace from enemies, and political greatness.

[2] *ANET*, p. 412.
[3] "The Book of Deuteronomy in Its Relation to Wisdom" (in Hebrew), *Jubilee Volume for Y. Kaufmann* (Jerusalem, 1960), pp. 104ff.

The linguistic tendency toward expansion and reiteration affects the organization of D's material.[4] The opening chapter (xii) of the code, with its frequent repetition of the list of offerings, is an outstanding example. The considerable variation in the naming of the offerings is best explained as a loose attempt in each case to embrace every possible offering:

Vs. 6 lists in exhaustive fashion: *a* burnt offerings, *b* sacrifices, *c* tithes, *d* heave offerings, *e* votive offerings, *f* freewill offerings, *g* firstlings.

Vs. 11 repeats *a–d* and then lists "All your votive offerings which you vow to the Lord."

Vss. 13, 14 repeat only *a,* the burnt offerings. It is likely that the other offerings are implied also. "Burnt offerings" and "sacrifices" are often mentioned together in general designations of sacrifices (Ex. x. 25, xviii. 12; Josh. xxii. 26, 28; I Sam. vi. 15, xv. 22; Jer. vii. 22).

Vs. 17 begins at *c,* the tithes, and enumerates them: grain, wine, and oil; it then mentions *d–g,* but in a different order, and for *e* there is a more general wording, "And any of thy votive offerings which thou vowest."

Vs. 26 has what is probably an all-inclusive reference, namely, "holy things" and "votive offerings."

A common but ineffective approach to this repetitiveness in xii has been to apply source analysis and unravel different strands of material.[5] Such a procedure invites the criticism of

[4] On the repetitive character of D's language, see S. R. Driver, *Deuteronomy,* ICC (3d ed., Edinburgh, 1902), pp. lxxxviiff.

[5] J. Hempel, *Die Schichten des Deuteronomiums* (Leipzig, 1914), p. 190, sets out three statements of the law of centralization (vss. 2–7, 8–12, and 13, 14, 17–19) and two permitting profane slaughter (vss. 15, 16, and 20–25) and postulates at least two series of laws belonging to different sources. He separates one series from another on the basis of differences in form and substance. Formally, vss. 2–7, 8–12 use the second person plural and align with the second person plural source in the historical introduction of Deut. i–iv, while vss. 13, 14, and 17–19 fit the second person singular source in Deut. iv–xi. Substantially, the

the Irishman who, on being asked the way to a certain place, replied, "I wouldn't start from here!" Although the recurring lists vary considerably in wording, their substance differs little; they do not reflect a legislator's drafting different legal enactments at different times. Rather, the setting is one of instruction, of repeating the same matter but saying it differently so that the hearer will absorb it. The use of the term "burnt offerings" as representative of the other offerings is an expedient to facilitate instruction. The lists suggest the enumerative language of the teacher rather than the competent draftmanship of the lawyer. A good example of enumerative language in the code is the list of superstitious practices in xviii. 9ff. While the other biblical codes contain some mention of such practices (Ex. xxii. 17, *18;* Lev. xviii. 21, xix. 26, 31, xx. 6, 27), the enumeration in D is more detailed, no less than nine being listed.[6]

Motive Clauses

The D laws contain a proliferation of clauses commending the laws to the addressee. These are the "motive" clauses—so

---

law of cultic centralization in vss. 13, 14, 17–19 is the fundamental one. That law is the basis of vss. 2–7, which urge cultic unity as a defense against alien worship, and vss. 8–12, which contrast cultic unity with the previous homeless situation of Israel. A. Welch, *The Code of Deuteronomy* (London, 1924), pp. 47ff., sees different legal sections in Deut. xii that reflect different historical conditions. Thus, vss. 13–19, forbidding the people to sacrifice at every place, reflect a time when Israel was settled in Canaan but the Canaanites were still strong enough to have their own altars. Vss. 8–12 condemn laxity in worship and reflect an unsettled condition in Israel. Vss. 1–7, commanding the destruction of heathen places, reflect a time when the Canaanites had been overrun and Israel was master of the land.

[6] J. A. Wilson, *The Culture of Ancient Egypt* (Chicago, 1956), p. 263, draws attention to the enumerative lists in the exercises of Egyptian schoolboys.

G. von Rad, *Deuteronomy* (Eng. ed. London, 1956), p. 92, also argues that the varying enumerations of the offerings in xii signify "all of them."

called because they attempt to motivate the listener in accordance with the legal and moral instruction being given. The motive clauses, uttered in the same breath as the laws and not as later hortatory attachments, indicate a broad context of instruction as D's setting for the presentation of its laws. In Proverbs, the many motive clauses serve the same didactic function.[7]

The sage in Proverbs often commends wisdom to his disciples: "Hear, my son, thy father's instruction and reject not thy mother's teaching; for they are a fair garland for thy head and pendants for thy neck" (Prov. i. 8, 9). Or he explains why the voice of wisdom enjoins obedience: "My son, be attentive to my wisdom . . . that thou mayest keep discretion" (Prov. v. 1, 2). Or he indicates the reward of his teaching: "My son, do not forget my teaching, but let thine heart keep my commandments; for length of days and years of life and abundant welfare will they give thee" (Prov. iii. 1, 2).

In D the clauses often state the basis for the laws. Frequently they are attached to unenforceable laws, that is, laws whose observance cannot be compelled under threat of a stated penalty, either for lack of an enforcing agency or because such compulsion in not in question. Examples explaining the basis of a law are: "Be careful not to eat the blood for the blood is the life" (xii. 23); and, "No man shall take a mill or upper millstone in pledge, for he would be taking a life in pledge" (xxiv. 6). Numerous examples also appear in those laws that mention Israel's experience in Egypt. The command to eat unleavened bread is based upon the fact that, "in hurried flight thou camest forth from the land of Egypt" (xvi. 3).

Some motive clauses of the explanatory type are attached

[7] B. Gemser, "The Importance of the Motive Clause in Old Testament Law," *SVT*, 1 (1953), 64ff., suggests that the motive clause of Ex. xxiii. 8 about a bribe is a proverbial saying of considerable antiquity that points to a close relationship between law and wisdom.

to laws that are enforceable. Normally, legislation proper (statutes with detailed orders and enforceable sanctions) dispenses with explanations as to why the legislation is given. The laws in xxii on adultery and seduction are intended to be legislation in the narrow, precise sense, but they also have motive clauses. The reason is that D is commending reforming legislation. In the law on adultery (xxii. 22), the redundant "even both of them shall die" indicates that the previous law punished by death only the man.[8]

Two other types of motive clause in D are that which promises a reward for keeping the law, and that which explains the purpose of keeping it. Often these clauses are introduced by the particle לְמַעַן ("in order that"). Examples of the reward type are:

Thou shalt not eat it [the blood]; in order that it may go well with thee and with thy children after thee (xii. 25).

And when he [the king] sits on the throne of his kingdom, he shall write for himself in a book a copy of this law . . . and he shall read in it . . . keeping all the words of this law . . . that his heart may not be lifted up . . . that he may not turn aside from the commandment . . . in order that he may continue long in his kingdom, he and his children, in Israel (xvii. 18–20).

A full and just weight thou shalt have, a full and just measure thou shalt have; in order that thy days may be prolonged (xxv. 15).

These laws all promise the familiar wisdom reward of well-being and long life. Closely related is the promise of material well-being and prosperity in the following laws:

At the end of every three years thou shalt bring forth all the tithe of thy produce . . . and the Levite . . . the sojourner, the fatherless, and the widow . . . shall come and eat . . . in order

[8] For evidence that this is the first law in Hebrew legal history to demand the death of both the adulterer and the adulteress, see D. Daube, "Concerning Methods of Bible Criticism," *AO*, 17 (1949), 93.

that the Lord thy God may bless thee in all the work of thine
hands (xiv. 28, 29).

Justice, justice thou shalt follow in order that thou mayest live
and inherit the land (xvi. 20).

To a foreigner thou mayest lend upon interest, but to thy
brother thou shalt not lend upon interest; in order that the Lord
thy God may bless thee in all that thou undertakest (xxiii.
21, 20).

The particle לְמַעַן also introduces motive clauses that express
the purpose of obedience to the laws in terms similar to
wisdom instruction. The sages point out the purpose of their
teaching: "That men may know wisdom and instruction, understand words of insight, receive instruction in wise dealing,
righteousness, justice, and equity" (Prov. i. 2ff.). Similarly, in
two D laws (the annual tithe, xiv. 23, and the king, xvii. 19)
learning the fear of Yahweh is the expressed purpose.

In general, the motive clauses in D are attached to unenforceable rather than enforceable laws. A good illustration of
this general rule is xvii. The law concerning the idolater and
the law concerning the supreme authority's decision which
must be obeyed could be enforceable under certain conditions; the only motive clause in each case is the nonformal
one that the evil be purged. The law concerning the king, on
the other hand, is unenforceable, and the number of motive
clauses is large.

Forms of Legislation

In different areas of human engagement things are differently expressed, even where their concerns overlap. Philo-
sophical discourse differs from that of politics, even when the
subject of discussion is, for example, freedom. Legal discourse
is different again. An examination of language constructions
leads to a recognition of the human situations that produced

them. In his introductory chapter to *Forms of Roman Legislation* (Oxford, 1956), David Daube stresses the point that a study of the forms of language reveals the social data underlying them. Form criticism, he claims, takes its cue from two observations. First, especially in ancient literature because of its oral roots, literary forms are the product not so much of individual writers as of communal experience and communal need. Hymns, war cries, riddles, legends, and so on have each their fixed, peculiar style, fashioned by ancient society's requirements. Secondly, once established, forms lead a sturdy life of their own, even when removed from their original settings in life. In a Pauline epistle one form still shows its origin in catechetical teaching, another in academic exegesis of scripture, and a third in liturgy. Form criticism may be used as a tool to go beyond source criticism to the elements of social life in antiquity from which, ultimately, a piece of literature derives its shape or form.

Biblical scholars have been much preoccupied with two general forms of legislation, the apodeictic and the casuistic, or conditional, forms. The conditional form—"If a man does such and such, then . . ."—corresponds to a setting where there is need for careful legal regulations that encompass a problematical situation and its solution. It is an indispensable form for the practical, exact needs of any secular jurisdiction, but it is out of place where secular justice is powerless to intervene. This area is where the apodeictic forms— the prohibition, the positive duty, the curse—must be used. These forms can be applied to the most common moral and religious offenses but are useless for the needs of ordinary, exact jurisdiction.[9] The D code contains a mixture of the

[9] A. Alt's essay, "Die Ursprünge des israelitischen Rechts," *Kleine Schriften zur Geschichte des Volkes Israel*, I (München, 1953), 278ff., stimulated much discussion, especially his conclusion that the apodeictic form was peculiarly Israelite. This view is refuted by examples of the apodeictic form in other Near Eastern literature. See R. Kilian,

conditional and the apodeictic, often within the same law. This mixing together of forms indicates how intimately law, religion, wisdom, and morality are interwoven in D and underlines the point that the setting is instruction in wide ranging subject matter.

There is one legal form that is used consistently in the D laws. Where a positive act is enjoined, it is coupled with a negative warning or prohibition. Positively, xii. 2, 3 enjoin the destruction of foreign places of worship, and xii. 4 gives the negative warning, "You shall not do so to the Lord your God." Positive commands concerning the chosen place of worship continue in xii. 5–7, and xii. 8 gives the negative counterpart, "You shall not do according to all that we are doing here." Expansively, xii. 20–22 permit the eating of flesh: "When . . . thou sayest, 'I will eat flesh . . .' thou mayest eat as much flesh as thou desirest. If the place . . . is too far . . . thou mayest eat within thy towns as much as thou desirest. Just as the gazelle or the hart is eaten so thou mayest eat of it, the unclean and clean alike may eat of it." The almost garrulous negative counterpart follows: "Only be sure thou dost not eat the blood . . . thou shalt not eat the life with the flesh. Thou shalt not eat it . . . thou shalt not eat it." Even within this series of prohibitions there is an inclination to insert a positive injunction; thus, in vs. 24: "Thou shalt pour it out upon the earth like water."

"Apodiktisches und kasuistisches Recht im Licht ägyptischer Analogien," *BZ*, 7 (1963), 185–202; S. Gevirtz, "West-Semitic Curses and the Problem of the Origins of Hebrew Law," *VT*, 11 (1961), 137ff.

D. Daube's thesis, based on Roman law, is that the conditional form, "If a man murders another man, he shall be put to death," predominates in early legislation, whereas later the form, "Whoever murders a man shall be put to death," is equally common, this change reflecting an evolution from folk law to a legal system; see his *Forms of Roman Legislation* (Oxford, 1956), pp. 6–8. Daube's discussion of the differences between the conditional and apodeictic forms in biblical law is found in "Some Forms of O.T. Legislation," *Proceedings of the Oxford Society of Historical Theology*, 1945, pp. 36–46.

Some further examples of this consistent formulation of law in D are: "Everything that I command you you shall be careful to do; thou shalt not add to it or take from it" (xiii. 1; *xii. 32*). The negative warning comes first in xiii. 4, 5 (*3, 4*), "Thou shalt not listen to that prophet," followed by the positive injunction, "After the Lord your God you shall walk and him you shall fear." A sequence of positive commands alternating with prohibitions occurs in xv. 19–23: "Every firstling male . . . thou shalt consecrate . . . thou shalt do no work . . . thou shalt eat it . . . but if it has any blemish thou shalt not sacrifice it . . . thou shalt eat it within thy towns . . . only thou shalt not eat its blood, thou shalt pour it out." Finally, there is a reworking in xxii. 1–4 of an earlier law in Ex. xxiii. 4 in which the distinctiveness of D's style is readily seen. The Ex. xxiii version reads, "If thou meetest thine enemy's ox or his ass going astray, thou shalt bring it back to him"; this D recasts as, "Thou shalt *not* see the ox of thy brother or his sheep go astray and hide thyself from them; thou shalt take them back to thy brother."

This positive-negative formulation of rules is also found in the domain of didactic counsel: "Trust in the Lord with all thine heart, and do not rely on thine own insight" (Prov. iii. 5); "Be not wise in thine own eyes; fear the Lord, and turn away from evil" (Prov. iii. 7). The instruction of Ptah-hotep advises:

If thou art seeking out the nature of a friend . . . draw near to him and deal with him alone. . . . Reason with him after a while. Test his heart with a bit of talk. If . . . he should do something with which thou art displeased, behold, he is still a friend. Do not answer in a state of turmoil, do not remove thyself from him; do not trample him down.[10]

The sages proffer advice on what should and should not be done and on the behavior of the wise man and the fool. Positive attitudes, directions, and duties, all with their an-

[10] *ANET,* p. 414.

titheses, are characteristic traits of wisdom rules and D laws. Both are concerned with the correct limits of behavior. D addresses itself to the "dilemma" situation in relation to straying animals (xxii. 1–4): "Thou shalt *not* see thy brother's ox . . . and hide thyself . . . if he is *not* near or thou dost *not* know him . . . thou shalt bring it home to thine house." In like fashion, D describes what a man must do if he comes upon a bird's nest by chance (xxii. 6, 7): "If thou comest upon a bird's nest before thee on the way . . . and the mother sitting upon the young or upon the eggs, thou shalt *not* take the mother with the young; thou shalt let the mother go, but the young thou mayest take to thyself." The fact that the main form of law in D so closely resembles the balanced counsel of the sages is added proof that the D legislator was well acquainted with the sage-student setting.

Another form found in the D laws also reflects wisdom influence. This is the "public example" form—"All Israel shall hear, and fear, and never again do this evil thing in thy midst (xiii. 12, *11* ;*cf.* xvii. 13, xix. 20, xxi. 21). The offenses to which this form is applied are instigation to idolatry, disobedience to high authority, false witness, and disobedience to parents. A law concerning the latter transgression reads:

If a man has a stubborn and rebellious son, who will not obey the voice of his father or the voice of his mother, and, though they chastise him, will not give heed to them, then his father and his mother shall take hold of him and bring him out to the elders . . . and they shall say to the elders of his city, "This our son is stubborn and rebellious, he will not obey our voice; he is a glutton and a drunkard." Then all the men of the city shall stone him to death with stones; so thou shalt purge the evil from thy midst; *and all Israel shall hear, and fear* (xxi. 18–21).

In each law, as in the one quoted, the offense is described in terms of a single culprit, whose fate is spelt out. The intention behind this form is to offer each case as an example to a public which must take note and resolve not to imitate it.

D's use of specific cases to illustrate an offense has parallels in the wisdom literature. The destruction of the young man by the harlot is extravagantly described in Prov. vii. 22ff., the design being to deter others from following his example:

All at once he follows her, as an ox goes to the slaughter, . . . as a bird rushes into a snare; he does not know that it will cost him his life. . . . *And now, O sons, listen to me.* . . . Let not thine heart turn aside to her ways, do not stray into her paths; for many a victim has she laid low; yea, all her slain are a mighty host.

As in the D laws, the emphasis is on the individual offender and his offense rather than the category of offenders and what their offenses have in common. The general aspect is less emphasized so that the more striking case of an individual example may exert a deterrent effect.

David Daube discusses a legal form that occurs only in D.[11] Four laws begin with, "If there be found":

If there be found . . . a man or woman that doeth evil . . . and goeth and serveth other gods . . . the sun or moon or any of the host of heaven (xvii. 2ff.).

If there be found one slain . . . lying fallen in the field, and it be not known who hath slain him (xxi. 1).

If there be found a man lying with a woman married to a husband (xxii. 22).

If there be found a man stealing any of his brethren of the children of Israel (xxiv. 7).

11 "To Be Found Doing Wrong," *Studi in onore di Volterra*, II (Rome, 1969), 3ff. The translations that follow are Daube's.

Daube discusses another form unique to D, "thou canst not do so-and-so" or "he cannot do so-and-so" (xii. 17, xvi. 5, xvii. 15, xxi. 16, xxii. 3, 19, xxiv. 4), and argues that the form stands halfway between wisdom advice and statutory injunction proper. See "The Culture of Deuteronomy," *Orita* (Ibadan), 3 (1969), 41–43.

Closely allied with these is: "There shall not be found among thee any one making his son or daughter to pass through the fire" (xviii. 10).

This form is not used to describe the situation of a person caught red-handed. This use is ruled out because in the case of the untraced homicide a flagrant act is not in question, and in the case of the idolator an enquiry has to be instituted to determine who the culprit is. According to Daube, in using this form the D lawgiver,

shifts the emphasis from the fearfulness of the crime to the fearfulness of the resulting appearance in the eyes of the beholder— God, above all. God is thought of as observing, watching, and what the warning is directed against, in strictness, is not the crime but the inadequacy he will come upon if the crime is committed. The people should be able to stand up to his searching look, the thing to be avoided is the blemish left by a wrong.[12]

One should think of the corpse that horrifies the beholder, spoils the appearance of the land, and requires a special ceremony to remove the blot.

Daube underlines the shame-cultural background of the D laws, pointing out that in the Pentateuch the only law in which the punishment consists of public degradation is Deut. xxv. 5–10 (concerning the man who, because he refuses to perpetuate his dead brother's name, is publicly humiliated by the brother's widow). The D laws reflect a social group whose members are sensitive to one another's behavior, and Daube identifies the social group in ancient Israel that exhibits marked shame-cultural development as the wisdom circles. This group shows a preoccupation with the consequences of behavior, particularly in relation to the student of wisdom who seeks the approval of his teachers and peers as he strives toward success in life.

Daube's insight into the shame-cultural aspect of D clarifies some of the peculiar tendencies in the D laws. It explains D's bias regarding such things as the shaming of parents (xxi.

[12] "To Be Found Doing Wrong," p. 7.

18–21), the indignity of excessive punishment (xxv. 1–3), the immodesty of the woman who grasps a man's genitals in a fight (xxv. 11, 12), and the insult to a virgin of Israel whose name is demeaned by certain accusations (xxii. 13–21). The shaming aspect in all these instances is prominent. Light is also cast on the nature of punishment in the D laws. Because the tendency of the laws is to focus attention on the public aspect of wrongdoing, sanctions become less dependent on an administered system of penalties and more dependent on social and religious pressures within the community.

Parallelism and Symmetry in the Laws

Another indication of the peculiar character of the D laws lies in the care that is taken in the drafting of each law. Care in legal drafting is normally associated with the accurate circumscribing of a law's provisions, but in D it is shown by the duplication of statements. D's repetitions are reminiscent of the stylistic, synonymous parallelism of wisdom counsel. In Proverbs a common synonymous parallelism is of the kind "My son, if thou hast become surety for thy neighbor, hast given thy pledge for a stranger" (Prov. vi. 1). Some examples of parallels (//) in the D laws are:

That thou be not ensnared to follow them // that thou dost not inquire about their gods, saying, "How did these nations serve their gods?" (xii. 30)

And if the way is too long for thee // because the place is too far from thee (xiv. 24).

Whatever thy appetite desireth // whatever thy appetite craveth (xiv. 26).

Thou shalt not harden thine heart // and thou shalt not shut thine hand against thy poor brother (xv. 7).

Then thou shalt do according to what they declare to thee // and thou shalt be careful to do according to all that they direct thee; according to the instructions which they give thee // and according to the decision which they pronounce to thee (xvii. 10, 11).

The law of the bird's nest (xxii. 6, 7) has a striking parallelism of a slightly different kind; everything is run off in pairs:

a) In any tree or on the ground.

b) With young ones or eggs . . . upon the young or upon the eggs.

c) Thou shalt not take the mother with the young; thou shalt let the mother go, but the young thou mayest take to thyself.

d) That it may go well with thee, and that thou mayest live long.

The general effect of this parallelism is that the law has a balanced symmetrical structure. Another example is the law on weights and measures (xxv. 13–16):

a) Thou shalt not have in thy bag two kinds of weights, a large and a small. Thou shalt not have in thine house two kinds of measures, a large and a small.

b) A full and just weight thou shalt have, a full and just measure thou shalt have.

c) That thy days may be prolonged in the land which the Lord thy God gives thee.

d) For all who do such things, all who act dishonestly, are an abomination to the Lord thy God.

The reward clause in *c* is related to the positive command in *b*, and the condemnatory clause in *d* is related to the prohibition in *a*.[13]

13 *Cf.* Deut. v. 16: "[*a*] Honor thy father and thy mother, [*b*] as the Lord thy God commanded thee; [*c*] that thy days may be prolonged, [*d*] and that it may go well with thee, in the land which the Lord thy God gives thee."

S. Bertman, "Symmetrical Design in the Book of Ruth," *JBL*, 84 (1965), 165ff., describes a literary design in the presentation of the story of Ruth: "Elements of content, either analogous or contrasting, stand over against each other in the structure of the story and appear thereby to counterbalance one another." The motivation for such

Many D laws manifest a general disposition of their parts (sentences, phrases, words) that conveys an impression of symmetry of structure. Inevitably the process of indicating such symmetry involves an element of arbitrariness. In the following laws, symmetry is sought in the relationship between the parts, while parallelism is present within the parts.

Deut. xxii. 1, 2:

a) Thou shalt not see thy brother's ox or his sheep go astray, and hide thyself from them.

b) Thou shalt take them back to thy brother.

c) And if he is not near thee // or if thou dost not know him, thou shalt bring it home to thine house // and it shall be with thee.

d) Until thy brother seeks it; then thou shalt restore it to him.

Here, *a* is related to *b* in the same way as *c* is to *d*. A comparison between D's law and the similar law in Ex. xxiii. 4, "If thou meetest thine enemy's ox or his ass going astray, thou shalt bring it back to him," underlines D's greater symmetry of structure.

Deut. xxiv. 10–13:

a) When thou makest thy neighbor a loan of any sort, thou shalt not go into his house to fetch his pledge.

b) Thou shalt stand outside, and the man to whom thou makest the loan shall bring the pledge out to thee.

c) And if he is a poor man, thou shalt not sleep in his pledge.

d) When the sun goes down, thou shalt restore to him the pledge that he may sleep in his cloak and bless thee // and it shall be righteousness to thee before the Lord thy God.

The symmetry in this law is best seen in terms of the typical D positive-negative formulation: *a* has its positive counterpart in *b*, *c* its positive counterpart in *d*.

---

composition, he suggests, may be related to that which produces the parallelism of Hebrew poetry.

W. L. Moran, "The Literary Connection between Lv 11, 13–19 and Dt 14, 12–18," *CBQ*, 28 (1966), 275, refers to the greater symmetry of D (in contrast, for example, to Lev.) as a general characteristic.

To recognize D's stylistic parallelisms is to remove the need, felt by many critics,[14] to excise from the text statements regarded as editorial additions. An example of such a passage is xviii. 1–5, on the dues of the Levites, which many critics have argued is overladen with additions from the notice in x. 8ff. about the Levites. Additions in one sense they may be, but they are original to D's intention. The law as it stands may be set down as follows:

a) The levitical priests // all the tribe of Levi, shall have no portion // inheritance with Israel.

b) Fire-offerings to the Lord // and his dues they shall eat.

c) They shall have no inheritance among their brethren // the Lord is their inheritance, as he promised them.

d) And this shall be the priests' due from the people, from those offering a sacrifice . . . // first fruits of grain [etc.].

Part *a* is related to *c*, while *b*, a general statement about the dues of the priests, is related to *d*, which details them. The negative statement in *a* is matched by the counterpart positive statement in *b*. In *c* the same positive-negative pattern is clear.

Despite the artificial way in which the structure of the previously quoted laws is sketched, it is apparent that such features are not fortuitous and that much stylistic care is given to the writing of the laws. A comparison is invited with the rhetorical patterns found in the proverbial literature.[15] J. Morgenstern suggests that some of the laws in the book of

[14] For example, C. Steuernagel, *Das Deuteronomium* (2d ed., Göttingen, 1923), pp. 119–21; F. Horst, *Gottes Recht* (Munich, 1961), pp. 142ff. J. Emerton, "Priests and Levites in Deuteronomy," *VT*, 12 (1962), 133ff., refutes a theory by G. E. Wright (in a short note in *VT*, 4 [1954], 325ff.), who distinguishes between the term "priests" and the term "Levites" as used by D. Emerton convincingly argues for the identity of "all the tribe of Levi" with "the priests, the Levites" in Deut. xviii. 1.

[15] See J. Muilenburg on rhetorical patterns in the Old Testament: "Hebrew Rhetoric: Repetition and Style," *SVT*, 1 (1953), 97ff.; and "Form Criticism and Beyond," *JBL*, 88 (1969), 1–18.

the Covenant share with Proverbs a definite metrical form, synthetic parallelism, and subject matter.[16] For example, Ex. xxiii. 1, "Thou shalt not repeat an unfounded rumor; neither shalt thou set thy hand with a corrupt person to become a false witness" (Morgenstern's translation), has a 4/3/3 metrical form in Hebrew, and in a manner characteristic of biblical synthetic parallelism moves from a milder matter, false rumor, to a severer one, false testimony, in order to achieve a climactic effect.[17] Warnings against false witness are found throughout Proverbs. It is likely that D's stylistic patterns are also associated with the cultivation of language and style in an academic, wisdom setting.

Summary

The D laws are characterized by consistent language and style. This consistency is observed in the commonly used positive-negative formulation of the laws and in the care with which each law is drafted. Both the expansive and repetitive nature of D's language and the special forms of legislation employed by him suggest his familiarity with an academic setting of instruction in matters of law, morality, wisdom, and religion. A puzzle arises when D's consistency in drafting, in language, and in form is set beside his apparent unconcern about the arrangement of his laws and his seemingly unsatisfactory method of repeating a law, or part of a law, at different points in the code.

The general aim of the laws' motive clauses is to commend the laws. It should not be forgotten that the attribution of the legislation to Moses is a major attempt at commenda-

---

[16] "The Book of the Covenant (Part Four)," *HUCA,* 33 (1962), 90ff. Some of Morgenstern's examples are unconvincing because of severe textual surgery. Gemser, pp. 50 and 64, suggests that certain motive clauses in the laws exhibit a rhythmic form, e.g., in Ex. xx. 7, xxii. 20 (*21*), Deut. xxiv. 6.

[17] *Cf.* a similar effect in Prov. xxvi. 3, "A whip for the horse, a bridle for the ass, and a rod for the back of fools."

tion. The tone of the laws suggests that the code is the work of someone who wishes reform; the constant use of motive clauses, and particularly their use in laws that could be enforced, suggests the reformer's lack of enforcing power and hence his distance from political power.

Because the laws are so diverse in their interests, it is difficult to assess the purpose of the legislation. The motive clauses emphasize the diversity. They can be seen as a manifestation of the legislator's deeper view of things. They reveal his motivations, his ideological slant, the reasons for his laws, and his historical, religious, and political interests. The laws therefore reveal much more than might be supposed because of their apparently haphazard presentation, which gives an impression of incoherence and lack of depth. Von Rad draws attention to the broad range of legal and nonlegal subjects encompassed by D and points to its strong eclectic stamp.[18] The expansive, eclectic background of the D laws requires further examination in order to determine the relationship between the laws' diversity and their arrangement in the code.

[18] *Studies,* p. 23.

3. The Mishpatim and the Deuteronomic Laws

One recognized source of the D laws is the code of laws contained in Ex. xxi. 2–xxiii. 19, the book of the Covenant, or Mishpatim (M). D's relationship to M is complicated, both in the degree of similarity between the subject matter of D and that of M [1] and in the degree of similarity between the intentions of D and M. D omits certain laws that are in M, and those that he includes often appear in a different form and at a different place in his code. The peculiarities of language, form, and content found in D are not exhibited by M, which lacks the ideological coloring of D as well as the latter's eclectic tendency to embrace many subjects and bring in the past history of Israel.[2] The intentions of D also vary from those of M. The D code is not intended to be a more up-to-date version of M. [3] Rather, D uses M in an eclectic fashion; M serves as legal tradition for the D laws, and other, nonlegal elements, for example the past traditions of Israelite life, are

[1] There is a difficulty in determining which laws in D correspond to laws in M. See the lists of parallel laws in S. R. Driver, *Deuteronomy*, ICC (3d ed., Edinburgh, 1902), pp. iv–vii, and in G. von Rad, *Deuteronomy* (London, 1966), p. 13. Von Rad points out that his number of parallel cases could be reduced or increased.

[2] Two similar laws that refer to the sojourn in Egypt (Ex. xxii. 20–23; *21–24* and xxiii. 9) are exceptions. These two laws stand at the head of two related series of laws in M, and D in turn is influenced by this M pattern of arrangement.

[3] See von Rad, *Deuteronomy*, p. 13; *cf.* O. Eissfeldt, *The Old Testament: An Introduction* (Eng. ed., Oxford, 1965), pp. 220ff.

combined with the earlier legal material. D's purpose is to present a normative standard of instruction which is partly worked out by a study of literary traditions about Israel's past. The incorporation of the earlier M laws is one means of contributing to the normative value of the D code. These differences in content and intention can be illustrated by examining some examples of D's use of the M laws.

The Release of Slaves

Ex. xxi. 2–6: (2) When thou buyest a Hebrew slave, he shall serve six years, and in the seventh he shall go out free, for nothing. (3) If he comes in single, he shall go out single; if he comes in married, then his wife shall go out with him. (4) If his master gives him a wife and she bears him sons or daughters, the wife and her children shall be her master's and he shall go out alone. (5) But if the slave plainly says, "I love my master, my wife, and my children; I will not go out free," (6) then his master shall bring him to God, and he shall bring him to the door or the doorpost; and his master shall bore his ear through with an awl; and he shall serve him for life.

Deut. xv. 12–18: (12) If thy brother, a Hebrew man, or a Hebrew woman, is sold to thee, he shall serve thee six years, and in the seventh year thou shalt let him go free from thee. (13) And when thou lettest him go free from thee, thou shalt not let him go empty-handed; (14) thou shalt furnish him liberally out of thy flock, out of thy threshing floor, and out of thy wine press; as the Lord thy God has blessed thee, thou shalt give to him. (15) Thou shalt remember that thou wast a slave in the land of Egypt, and the Lord thy God redeemed thee; therefore I command thee this today. (16) But if he says to thee, "I will not go out from thee," because he loves thee and thy household, since he fares well with thee, (17) then thou shalt take an awl, and thrust it through his ear into the door, and he shall be thy bondman for ever. And to thy bondwoman thou shalt do likewise. (18) It shall not seem hard to thee, when thou lettest him go free from thee; for at half the cost of a hired servant he has served thee six years. So the Lord thy God will bless thee in all that thou doest.

In both M and D, a male slave is to be released after six years' service. M then treats the case where a master gives a wife to a male slave and children are born of the union. In M, only the male slave is to be released at the end of the six-year period; the wife and children remain with the master. Thus far in M there is no independent reference to a female slave. In vss. 7ff., however, M considers the release of a female slave, or rather a slave concubine. In D, a female slave is to be released in the same manner as a male slave. D is silent about the case of a slave's marrying during his period of service. The question of whether the wife given to a male slave accompanies him at the time of his release or must wait until she has served six years is a matter of interpretation. The correct interpretation is probably that she accompanies him, for when the male slave in D wishes to continue residence with his master he speaks only of loving the master and his house and does not mention, as is the case in M, his wife or family. The implication is that if such a slave has been given a wife, she is now included in his destiny. The relationship between the two laws at this point is complex.

The two laws concern different matters. M deals first with a male slave, then with a wife given to him and children born to them, and finally with a slave concubine. D deals only with the male and female slave. Further, M confines itself to the enforceable, while D reveals the tendency that has been noted earlier to concentrate on the unenforceable aspects of a law. This means that D still accepts the M rule (extending it to include female slaves) that the obligation to release slaves after six years is binding, but the emphasis has shifted to matters outside the jurisdiction of the courts, namely, generous provision for a released slave (not considered in M) [4] or his voluntary continuation with the

---

[4] D's concern with charity is not a normal legal concern. D stipulates that a departing slave should be well provided for, with sheep, grain, and wine. This spirit of largesse is reminiscent of the social idealism

master. In M, the male slave who is given a wife by his master and who would have to leave without her after six years can invoke a rule permitting him to recognize his attachment to his family. This rule gives him the option of individual freedom or permanent attachment to his master and family. In D, it is likely that this situation of a slave's being released without his wife no longer applies. However, D retains an interest in the effect of this option rule by recognizing that permanent bondage with security may be preferable to freedom with penury. Hence D holds out the offer to either male or female slave of permanent attachment to the master's household. D's law shows a typical trait: there is an implicit appeal to the addressee's standing in life, where rank imposes high-minded obligations. The change of address, from the more formal third person in M to the less formal second person in D, underlines the point.

Scholars have seen a difference between the two laws in the ceremony performed when a slave opts for perpetuity of service. In M, the master brings the slave to God, to Elohim,[5] and at a door or doorpost bores his ear with an awl. This is generally interpreted to mean that the slave is brought to the sanctuary where justice is administered, and then led to the doorway (whether of the sanctuary or the master's house is not clear),[6] where the master bores his ear; in other words,

---

and humanitarianism of wisdom circles in their concern for the oppressed and downtrodden. Job fears the "crime" of rejecting the cause of his male and female servants (Job xxxi. 13). *Cf.* F. C. Fensham, "Widow, Orphan and the Poor in Ancient Near Eastern Legal and Wisdom Literature," *JNES,* 21 (1962), 129ff.

[5] For the use of Elohim in M, see: C. H. Gordon, "Elohim in Its Reputed Meaning of Rulers, Judges," *JBL,* 54 (1935), 139, who suggests the meaning "household gods"; and A. Draffhorn, "Ilani/Elohim," *JBL,* 76 (1957), who suggests a parallel with the use of the term Ilani, "gods," in the Nuzi legal texts.

[6] There is probably an interpolation in Ex. xxi. 6. The repetition "And his master shall bring him to God, and he shall bring him to the door" suggests this, for such repetitions are not normal in M. The

the ceremony in M is a public, official one of a religious kind, whereas in D it is solely domestic, being performed entirely at the master's own home. The judicial, religious ceremony incorporated in the M version has fallen into disuse. However, the difference between the ceremonies in the D and M laws may not be as distinct as such an interpretation would suggest. The "bringing to God" in Ex. xxi. 6 may be paralleled in D. In vi. 9, xi. 20 God's commandments are to be written on the doorposts of the house, and it is conceivable that D, understanding M's reference to God in this way, is aware of the religious element involved when his law refers to the slave's branding at the doorpost.

Slave Concubines, Captive Maid, Unloved Wife

Ex. xxi. 7–11: (7) When a man sells his daughter as a slave, she shall not go out as the male slaves do. (8) If she does not please her master, who has not designated her for himself, then he shall let her be redeemed; he shall have no right to sell her to a foreign people, since he has dealt faithlessly with her. (9) If he designates her for his son, he shall deal with her as with a daughter. (10) If he takes another wife to himself, he shall not diminish her food, her clothing, or her marital rights. (11) And if he does not do these three things for her, she shall go out for nothing, without payment of money.

Deut. xxi. 10–14: (10) When thou goest forth to war against thine enemies, and the Lord thy God gives them into thine hands, and thou takest them captive, (11) and seest among the captives a beautiful woman, and thou hast desire for her and wouldest take her for thyself as wife, (12) then thou shalt bring her home to thine house, and she shall shave her head and pare her nails. (13) And she shall put off her captive's garb, and shall remain in thine house and bewail her father and her mother a full month; after that thou mayest go in to her, and be her husband, and she shall be thy wife. (14) Then, if thou hast no delight in her, thou shalt let her go where she will; but thou shalt not sell her for money,

---

implication is that the domestic ceremony has been added to the religious, legal one.

thou shalt not treat her as a slave, since thou hast humiliated her.

Deut. xxi. 15–17: (15) If a man has two wives, the one loved and the other disliked, and they have borne him children, both the loved and the disliked, and if the first-born son is hers that is disliked, (16) then on the day when he assigns his possessions as an inheritance to his sons, he may not treat the son of the loved as the first-born in preference to the son of the disliked, who is the first-born, (17) but he shall acknowledge the first-born, the son of the disliked, by giving him a double portion of all that he has, for he is the first issue of his strength; the right of the first-born is his.

Three conditions govern the release of slave concubines in M. First, if a woman is sold to a master but he finds her displeasing and does not designate her to himself,[7] but allows her to be ransomed, he cannot sell her to a foreign people.[8]

[7] This is the reading of MT, אֲשֶׁר לֹא יְעָדָהּ. If לוֹ is read instead of לֹא, then this ruling in the case of a master's taking a concubine would contradict the final ruling (vs. 11), where a master must uphold the rights of any concubine he has taken and, if he fails, must release her without payment and not give her to be ransomed as in vs. 8. The reading לוֹ should not be dismissed altogether, however. It is possible that vs. 11 represents a coda that has been added, not after the ruling in vs. 8, where logically it should have appeared, but at the end of the existing code of provisions on the release of slaves, slave concubines, etc. On this method of adding new rules, see D. Daube, *Studies in Biblical Law* (Cambridge, Eng., 1947), pp. 74ff.

U. Cassuto, *Exodus* (Eng. ed., Jerusalem, 1967), p. 268, thinks the לֹא is not the negative particle but א used for the long final vowel.

[8] Cassuto, *Exodus,* unconvincingly limits the meaning of a "foreign people" to a "strange family." He suggests that the term "people" in the phrase has an archaic significance. Equally doubtful is S. M. Paul's view, following Cassuto, that עַם נָכְרִי means "outsiders," i.e., anyone not a member of the nuclear family. On this basis, where the expression is almost explained away, the unsatisfactory implication is that the girl's original purchaser would have to sell her to someone within the nuclear family. The fact that she can be put up for ransom, but not to a "foreign people," suggests the less rigorous limiting condition that she not be sold abroad. The use of the term "Hebrew" in this law would possibly contrast with "foreign people." See Paul, "Exod. 21:10: A Threefold Maintenance Clause," *JNES*, 28 (1969), 48–53.

Second, if the buyer designates her to his son she must be treated as a free maiden according to the rule applying to such. Third, if the master takes a second concubine and does not uphold the first concubine's rights of food, clothing, and cohabitation,[9] she must be released without ransom.

Since the D laws are related to the M laws in a complex manner, there is a strong possibility that the M rules concerning the slave concubine influence the two D laws that are laid down consecutively in xxi. 10–17. In Ex. xxi. 8 the master who buys a woman but finds her ill-pleasing and does not designate her, but allows her to be ransomed, has no right to sell her to a foreign people since he is dealing faithlessly with her. The rule concerns a woman still a virgin if the masoretic text, "Who has not designated her," is followed. The master presumably could have designated her to a slave, but the rule deals with the situation in which she is to be ransomed and imposes a restriction on the master not to sell her to a foreign people. D deals with the case of a foreign captive woman who is *prima facie* a slave and who could have been sold by her owner if he had not married her. By virtue of the marriage, however, the Hebrew master must accord her special treatment. As in Ex. xxi. 8, the D law concerns a slave woman who displeases the man. But since in D she is married to him, he may divorce her but he must not sell her for money, thereby treating her as an article of trade, because he has humiliated her. This decision of D appears to be influenced by the rule in Ex. xxi. 11, under which a woman who is denied her rights as a man's concubine must be released without payment of money.

The influence of the M rules on the D laws on marriage to a captive maid and on the unloved wife is confirmed by another remarkable, if indirect, connection between them.

[9] On the translation of the terms of the concubine's rights, see R. North, "Flesh, Covering and Response," *VT*, 5 (1955), 206. For the rendering "food, clothing, and oil" see Paul.

R. Yaron has drawn attention to the narrow scope of D's law concerning the unloved wife; it deals only with inheritance rights when there are two wives and is silent on the position when there is but one.[10] The narrow scope of the law can, in part, be attributed to the influence of the M rule in which a master who takes a second concubine must not diminish the food, clothing, and marital rights of the first. The D law is applying the same principle. The most important nexus is the intention of the D law to uphold the rights of the son born of the unloved wife. In doing this, the law indirectly prevents the diminution of the rights of the unloved wife and in this respect corresponds to the intention of the M rule to uphold the rights of the slave concubine whose master takes a second concubine.[11] The first slave concubine of M corresponds to the unloved wife of D, since according to the M rule she is liable to be thrust aside by the newly favored concubine and deprived of her rights.

A similar technical phrase is used in the D law on the unloved wife and her son and in the M law on the concubine designated by her buyer for his son, suggesting that there may be a minor linguistic nexus between the two. M refers to the rule relating to free maidens (משפט הבנות), while D refers to the rule relating to the first-born (משפט הבכורה).

The M law in which a slave concubine is given full marital status if her master disposes of her to his son represents a stage in the breakdown of the practice of concubinage. The other M laws on the subject also lay particular obligations on the master and work in favor of a more humane treatment for concubines. The terms of the D law on the foreign

[10] *Gifts in Contemplation of Death in Jewish and Roman Law* (Oxford, 1960), p. 9.

[11] It is noteworthy that in the case of Bathsheba and Solomon the mother's rights are associated with her son's inheritance (I Kings i. 11–21). In the Middle Assyrian laws, a wife's maintenance, after her husband's death, is to be provided for by her sons. See G. R. Driver and J. Miles, *The Assyrian Laws* (Oxford, 1935), pp. 229–32, 415.

captive maid indicate that she is to be accorded a status more like that of a full wife than of a concubine: she must submit to an elaborate ceremony; there is to be a period of waiting in honor of her parents—a remarkable example of D's "international" wisdom outlook; and she is to have the right of freedom if she is divorced.[12]

It has been submitted that certain D laws owe something to a reworking of elements in some M laws. However, especially in the two D laws on the captive maid and the son of the unloved wife, the connections with M are indirect. D's eclectic method of compiling his laws explains the divergence from M. The law on the inheritance rights of the unloved wife's son may serve as illustration. This law derives its particular cast from its connection with the rule in Ex. xxi. 10. The concern is not only with the rights of the first-born son but also with those of the unloved wife. Another link is also to be noted, but it is associated with a different, early tradition and explains the reference in the law to the *loved* and the *unloved* wife. A law on the inheritance rights of the first-born son of a man with two wives could simply state the position without indicating the contrast between the loved and the unloved wife. The D law is narrow, its concern with inheritance rights being limited not just to a situation in which there are two wives but to one in which one wife is loved and the other unloved. The explanation for this narrowness is that D's law is constructed in relation to the Genesis tradition about Jacob's wives: Rachel, whom

[12] In Assyria, war captives were treated by their masters as slave girls, concubines, or full wives. *Ibid.*, pp. 127ff.

In Ex. xxi. 7, xxiii. 12 אָמָה means a concubine. In D, אָמָה (v. 14, 21, xii. 12, 18, xv. 17, xvi. 11, 14) has the general meaning of maidservant, whose primary attachment is possibly to the mistress of the house, as in Ps. cxxiii. 2, Is. xxiv. 2, and Prov. xxx. 23.

For discussion of the terms אָמָה and שִׁפְחָה, and for the view that the latter, usually the maidservant attached to the mistress of the house, would be more accurate in D, see the short note by A. Jepsen, *VT*, 8 (1958), 293–97.

Jacob loved, and Leah, whose womb was opened first because the Lord saw that she was unloved (Gen. xxix. 31).
Reuben was the first-born son, and in Gen. xlix the aged
Jacob addresses Reuben first and acknowledges him, the first-
born of the unloved wife, as his first-born.[13] Moreover Jacob
refers to Reuben as the "first-fruits of my strength," exactly
the phrase used in the D law to justify the double share that
the first-born of the unloved wife is to receive.

D revises both an earlier M law and an earlier narrative
tradition to produce his own law. This example is but one
of many in which his eclectic method is visible. The intention of such a method is to survey comprehensively past traditions, legal and nonlegal, and to produce a code of laws
that will appear to stem from antiquity.

Two Series of Laws in the Mishpatim

D's method of drafting laws is based on one that has been
applied to certain laws in the M code. The arrangement of
the M laws in Ex. xxii. 20–30 (*21–31*) and xxiii. 9–19 is striking. Ex. xxii. 20 (*21*) concerns the oppression of the sojourner, so too does Ex. xxiii. 9. In fact, if the laws in xxii.
20–30 (*21–31*) are compared with those in xxiii. 9–19, the
laws in one list have, in sequence, laws affiliated to them in
the other list. The pattern of correspondence that emerges is
as follows:

   1a) xxii. 20–23 (*21–24*). Oppression of sojourner ("for you
      were sojourners in the land of Egypt"), widow, orphan.

---

[13] Jacob's statement to Reuben, "Thou art my first-born," is a normal
way of legally acknowledging a person's status. See D. Daube, *Studies in
Biblical Law*, pp. 7ff., for examples from both biblical and ancient
Near Eastern codes. See also, R. Yaron, *Introduction to the Law of
the Aramaic Papyri* (Oxford, 1961), p. 46, for an example from Elephan-
tine. On "to acknowledge" as a technical legal term, used, for example,
in the D law on the first-born, see D. Daube and R. Yaron, "Jacob's
Reception by Laban," *JSS,* 1 (1956), 60–62.

1b) xxiii. 9. Oppression of sojourner ("for you were sojourners in the land of Egypt").

2a) xxii. 24–26 (*25–27*). Protection of the poor from loans
at interest and from oppressive pledging.

2b) xxiii. 10–12. Seventh year release of the land's produce for the poor and sabbath rest for the bondmaid's
son and for the sojourner.

3a) xxii. 27 (*28*). No cursing God or the ruler of the people.

3b) xxiii. 13. To heed all that has been said, no names of
other gods to be mentioned.

4a) xxii. 28 (*29*). No delay in offering from harvest, wine,
and olive press, first-born males for Yahweh.

4b) xxiii. 14–17. Three feasts of the year, males to appear
at each.

5a) xxii. 29 (*30*). First-born of oxen and sheep to be
sacrificed on eighth day.

5b) xxiii. 18, 19a. No leaven with blood of sacrifice, and
fat of feast not to remain overnight; first-fruits to be
brought to house of Yahweh.

6a) xxii. 30 (*31*). Men holy to Yahweh—not to eat flesh
torn by beasts but to cast it to dogs.

6b) xxiii. 19b. Kid not to be boiled in mother's milk.

That the pattern is one of correspondence is confirmed by
observing how D reworks these M laws in his code. Thus the
D law on the poor and seventh year release of debts (xv. 1–
11) is a further development of the association between the
release of the land's produce for the poor in the seventh
year (2b) and the prohibitions against lending at interest and
oppressive pledging (2a). The law on torn animal flesh (6a)
and the law on the kid in the mother's milk (6b) are brought
together in Deut. xiv. 21. These two examples of what D
does with the M laws provide excellent illustrations of D's
eclectic method. D combines the laws, either by juxtaposing

them or by fusing an element of one law with part of another, in the same manner as we saw him combining an earlier law and an earlier narrative tradition.

If the arrangement rather than the history of the laws in M is considered, several observations may be made. First, the fact that one series of laws is placed after another series proves nothing about the date of the laws, since those in the second series could predate corresponding laws in the first series.[14] Second, the correspondence between the laws in the two series is fairly loose. Consider, for example, the broad concern with the rights of the poor and oppressed. It is because they both address this issue (the association between a seventh fallow year and a seventh day rest from work is another reason) that, within the second series itself, the law on the sabbath rest for the bondmaid's son and the sojourner follows the law on the release of the land for the poor (2b). Further, this is why both of these laws are aligned with laws in the first series on lending to the poor and on taking a poor man's garment in pledge (2a).

Third, it is likely that the lawgiver who set down these laws was aware of their unenforceable nature. No practical system of law known to him could enforce such laws should they go unheeded. The laws in both series are concerned with matters too complex for normal human jurisdiction to control. No enforceable penalties are mentioned. The prohibition against oppressing the sojourner embodies a moral appeal to Israel's past situation in Egypt. The oppressor of the widow and orphan is threatened with divine punishment. In contrast, all the laws preceding Ex. xxii. 20 (*21*), the first law of the first series, were probably enforceable, legal

[14] For possible reasons why other laws (Ex. xxiii. 1–8) come between the two series, see D. Daube's discussion about early lawgivers' reluctance to interfere with an established written code (*Studies in Biblical Law*, pp. 74ff.). In the case of the M double series, the implication would be that when the second series was being set down the laws in Ex. xxiii. 1–8 were already written down in their present position following the first series.

machinery was available to handle the situations they govern (Ex. xxi. 2–Ex. xxii. 19, 20).

Such unenforceable laws in the two series reflect, on the part of their drafter, overlapping interests in religion, morality, justice, and social behavior. They do not reflect special interests—for example, those of the priests, even though cultic laws are included. It would be rash to suggest that they stem from wisdom circles. However, the scribal method used in presenting the second series in loose correspondence to the first does reflect the scribal practice of the sages more than competent legal drafting, where one expects similar laws to be placed together. J. Morgenstern indicates the stylistic affinity between some of the laws in this part of M and the biblical proverbs.[15] Moreover the listing of a series of laws to correspond to another series has mnemonic advantages useful in instruction. The M scribe's concern with mnemonic technique may reflect classroom experience. The loose pattern of correspondence between the laws in the two series compares with a similar loose association in the arrangement of individual biblical proverbs. For example, in Prov. xxvi the first two proverbs are formally associated by their use of nature similes and the achievement of a climactic effect in the third part of each proverb. The latter feature is carried over into the next proverb, about the fool, "A whip for the horse, a bridle for the ass, and a rod for the back of fools." Then follow many proverbs concerning the ways of the fool (xxvi. 4–12). These in turn are followed by proverbs about the sluggard. It may be, therefore, that after the first series was set down in its present form (how the laws in this series came to be in this order is another question, not touched on here), a scribe then set down other laws in a sequence determined by association with the pattern of the first series.

[15] "The Book of the Covenant (Part Four)," *HUCA,* 33 (1962), 90ff.

Summary

The foregoing discussion has refrained from any systematic study of the relationship between the D and M laws. The reasons for this are threefold. First, the relationship is not just one of earlier laws being reinterpreted, or even misinterpreted, for later legal purposes, but a more complicated one. Second, evidence will be offered below of the special character of the D laws. The M laws are made to serve the dual purpose of providing instructional material and producing a code of laws which supposedly comes out of antiquity. The eclectic manner in which D uses the M laws supplies the hitherto missing factor in analyzing the relationships involved. For this reason a proper study of the problem requires a study of the D laws. The third reason is that D does not deal with the M code in a systematic way.[16] However, it can be demonstrated that the M laws are made to fit D's scheme of arrangement.

The method of arrangement used by M reveals something about the method used by D in presenting his laws. The fact that some of the laws from the double M series appear in Deut. xxiii and xxiv [17] suggests that D may have been prompted to present a double series of his own. This is, in fact, the case; it will be demonstrated that just as the two M lists begin with a law on the sojourner and an appeal to remember the time in Egypt, so the D double series issues from a two-part law (Deut. xxiii. 8, 7) on not abhorring the Edomite and not abhorring the Egyptian. This two-part law gives rise to a series of laws in Deut. xxiii with Edomite allusions and another series in Deut. xxiv with Egyptian allusions.

[16] See the lists in Driver, *Deuteronomy*, ICC, and von Rad, *Deuteronomy*.

[17] For example, Ex. xxii. 24, 25 (lending at interest) appears in Deut. xxiii. 20, 21 (*19, 20*); Ex. xxii. 25, 26 (pledges) in Deut. xxiv, 10–13; and Ex. xxii. 20–23 (*21–24*), xxiii. 9 (justice for the stranger, widow, orphan) in Deut. xxiv. 17ff.

The M method also illuminates what has been a major problem in the study of the D laws, namely, the apparently haphazard order in which they are set down. Two examples will illustrate the difficulty. A law on straying animals is followed by laws on transvestite practice, a bird's nest, and the parapet for a new house (Deut. xxii. 1–8). Another sequence sets a law on the fugitive slave before laws on cultic prostitution and lending (Deut. xxiii. 16–21; *15–20*). Such an ordering of laws presents a chaotic aspect. The scholarly opinion has been that while some semblance of order can be seen in the laws in the earlier chapters of the code, there is none in the later.[18] The explanation offered for the disorder, especially in the later laws, is that editorial redactions added laws without regard for their relationship to preceding ones.[19] The following chapters propose a solution to this problem of order in the D laws. It is not a matter of editorial redactions. Rather, the laws are all assembled by one hand and demonstrate a remarkable system of order and presentation. The system is similar to the arrangement of the M double series, in which the second list represents a repeated sequence of laws similar in content to the first.

[18] Driver, *Deuteronomy*, ICC, pp. 135, 136. A. Welch, *The Code of Deuteronomy* (London, 1924), p. 23: "For while any order into which the laws may be placed is sure to be unsatisfactory, none can be quite so bad as the order in which they appear in Deuteronomy today." R. Pfeiffer, *Introduction to the Old Testament* (New York, 1948), p. 232: "The disorder is so extreme that one would almost call it deliberate, unless it arose as a result of successive additions of new material." E. W. Nicholson, *Deuteronomy and Tradition* (Oxford, 1967), p. 33: "This lack of order in xii–xxvi has so far defied solution."

[19] Some researchers note the affinity of these "added" laws with preceding ones in the code and accordingly speak of different editorial strands. See, for example, J. Hempel, *Die Schichten des Deuteronomiums* (Leipzig, 1914), p. 226; C. Steuernagel, *Die Entstehung des deuteronomischen Gesetzes* (Berlin, 1901), p. 48.

4. Initial Presentation:
xii. 1–xvi. 17

A study of the method of presentation of the D laws demonstrates new areas of meaning. D's technique for drafting laws involves the expansion of material presented at the beginning of his code with material taken from earlier M laws or earlier narrative traditions. The process is an eclectic one. Material is brought together by a process of association, combined, and presented in the form of "law." The resulting laws are diverse, artificial, and, because of the infusion of early material, seemingly ancient.

The use of early traditions pervades the D code and extends beyond those laws that explicitly recall earlier traditions; for example, the law on leprosy (xxiv. 8, 9), "Remember what the Lord thy God did to Miriam," recalls the story in Num. xii. The significance of the historical notices in the D laws is not generally appreciated. A. Weiser describes the Deuteronomic historical writings (Joshua–Kings) as a presentation and interpretation of past events according to standards set in the D laws.[1] As the first step in such an interpretation, the D laws themselves present and interpret past events in Genesis–Numbers according to the D standpoint.[2]

---

[1] *The Old Testament: Its Formation and Development* (Eng. ed., New York, 1961), p. 335. R. A. Carlson, *David, the Chosen King* (Uppsala, 1964), pp. 180ff., suggests that the ordering of material in II Sam. x–xx agrees with the arrangement of the laws in Deut. xxii. 13ff.

[2] *Cf.* M. Greenberg's point that the laws in Ezek. xl–xlviii are de-

Affinities between the D laws and wisdom instruction have been noted. The process involved in the compilation of the D code parallels that used by the scribes in compiling the book of Proverbs. The listing of diverse proverbs—often one is linked to another by some form of association—is clearly eclectic in character. This simple listing may be explained by the notion that to lay up these words of the wise is to acquire wisdom. In D, the process of gathering material and working with it is much more complex. The eclectic character of the D laws lies not only in the presentation of diverse subject matter but also in the composition of individual laws. D's choice of method may be explained by his feeling that a combination of different strands of tradition yielded a deeper and more authoritative tradition. An alternative explanation may be that D was attempting to produce an authoritative work that included, summarized, and venerated past traditions. The artificiality of the product is the result of D's attempt to present his seventh-century viewpoint in Mosaic form.

Opening Laws of the Code: xii. 1–28

Chapter 2 has examined the special character of the opening section of the laws and argued that the frequent repetition of rules for sacrifice and worship does not suggest a heterogeneous code of rules, composed at different times and places, but rather reflects a setting of instruction. Matters are repeated, especially in this opening part of the instruction, in order to fix the teaching in the mind of the hearer. The repetitions occur within a very limited subject matter and mark the beginning of a process of expansion that is carried through the rest of the law code. It is clear that the laws increase greatly in number in the later chapters of the code. It is also noteworthy that the didactic, hortatory comments on the laws are extensive to begin with but not so prominent

---

signed to set right wrongs in Israel's past life—"Idealism and Practicality in Numbers 35:4–5 and Ezekiel 48," *JAOS,* 88 (1968), 64.

later. A teacher would be inclined to impart a greater number of laws, and with less commentary, only after an initial attempt to lay down a careful basis of instruction.[3]

Instigation to Idolatry: xii. 29–xiii. 19 (*18*)

(29) When the Lord thy God cuts off before thee the nations whom thou goest in to dispossess, and thou dispossessest them and dwellest in their land, (30) take heed lest thou be ensnared to follow them, after they have been destroyed before thee, and lest thou seekest to inquire about their gods, saying, "How did these nations serve their gods?—that I also may do likewise." (31) Thou shalt not do so to the Lord thy God; for every abominable thing which the Lord hates they have done for their gods; for they even burn their sons and their daughters in the fire to their gods.

(1, *32*) Everything that I command you, you shall be careful to do; thou shalt not add to it or take from it.

(2, *1*) If a prophet arises among thee, or a dreamer of dreams, and gives thee a sign or a wonder, (3, *2*) and the sign or wonder which he tells thee comes to pass, and if he says, "Let us go after other gods," which thou hast not known, "and let us serve them," (4, *3*) thou shalt not listen to the words of that prophet or to that dreamer of dreams; for the Lord your God is testing you, to know whether you love the Lord your God with all your heart and with all your soul. (5, *4*) You shall walk after the Lord your God and fear him, and keep his commandments and obey his voice, and you shall serve him and cleave to him. (6, *5*) But that prophet or that dreamer of dreams shall be put to death, because

---

[3] The general, formal affinity with the book of Proverbs may be noteworthy. The first collection of proverbs (i–ix) is distinguished by the fact that it contains didactic pieces of greater length than elsewhere in the book; contrast this collection, for example, with that in x–xxii, which consists of single proverbs. *Cf.* O. Eissfeldt, *The Old Testament: An Introduction* (Eng. ed., Oxford, 1965), pp. 472ff. Carlson, pp. 154ff. suggests that Prov. i–ix should no longer be regarded as the most recent section of Proverbs.

See Chapter 6 below for discussion of the laws on the centralization of the cult in xii, and their underlying viewpoint, and Chapter 5 for discussion of an earlier tradition that colors the presentation of the laws on eating meat in xii.

he has taught rebellion against the Lord your God, who brought you out of the land of Egypt and redeemed thee out of the house of bondage, to make thee leave the way in which the Lord thy God commanded thee to walk. So thou shalt purge the evil from the midst of thee.

(7, *6*) If thy brother, the son of thy mother, or thy son, or thy daughter or the wife of thy bosom, or thy friend who is as thine own soul, entices thee secretly, saying, "Let us go and serve other gods," which neither thou nor thy fathers have known, (8, *7*) some of the gods of the peoples that are round about you, whether near thee or far off from thee, from the one end of the earth to the other, (9, *8*) thou shalt not yield to him or listen to him, nor shalt thine eye pity him, nor shalt thou spare him, nor shalt thou conceal him; (10, *9*) but thou shalt kill him; thine hand shall be first against him to put him to death, and afterwards the hand of all the people. (11, *10*) Thou shalt stone him to death with stones, because he sought to draw thee away from the Lord thy God, who brought thee out of the land of Egypt, out of the house of bondage. (12, *11*) And all Israel shall hear and fear, and never again do any such wickedness as this in thy midst.

(13, *12*) If thou hearest in one of thy cities, which the Lord thy God gives thee to dwell there, (14, *13*) that certain base fellows have gone out among thee and have drawn away the inhabitants of the city, saying, "Let us go and serve other gods," which you have not known, (15, *14*) then thou shalt inquire and make search and ask diligently; and behold, if it be true and certain that such an abominable thing has been done in thy midst (16, *15*) thou shalt surely put the inhabitants of that city to the sword, destroying it utterly, all who are in it and its cattle, with the edge of the sword. (17, *16*) Thou shalt gather all its spoil into the midst of its open square, and burn the city and all its spoil with fire, as a whole burnt offering to the Lord thy God; it shall be a heap for ever, it shall not be built again. (18, *17*) None of the devoted things shall cleave to thine hand; that the Lord may turn from the fierceness of his anger, and show thee mercy, and have compassion on thee, and multiply thee, as he swore to thy fathers, (19, *18*) if thou obeyest the voice of the Lord thy God, keeping all his commandments which I command thee this day, and doing what is right in the sight of the Lord thy God.

A general exhortation to keep all the commandments constitutes the formal opening of the D code (xii. 1), and, because D systematically repeats previously presented material,
a similar exhortation is given in xii. 28. This pattern of repetition is clear again in the laws on instigation to idolatry. At
the beginning of the code (xii. 2–4), D commands the destruction of the places and relics of worship of the nations disin-
herited by Israel. The instigation laws (xii. 29–xiii. 19, *18*)
again take up the subject of the danger to Israel of the
abominable practices of these nations. D's method recalls that
of the M double series, where laws are presented in parallel
sequences.

In xii. 2–4 and xii. 29–31 there are similarities both in the
characteristic positive-negative formulation as well as in the
concern with idolatrous practices. Thus, vss. 2, 3 and vs. 30
are both positive commands: "You shall utterly destroy . . .
all the places . . . and tear down their altars . . . and destroy their name out of that place" and "Take heed lest thou
be ensnared to follow them . . . and lest thou seekest to
inquire about their gods." In turn, vs. 4 and vs. 31 are prohibitions: "You (thou) shall not do so to the Lord your (thy)
God." This general prohibition in vs. 31 is followed by two
motive clauses. These clauses illustrate how the lawgiver fills
out his instruction and carries forward the body of knowledge
he is imparting.

There follow then three laws on instigation to idolatry (xiii.
2–19; *1–18*). The instigators in each case—the prophet or
dreamer of dreams, the intimate relative or friend, and the
certain worthless men of an Israelite city—with their calls to
serve other gods, are guilty of inciting idolatry. These three
laws, which continue from xii. 29–31 the subject of instigation to idolatry and ensnaring others to serve the gods of
peoples near or far (xiii. 8, 7), can be considered an extension
of the revision and expansion of xii. 2–4, the law calling for
the extermination of the places and ways of worship of these

other gods. This reversion illustrates the D method, under which earlier material is reverted to, to be expanded and elaborated upon. The D style of writing, observable in other, nonlegal parts of the book, where a theme is reiterated and expanded upon,[4] is recognizable in this legal instruction.

The main subjects of xii are sacrifice and feasting. Descriptions of the sacrifices and offerings vary in terminology and in the numbers listed; so too does the language vary in the recurring commands about the chosen place. The same features of concentration and variation are found in xii. 29–xiii. 19, *18*. The subject is idolatry; in the recurring formula used by the instigators, and in the appended comments, the language varies:

"Let us go after other gods," which thou hast not known, "and let us serve them" (vs. 3, 2);

"Let us go and serve other gods," which neither thou nor thy fathers have known, some of the gods of the peoples that are round about you, whether near thee or far off from thee, from the one end of the earth to the other (vss. 7, 8; *6, 7*);

"Let us go and serve other gods," which you have not known (vs. 14, *13*).

At this stage in the instruction, the laws imparted are few and the hortatory comment extensive. The variations in language correspond not to different source materials but to the broad and flexible use of language appropriate to instruction.[5]

The law in xiii. 1 (*xii. 32*) states, "Everything that I command you you shall be careful to do; thou shalt not add to it or take from it." Although this law appears to be out of place, coming between the law on the idolatrous practices of other nations and the law on the prophet and dreamer of

---

[4] See S. R. Driver, *Deuteronomy*, ICC (3d ed., Edinburgh, 1902), pp. lxxxviiff.

[5] On this flexible element in D's language, see B. S. Childs, "Deuteronomic Formulae of the Exodus Traditions," *SVT*, 16 (1967), 30–39.

dreams,[6] it is not, for a similar exhortation occurs in iv. 1, 2, in the context of the apostasy to Baal at Peor. There, the positive exhortation is to keep all the commands which Moses (speaking in the first person) is giving, and this is followed, as in xiii. 1 (*xii. 32*), by D's typical negative counterpart, "You shall not add to the word which I command you, nor take from it." [7] The fact that D has already issued such an exhortation in a context of idolatry suggests that this is the reason why he repeats it in the context of idolatry in xiii. 1 (*xii. 32*). What D does, and this is typical of his eclectic method, is to bring in words of counsel previously given and to add this counsel to new, but similar, subject matter. D presents laws systematically in so far as the sequence is dependent upon previous laws in the code. At the same time, however, he interweaves material from other sources, either his own previously given material or earlier traditions.

The significance of xiii. 1 (*xii. 32*), as of iv. 1, 2, derives from the law on the prophet in xviii. 15–22. (The law in xviii will be shown to "revise" the law on the prophet in xiii.) In xviii, a prophet like Moses is to be raised up, and obedience to what he says is commanded. Like Moses, this

[6] M. Greenberg suggests that the prohibition against adding and subtracting appears at xiii. 1 (*xii. 32*) because the preceding reference to Molech worship (in xii. 31) had been understood as commanded by God (he cites the interesting text in Ezek. xx. 25, 26). Such an understanding had, therefore, constituted a false addition to the law. He points out how, in the Christian division of verses, xii. 32, the prohibition against adding and subtracting, is linked with the preceding prohibition against idolatry. See "Ezekiel 20 and the Spiritual Exile" (in Hebrew), *Israel Society for Biblical Research, 'Oz le-David,* 15 (Jerusalem, 1964), 437.

[7] While the wording of the two prohibitions is alike, there is the you/thou variation in xiii. 1 (*xii. 32*). Owing to the distinctive Deuteronomic positive/negative formulation of the law, it cannot be argued that the second person singular is original and the second person plural not. The xiii. 1 (*xii. 32*) plural form in a decidedly singular context is one indication that D is repeating the similar law of iv. 2, which is entirely in the plural form.

prophet stands above the law of xiii. 1 (*xii. 32*) on not adding or subtracting from the given commands. A true prophet may add to the commands, as Moses is now doing. However, there is the danger of a false prophet giving commands that have not Yahweh's authority (xviii. 20), as the false prophet or dreamer of dreams does in xiii. 2ff. (*1ff.*) in commanding the worship of other gods. The significance of the law in xiii. 1 (*xii. 32*) is, therefore, that only what the prophet Moses is commanding should be obeyed, not the "additions" or "subtractions" of the false prophet and his like.

A clue to D's concerns in the three laws on instigation to idolatry may lie in the tradition of the apostasy to Baal at Peor. This tradition is mentioned in Deut. iv. 3, 4, and a full account is found in Num. xxii–xxiv, xxv, and xxxi. The account in Numbers, as G. B. Gray shows,[8] is ambiguous in many respects, but the fact that D knew some such tradition seems certain, and that the tradition is in his mind in the law of xiii. 1 ([*xii. 32*] on not adding to or subtracting from the commandments) seems highly probable.

In the D law, a prophet or dreamer of dreams may be able to produce signs or wonders but this is no guarantee that his words are about Israel's God. They may be about foreign gods. Balaam is a prophet (Num. xxiv. 2ff.) and a dreamer of dreams.[9] He is also a diviner, who would be able to perform signs and wonders (Num. xxii. 7). He is a foreigner, who is contacted by Israel's God when the Moabites and Midianites seek him to curse Israel. In language akin to that of Deut. iv. 1, 2 and xiii. 1 (*xii. 32*) he tells them how he cannot go beyond the command of the Lord his God to do less or more (Num. xxii. 18). Only the word that God puts in his mouth must he speak (Num. xxii. 35, 38). This statement resembles the law on the prophet in Deut. xviii. 15–22: God will put

---

[8] *Numbers,* ICC (Edinburgh, 1903), pp. 307ff.

[9] Balaam receives word from Yahweh by night, which suggests by dreams (Num. xxii. 8–13, 19, 20).

words in the mouth of the true prophet and only these must he speak.

However, Balaam also appears in a less favorable light in Numbers. He arouses the anger of God (Num. xxii. 22), although it is not clear why. The emphasis on Balaam's acknowledging only the word that God has spoken to him (Num. xxii. 20, 35, xxiii. 12) contrasts with his normal practice of acknowledging the words of other gods. He is, after all, a foreigner whose way is opposed (Num. xxii. 32). Moreover, it is at the high places of Baal that he beholds the Israelites, and that he worships (Num. xxii. 41, xxiii. 1ff.). D, keenly aware of the intricacies of idolatry, probably found much to reflect upon in the Balaam tradition. His depiction of the prophet who is able to display divine powers but does not follow the words of Israel's God could be based on this tradition.

Balaam was eventually put to death by the Israelites because, it is implied,[10] he had a hand in the apostasy to the Baal of Peor (Num. xxxi. 8, 16). This apostasy is described in Num. xxv. 1ff. The Israelites had worshiped foreign gods, and Moses commanded the judges to slay the culprits. The account of an incident that occurred after the judgment on the idolaters describes how an Israelite brought a Midianite woman into his family and how both were slain for an offense which, although it is not recorded in detail, is associated with the apostasy to foreign gods. D's didactic use of the tradition associated with this incident may underlie his remarkable piece of legislation that demands punishment by death for instigation to apostasy within a family by a man's brother, son, daughter, wife, or close friend.

A combination of factors suggests the influence of the traditions concerning Balaam and the apostasy to foreign gods on these D laws. D's awareness of the apostasy at Peor is explicit in iv. 3 and strongly implied in xiii. 1 (*xii.* 32). The description of Balaam in the traditions—one who is like a

10 The Hebrew of Num. xxxi. 16 is obscure.

prophet or dreamer of dreams under the power of Israel's God but is also an instigator to worship of foreign gods—also characterizes the prophet or dreamer of dreams in D who is condemned to death. In D, the prophet's activity diverges from the "way," and this "way" is associated with the exodus from Egypt (xiii. 6, 5). Balaam's actions belong to the same period; his attempt to curse Israel at that time is condemned in xxiii. 5 (4).

For the background to D's unique law of apostasy within a family, the incident, also associated with Balaam, concerning the Israelite and the Midianite woman is suggestive. D has possibly reshaped this story into a law designed for didactic, deterrent purposes. The account in Num. xxv of the more general apostasy when the Israelites were executed for worshiping foreign gods records that a public example was made of the idolaters (vs. 4). D's law concludes with a statement of public warning that all Israel hear and fear the example cited in the law.

In the case of the final law, that concerning instigation within a city, there is no specific link with the earlier traditions. A generalizing tendency, based both on such traditions and on D's own concerns, could account for this law.[11]

Body Marks for the Dead: xiv. 1, 2

(1) You are the sons of the Lord your God; you shall not cut yourselves or make any baldness on your foreheads for the dead. (2) For thou art a people holy to the Lord thy God, and the

[11] M. Weinfeld, *Deuteronomy and the Deuteronomic School* (Oxford, 1972), pp. 91–100, presents an impressive list of correlations (especially in language) between the idolatry laws in xiii and the material relating to seditious, political acts in the Assyrian state treaties, especially the seventh century B.C. Esarhaddon treaty. However, in accounting for the religious concerns of the D material as against the political concerns of the Assyrian material it is not sufficient to draw attention, as Weinfeld does, to political elements (p. 92) in the biblical material and religious elements (p. 85) in the Assyrian. D's reflection on native Israelite history, probably the Balaam traditions, is a key factor in the presentation of his idolatry laws.

Lord has chosen thee to be a people for his own possession, out of all the peoples that are on the face of the earth.

Interpreters have connected this law with the food laws that come after it in D's code, despite the fact that there is no specific association other than a common concern that Israel should be a people specially related to Yahweh, keeping itself free from certain contaminations. Two factors have encouraged interpreters to see a connection. First, the traditional chapter division separates the law on body marks for the dead from the preceding idolatry laws and places it before the food laws. Second, that part of the motive clause which states that Israel is a people holy to God is repeated in xiv. 21a, after the prohibition against eating an animal corpse. It is possible to read this motive clause as referring not only to this prohibition but also to all the preceding food laws (xiv. 3–20).[12]

The original connection of this law concerning the dead, however, is with the preceding laws on instigation to idolatry. In xiii. 16ff. (*15*ff.) there are instructions about submitting the inhabitants of an idolatrous city to the ban. All of them are to be struck dead with the sword. The motivation for D's mourning law may lie in his realization that the inhabitants of such a city, even though idolatrous and slain by the sword, may be mourned by fellow Israelites and that mourning for a brother, son, daughter, wife, or neighbor put to death for instigation to idolatry would be even more likely. His law would then mean that there must be no mourning of the idolaters in the customary manner, namely, by cutting the flesh and marking the forehead. The law does not pro-

---

[12] This motive clause, however, appears on each occasion after a law dealing specifically with the dead, a dead person (vs. 1) and a dead animal (vs. 21). In each case, moreover, there is an underlying contrast with a foreign element. In xiv. 1 there must be no mourning for the dead because they had worshiped foreign gods (see following discussion in the text); and in xiv. 21, while the Israelite must not eat the animal corpse the sojourner may eat it or it may be sold to the foreigner.

hibit the rites of mourning—indeed, they are the normal way of showing respect for the dead—but prohibits mourning for these idolaters. To mourn them would bring about contamination, since the magical rites establish a mysterious sympathy between the living and the dead.

A parallel in Jer. xvi supports this interpretation since it shows a concern similar to one voiced in Deut. xiii. In Jeremiah, there is a warning not to make marriages with an apostate people.[13] Jeremiah prophesies the extermination of the apostates, who will die by the sword and by famine. Mourning these apostates is prohibited (Jer. xvi. 5, 6) and, as in Deut. xiv. 1, there is to be no cutting oneself and making oneself bald for them. God denies his peace, mercy, and compassion to these people because they have served other gods and forsaken him and his law (Jer. xvi. 5, 11). A comparison may be made with the warning in D against contact after the ban with anything belonging to the apostates, so that God will turn from his anger and show compassion. The parallel between Jeremiah and D supports the assumption that D's mourning law is associated with the preceding idolatry laws. The disgrace attached to those who receive no mourning or burial is well described in Jer. xvi. 6–8, Ezek. xxiv. 15–23, Ps. lxxix. 3.[14]

D's mourning law is therefore part of the revision and expansion of xii. 2–4 (foreign worship). Interestingly, the words in the law about Israel being a people holy to God, his own possession out of all the peoples on the earth, occur also in vii. 6. There they are stated in the context of the command to destroy the idolatrous nations, to break down their altars, and to dash in pieces their pillars. The same command is repeated in xii. 2–4.

[13] The specific parallel to this warning is in Deut. vii. 3.

[14] Jer. xvi. 7, like Deut. xiv. 1, uses the singular participle "the dead," in reference to dead idolaters. Ezek. xxiv. 17 uses the plural participle again in reference to those not to be mourned.

Commentators have understood the D mourning law as a reference to the dead in general. A. Bertholet realizes that Jer. xvi indicates that the custom of cutting oneself and shaving one's forehead was normal mourning practice in Israel.[15] Failing, however, to notice the affinity between Deut. xiii. 13ff. (*12*ff.) and Jer. xvi, he regards the D law as later than Jeremiah and probably dependent upon the law in Lev. xix. 28. The Leviticus law, however, which is a general and quite differently worded prohibition against mourning marks on the body for the dead, has a basis different from the D law.

Food Laws: xiv. 3–21

(3) Thou shalt not eat any abominable thing. (4) These are the animals thou mayest eat: the ox, the sheep, the goat, the hart, the gazelle. . . . (21) You shall not eat anything that dies of itself; thou mayest give it to the alien who is within thy towns, that he may eat it, or thou mayest sell it to a foreigner; for thou art a people holy to the Lord thy God. Thou shalt not boil a kid in its mother's milk.

The section xii. 29–xiv. 2 (on idolatry) constitutes a re-survey and enlargement of the instruction in xii. 2–4 (on foreign worship). The food laws return to, and begin an expansion of, the subject matter of xii. 5–28: the requirements of offerings, tithes, and firstlings at the chosen place, the command to eat and rejoice there, and the permission to eat within the towns, or gates. These topics are enlarged upon throughout xiv. 3–xvi. 17, a section that begins with the food laws and ends with the feast laws. Although certain laws in this expansion section—the seventh year release of the debt and the release of slaves—might not appear to fit this revision pattern, they too arise from the resurvey of xii. 5–28, but in conjunction with a reworking of M laws.[16] The trigger

---

[15] *Kurzer Hand-Commentar zum Alten Testament, Deuteronomium* (Tübingen, 1899), p. 44. *Cf.* F. Horst, *Gottes Recht* (Munich, 1961), pp. 61, 62.

[16] As we have seen, D's debt release law reworks the M law on the release of the land's produce; D's slave law, unlike the M slave law,

for the food laws is the series of commands in xii about eating at the chosen place or within the gates. Specifically, the statements in xii. 15b, 22 about how, within the gates, the unclean and clean alike may eat flesh, such as that of the gazelle and the hart, leads to the development of laws on clean and unclean animals at xiv. 3ff.

A similar law occurs in Lev. xi. Driver points to a difference, however; the clean animals are only defined in Lev. xi. 3, while in D they are both defined (vs. 6) and exemplified (vss. 4, 5). This difference shows a development over time. Ordinarily, examples of things with something in common are recognized before there emerges a definition of what constitutes the common element. Once the definition is arrived at, the need to list the examples can be dispensed with. D, which lists examples of clean animals followed by a definition, reflects the middle stage of the process; Lev. xi, where the definition alone is found, the last.

Driver also identifies texts where the animals listed in D, other than the common domestic animals given first in the list, are also found.[17] Most of these texts are wisdom or poetical ones. It is possible that xiv. 4, which mentions the common clean domestic animals, belongs to an earlier stage of the law and that xiv. 5, which lists the less common animals, was added later. In view of D's wisdom affinities and the fact that other mentions of these animals occur largely in wisdom or poetical texts, this is not unlikely. Only a small group would be acquainted with the less common animals. R. Gordis points out that the frequent mention of game animals in wisdom material is an indication that only the upper

---

contains directions for the generous provision of food to a departing slave. D's interest in food is thus consistent with his revision pattern.

[17] *Deuteronomy*, ICC, p. 159. For a discussion of the relationship between both lists and arguments for the direct influence of Lev. xi on D, see W. L. Moran, "The Literary Connection between Lv. 11, 13–19 and Dt. 14, 12–18," *CBQ*, 28 (1966), 271–77. Moran does not deny the validity of M. Noth's view (*Leviticus* [Eng. ed., London, 1965], p. 91) that in general Deut. xiv. 3–21 is the earlier text.

classes would be in a position to eat such meat.[18] He even suggests that only these classes could afford to eat animal meat at
all. His observation may also apply to D and his circle of
pupils who belong to an educated class.

Annual Tithes: xiv. 22–27

(22) Thou shalt tithe all the yield of thy seed, which comes
forth from the field year by year. (23) And before the Lord thy
God, in the place which he will choose, to make his name dwell
there, thou shalt eat the tithe of thy grain, of thy wine, and of
thine oil, and the firstlings of thy herd and flock; that thou
mayest learn to fear the Lord thy God always. (24) And if the
way is too long for thee, so that thou art not able to bring the
tithe, when the Lord thy God blesses thee, because the place
is too far from thee, which the Lord thy God chooses, to set his
name there, (25) then thou shalt turn it into money, and bind
up the money in thine hand, and go to the place which the Lord
thy God chooses, (26) and spend the money for whatever thou
desirest, oxen, or sheep, or wine or strong drink, whatever thine
appetite craves; and thou shalt eat there before the Lord thy
God and rejoice, thou and thine household. (27) And thou shalt
not forsake the Levite who is within thy towns, for he has no
portion or inheritance with thee.

This law, concerning the annual tithes from the produce of
the field and the firstlings, continues the revision and enlargement of xii. 5–28. As we have seen, the food laws of xiv. 3–
21 are suggested by the permission of xii. 15 to eat flesh such
as the gazelle and the hart within the gates. Following this
permission is the contrasting prohibition in xii. 17 that the
tithes of the grain, wine, and oil, plus the firstlings, plus
certain other offerings, are not to be eaten within the gates.
In xiv. 22–27 D returns to the material of xii. 17 and formulates a command to eat the tithes and firstlings at the chosen
place. He then discusses the too distant location of the chosen
place, a problem previously touched on in xii. 21, where, in

[18] "Social Background in the Wisdom Literature," *HUCA,* 18 (1944),
92ff.

regard to the eating of nonsacred meat, permission is given
to eat it within the gates if the chosen place is too far.
In the tithe law in xiv. 22–27 permission to eat the tithes
and firstlings within the gates is not given, but the concession
is made that, if the place to which the tithes are to be taken is
too far off, their equivalent in money may be spent at the
chosen place on whatever is desired.

D's method of presenting legal instruction by the repetition
and expansion of previously stated material is again clear in
this law on the annual tithes, and the method explains an
apparent anomaly. The mention of the firstlings in the tithe
law appears to be out of place. C. Steuernagel suggests that
it is an insertion from the notice in xii. 17.[19] However, once
the D revision pattern is recognized, this command about the
firstlings can be seen to be not an insertion but a continuation of the instruction already given. The pattern is as follows: xii. 17 is a general law concerning the offerings at the
chosen place, with the tithes, firstlings, votive offerings, freewill offerings, and "hand" offerings all being mentioned. The
law in xiv. 22–27 takes up this law again, refers to the tithes
and the firstlings, but concentrates on the tithes. Eventually,
in xv. 19–23, after laws on the money debt and on slaves,
comes a particular law on the firstlings. Similarly, a general
concern with the Levites voiced in xii. 12, 18, 19 and xiv.
22ff. is narrowed to a law on them in xviii.

Triennial Tithe and Seventh Year Release of Debt:
xiv. 28–xv. 11

(28) At the end of every three years thou shalt bring forth
all the tithe of thy produce in the same year, and lay it up
within thy towns; (29) and the Levite, because he has no portion
or inheritance with thee, and the sojourner, the fatherless, and
the widow, who are within thy towns, shall come and eat and be
filled; that the Lord thy God may bless thee in all the work of
thine hands that thou doest.

[19] *Das Deuteronomium* (2d ed., Göttingen, 1923), p. 107.

(1) At the end of every seven years thou shalt grant a release. (2) And this is the manner of the release: every creditor shall release what he has lent to his neighbor; he shall not exact it of his neighbor, his brother, because the Lord's release has been proclaimed. (3) Of a foreigner thou mayest exact it; but whatever of thine is with thy brother thine hand shall release. (4) But there will be no poor among thee, for the Lord will bless thee in the land which the Lord thy God gives thee for an inheritance to possess, (5) if only thou wilt obey the voice of the Lord thy God, being careful to do all this commandment which I command thee this day. (6) For the Lord thy God will bless thee, as he promised thee, and thou shalt lend to many nations, but thou shalt not borrow; and thou shalt rule over many nations, but they shall not rule over thee.

(7) If there is among thee a poor man, one of thy brethren, in any of thy towns within thy land which the Lord thy God gives thee, thou shalt not harden thine heart or shut thine hand against thy poor brother, (8) but thou shalt open thine hand to him, and lend him sufficient for his need, whatever it may be. (9) Take heed lest there be a base thought in thine heart, and thou sayest, "The seventh year, the year of release is near," and thine eye be hostile to thy poor brother, and thou givest him nothing, and he cry to the Lord against thee, and it be sin in thee. (10) Thou shalt give to him freely, and thine heart shall not be grudging when thou givest to him; because for this the Lord thy God will bless thee in all thy work and in all that thou undertakest. (11) For the poor will never cease out of the land; therefore I command thee, Thou shalt open wide thine hand to thy brother, to the needy and to the poor, in the land.

A noticeable feature of D's presentation is that a law applying to the chosen place complements one applying to the other places in the land, which are termed "within the gates." [20] The annual tithe applies to the chosen place, while the triennial tithe applies within the gates. The same complementary relationship may be found in xii. 5–14 and xii. 15; xii. 17 and xii. 18; xii. 21 and xii. 26; xv. 20 and xv. 22; xviii. 1–5 and xviii. 6–8.

A triennial tithe is related to an annual tithe, but a rela-

[20] See Appendix.

tionship with the law on the seventh year release of debts can also be seen. Each law has the same formal opening: "At the end of *x* years." The relationship can be explained in terms of two earlier M laws, which D reworks. It is generally accepted that the D law concerning the release of the money debt in the seventh year is related to the earlier M law concerning the release of the land's produce for the poor in the seventh year.[21] What is not realized is that the author of the M laws associated the M law on release of produce (Ex. xxiii. 10, 11) with the corresponding law in his parallel list, namely, Ex. xxii. 24–26 (25–27), on lending to the poor and on oppressive pledging (see p. 63). Already in M, then, the seventh year release of the land's produce was associated with lending to the poor and taking a poor man's garment in pledge. The associative factor was the general concern of justice for the poor and the relief of their condition. D's law on the release of the money debt in the seventh year and on not withholding a loan from the poor is derived from a reworking of these earlier M laws.[22] The two M laws and the D law share a concern for the poor. D includes an expansive statement about how there will be no poor in the land and warns against refusing to lend to the poor because of the proximity of the seventh year.

[21] The M law uses the verb שָׁמַט, "to release," while the D law uses the action noun שְׁמִטָּה. The difference is significant. An action noun is usually formed at a stage later than the verb and is derived from it. Moreover, it is a stage that reveals a greater degree of reflection and abstraction than exists when only the verb is in use. Whether or not D is the first to use this action noun (it occurs nowhere else in the bible) cannot be determined. However, D's idealistic thinking, which is especially prominent in his release law, and his reflective activity in forming the law out of two earlier M laws, provide the sort of fertile conditions in which action nouns originate. On their formation in all areas of human engagement, see D. Daube, *Aspects of Roman Law* (Edinburgh, 1969), pp. 11–63.

[22] For remissions of commercial debts in Assyria, and official and royal acts proclaiming them, see under the heading *andurāru* in the *Assyrian Dictionary* (Chicago, 1968), I, A, pt. II, 115–17.

In spite of M's influence, however, D rejects part of the M law; there is no seventh year release of the land's produce in D. The replacement of the M institution by the seventh year release of the money debt probably reflects a more commercial way of life in D's time. But D does not reject the M law entirely. The laws concerning the annual and triennial tithes precede the D law concerning the money debt. Each year, a tenth of all the produce of the seed is to be eaten at the chosen place. Every three years this tithe is to be kept within the gates and given to the Levite, the sojourner, the widow, and the orphan. This triennial tithe for the poor thus appears to be a further development by D of the M law's intention to provide for the relief of the poor by a periodic release of the land's produce. No definite proof exists that the triennial tithe law is D's creation. Its terms, however, are unique to D. Moreover, the fact that it comes immediately before the D law on the release of the money debt, which itself stems from the M law, is a strong indication that D's triennial tithe law is related to this only partly rejected M law. There is certainly a considerable difference between the release of the whole produce of the land and the release of a tithe of the produce. Given the doctrinaire element and social idealism in his writing, D's thinking in terms of a tithe may perhaps be due to his notion of the abundance of material things (*cf.* Lev. xxv. 21), which would ensure that the tithe was sufficient for all the needs of the Levite and the poor, rather than to any idea that releasing the whole produce of the land would be impractical.

Slaves: xv. 12–18 (for a statement of the law, see p. 54)

The laws on the triennial tithe and debt release indicate how D is influenced by M laws as well as by the process of expanding upon his own earlier material. It is the expansion process that explains why D generally pays scant attention to the order and sequence of the M laws. In his slave law, however, D follows closely the sequence of laws in M. In M, a law on the sabbath comes after the law on the release of the produce of the land (Ex. xxiii. 10–12); in D, a law on slave release, and not one on the sabbath, comes after the law on the release of the money debt. This sequence in D can be easily accounted for. In the M law on the sabbath, the son of the bondmaid is singled out (along with the sojourner and animals) as deserving rest from work. This bondmaid's son is almost certainly the perpetual slave issuing from the union of a slave and the wife given him by his master, as described in the M law on slaves (Ex. xxi. 2–6). D has followed this connection and therefore reworks the M slave law at this point. Such a slave as the son of the bondmaid is not found in D because for D there could not exist the perpetual slave of M. The M ruling whereby the wife given to a slave and the children born to them do not go out with the slave at the end of six years is probably rejected by D. In the D code, both male and female slave may seek release after six years. Accordingly, the category of perpetual slave mentioned in Ex. xxi. 4 does not exist for D, and the special commendation in Ex. xxiii. 12 about the bondmaid's son requiring rest on the sabbath is not relevant. A second reason for the omission of the law on the sabbath at this point is that D already has such a law in v. 12ff. (It is interesting that D's law on the sabbath appeals to the memory of the slavery in Egypt, unlike the corresponding law in Ex. xx. 8ff., which refers to the creation of the world. This difference can be attributed to the influence on D of the other sabbath law in Ex. xxiii. 12, with its special interest in a slave's rest.) [23]

D thus moves straight into his slave law. While it is clear that the M law on slaves influences D's law, there are dif-

[23] The sabbath command is thus for the first time associated with the exodus; at least in explicit terms, the law on the release of slaves (Deut. xv) is similarly associated. The laws on the firstlings and on passover and matzoth have already in the JE tradition been associated with the exodus.

ferences. A main one is that D confines his law to the male and female slave, without touching, as M does, on the matter of a male slave's marrying while in service. D's narrower focus may be accounted for by his restricting himself to aspects of a matter previously touched on in his own presentation. In xii. 12, 18 the male and the female slave are mentioned in connection with a household's duties in sacrificial matters; they are thought of in terms of their working relationship to the household—and the same is true of the D slave law. In D's law, too, the slave speaks of loving his master and his house, which is different from Ex. xxi. 5, where the house is not mentioned.

Firstlings: xv. 19–23

(19) All the firstling males that are born of thy herd and flock thou shalt consecrate to the Lord thy God; thou shalt do no work with the firstlings of thy herd, nor shear the firstlings of thy flock. (20) Thou shalt eat it, thou and thy household, before the Lord thy God year by year at the place which the Lord will choose. (21) But if it has any blemish, if it is lame or blind, or has any serious blemish whatever, thou shalt not sacrifice it to the Lord thy God. (22) Thou shalt eat it within thy towns; the unclean and the clean alike may eat it, as though it were a gazelle or a hart. (23) Only thou shalt not eat its blood; thou shalt pour it out on the ground like water.

D's method is again clear: he returns to the notice on firstlings in xii. 17 and now presents a separate law concerning them. Its directions for the blemished firstlings are the same as those in xii. 15, 16, 20ff. The annual tithe law also alludes to them (xiv. 23) but does not deal with them fully.

The corresponding M law (Ex. xxii. 29, *30*) differs in some respects. First, D uses the generic term בקר, whereas M speaks specifically of the שור. D's tendency is toward the general statement of a law. However, D does specify certain rules for the firstlings of the ox and sheep—the two animals mentioned in M. Second, M speaks of giving the first-born to

God, whereas D uses the more technical term "to set apart." A reason for the difference in terminology may be that "to give," unlike "to set apart," suggests the indiscriminate giving of all firstlings to God. In fact, the M rule must at one time have intended this. Whereas M makes no distinction between types of firstlings, D distinguishes between blemished and unblemished. Perhaps, however, such a sharp contrast should not be drawn in this respect between M and D. The succeeding M law (Ex. xxii. 30, *31*) says, "You shall be men consecrated to me; therefore you shall not eat any flesh that is torn by beasts in the field," implying an awareness of what is fit for eating. The appearance of this law after the one on the firstlings does not warrant the view that the latter intended, at least at the time of the present redaction, the indiscriminate giving of all firstlings. Third, there is a difference concerning the time for handing over the firstlings. In M, they are handed over on the eighth day. This rule can no longer apply in D because the firstlings are neither to be worked nor sheared—a puzzling ruling if they are to be killed after a life of only eight days. Rather, they are to be presented year by year at the chosen place, but the exact time is not stated. The indication, however, since the law in D's code and in other codes (Ex. xiii. 2, 11ff., xxxiv. 18ff.) is closely joined with the law on matzoth, is that the firstlings were to be presented in the month of Abib.

The Three Annual Feasts: xvi. 1–17

(1) Observe the month of Abib, and keep the passover to the Lord thy God; for in the month of Abib the Lord thy God brought thee out of Egypt by night. (2) And thou shalt offer the passover sacrifice to the Lord thy God, from the flock or the herd, at the place which the Lord will choose, to make his name dwell there. (3) Thou shalt eat no leavened bread with it; seven days thou shalt eat it with unleavened bread, the bread of affliction—for thou camest out of the land of Egypt in hurried flight —that all the days of thy life thou mayest remember the day

when thou camest out of the land of Egypt. (4) No leaven shall be seen with thee in all thy territory for seven days; nor shall any of the flesh which thou sacrificest on the evening of the first day remain all night until morning. (5) Thou mayest not offer the passover sacrifice within any of thy towns which the Lord thy God gives thee; (6) but at the place which the Lord thy God will choose, to make his name dwell in it, there thou shalt offer the passover sacrifice, in the evening at the going down of the sun, at the time thou camest out of Egypt. (7) And thou shalt boil it and eat it at the place which the Lord thy God will choose; and in the morning thou shalt turn and go to thy tents. (8) For six days thou shalt eat unleavened bread; and on the seventh day there shall be a solemn assembly to the Lord thy God; thou shalt do no work on it.

(9) Thou shalt count seven weeks; begin to count the seven weeks from the time thou first put the sickle to the standing grain. (10) Then thou shalt keep the feast of weeks to the Lord thy God with the tribute of a freewill offering from thine hand, which thou shalt give as the Lord thy God blesses thee; (11) and thou shalt rejoice before the Lord thy God, thou and thy son and thy daughter, thy manservant and thy maidservant, the Levite who is within thy towns, the sojourner, the fatherless, and the widow who are in thy midst, at the place which the Lord thy God will choose, to make his name dwell there. (12) Thou shalt remember that thou wast a slave in Egypt; and thou shalt be careful to observe these statutes.

(13) Thou shalt keep the feast of booths seven days, when thou makest thine ingathering from thy threshing floor and thy wine press; (14) thou shalt rejoice in thy feast, thou and thy son and thy daughter, thy manservant and thy maidservant, the Levite, the sojourner, the fatherless, and the widow who are within thy towns. (15) For seven days thou shalt keep the feast to the Lord thy God at the place which the Lord will choose; because the Lord thy God will bless thee in all thy produce and in all the work of thine hands, so that thou wilt be altogether joyful.

(16) Three times a year all thy males shall appear before the Lord thy God at the place which he will choose: at the feast of unleavened bread, at the feast of weeks, and at the feast of booths. They shall not appear before the Lord empty-handed; (17) every man shall give as he is able, according to the blessing of the Lord thy God which he has given thee.

The three laws on the feasts of passover and matzoth, weeks, and booths conclude one series of laws based on an expansion of the material in xii. 5–28. Each feast is celebrated at the chosen place, and the specific section in xii which is being elaborated on at this point is xii. 26, 27: the demand to take the holy things and votive offerings to the chosen place. The significance of the fact that the feast laws conclude a revision of xii. 5–28 is that the offerings at these feasts probably consisted of the firstlings and the tithes of the grain, wine, and oil. Hence the laws on these dues in xiv. 22–27, xv. 19–23 can be considered as leading up to the presentation of the feast laws. In that they imply much of what has already been taught, the feast laws represent an end point in the expanded instruction of xii. 5–28. It is noteworthy that the concluding words of the passage—xvi. 16, 17—on how all males shall appear three times a year at the feasts, which are then named, constitute in themselves a summary statement about the requirements for the three feasts. In other words, the feast laws represent some kind of conclusion to preceding material, and xvi. 16, 17, in turn, are a concise summary of the feast laws. This summary character is further evidenced by the fact that xvi. 16, 17 are drawn from the similar commands in Ex. xxiii. 14–17, which in M do not serve a summary purpose.

It is widely agreed by scholars that D changes the character of the passover feast by combining it with the feast of unleavened bread.[24] In Ex. xii. 2ff., 21ff. the passover is private and domestic; in D it is public. One feature of D's passover has not been evaluated before. After eating the passover sacrifice, the people, in the morning, have "to turn and go to their tents" (xvi. 7). On this day there is a solemn assembly and no work is done. The pervasive idea here, which largely explains the unique character of D's passover, is his notion

---

[24] See, for example, R. de Vaux, *Ancient Israel: Its Life and Institutions* (2d Eng. ed., New York, 1965), pp. 485ff., and F. Horst, *Gottes Recht,* pp. 106, 107.

of Israel's "rest." Israel seeks a place of rest (xii. 9, xxv. 19), and secure settlement in the land will be that rest. D contains a speech by Moses about entering the land, and the laws are given with this *first* unique entry and settlement in mind. The passover law likewise deals with this special, first ever occasion—hence its change in character and its novelty.

On this occasion, all Israel, as it enters its rest, is to celebrate the passover at the chosen place of God's rest. The passover is combined with the feast of unleavened bread because both are re-enactments of the disturbance, unrest, and homelessness of Israel in Egypt and the exodus from there. This meaning already existed in the tradition. What is new in D is the symbolic significance given to the morning after, the turning to the tents. This action celebrates the first settlement and rest in the land. Whether D intends his passover to be re-enacted annually in this new form is not clear, for D is only concerned with the one future event of entering the land. Some evidence suggests that it is to be a single occasion. In xvi. 16 there is reference to the annual repetition of three feasts at the chosen place; the passover is *not* mentioned. Noting this, commentators have suggested that D is inconsistent in working with the older sources.[25] However, it is conceivable that D's emphasis on the particular event when Israel obtains settlement and security in the land implies a public celebration of the passover on this occasion but a private, domestic celebration thereafter.

The act of turning and going to the tents in D has an interesting parallel in Josh. xxii. 1ff. Joshua tells the Reubenites, Gadites, and Manassites that God has given rest to their brother Israelites and that they can now "turn and go to their tents" (exactly as in Deut. xvi. 7) and to their possession east of the Jordan—in sum, to their own "rest." [26] The idea in D

[25] See, for example, G. von Rad, *Deuteronomy* (Eng. ed., London, 1966), pp. 113, 114.
[26] "To turn" and "tents" have more than literal meanings. Driver,

is the same. This special passover will celebrate Israel's first
entry into the land and the securing of its rest there.[27] The
same notion of "rest" also underlies D's solemn assembly on
the seventh day, when no work is to be done. The thought of
the Chronicler offers an instructive parallel. Solomon, a man
of "rest," who because of this fact was allowed to build the
house of God (I Chron. xxii. 6ff.), held a solemn assembly on
the eighth day of its dedication (II Chron. vii. 9). The people
were then sent away to their "tents" (II Chron. vii. 10). This
journey to their homes is symbolic of Israel's entering its
"rest" (cf. I Chron. xxiii. 25). God's home, the temple, is
likewise his resting place (II Chron. vi. 41). It is interesting
to recall, because of D's notion of rest, how the sabbath law
of Ex. xxiii. 12 is not treated by D after his law on the release
of the money debt. M's sabbath law suggests instead D's treatment of the M slave release law. However, the idea of rest
implicit in the sabbath command seems to be revealed in
D's passover law. Two other affinities between the sabbath
law and D's passover law are noteworthy. First, D's sabbath
command in v. 12 has the same opening form as his passover
law; each begins with the infinitive absolute imperative:

Deuteronomy, ICC, p. 194, points out that פֶּסַח is a favorite word
with D. Noteworthy for D's context are Jer. vi. 4, about the day turning into night and doom (contrast the contrary situation implied in D
and Joshua); Deut. xxxi. 20, where Israel, having come into the land,
turns to other gods (punishment will be the loss of security); Job xxiv.
18, where no one turns to the vineyards of the wicked (the latter's
place in the land is without security). Likewise, the word "tents" in D
does not just represent a survival from Israel's nomadic existence, if
indeed it does at all (see H. J. Kraus, *Worship in Israel* [Eng. ed.,
Oxford, 1966], pp. 162ff.), but is also proverbial for a secure home or
place in the land. For this proverbial use, cf. Job viii. 22, xviii. 14,
xxix. 4; Prov. xiv. 11. For the interpretation of "tents" in Deut. xvi as
those of the ritual exodus into the desert at the New Year festival, see
J. B. Segal, *The Hebrew Passover* (Oxford, 1963), pp. 210, 211, cf.
p. 88.

[27] Cf. Josh. v. 10–12: the people's passover at Gilgal, the first in the
new land, and the end of the exodus.

"Keep the Sabbath day," and "Keep the month of Abib." [28]
Second, on the seventh day of passover there is an assembly
and, as on the seventh day of the week, no work is done. The
earlier JE legislation (Ex. xiii. 6) does not mention a rest
from work on the seventh day of matzoth. The explanation
of these affinities probably lies in D's method of creating
new laws, or new forms of old laws. One law is brought into
closer relation with another for this purpose. D's passover law
with its idea of rest is related to, and influenced by, the
sabbath law. D's tendency to create links between one law
and another is manifest in his attempt to associate events of
the exodus with as many laws as possible.[29]

Summary

The two main elements of the method by which D presents
laws are visible in the initial part of his code. D presents
legal material, then later returns to it and expands it. In this
expansion, material from other sources is also woven in.
These other sources are D's preceding historical and hortatory speeches, earlier traditions found in Genesis–Numbers,
and earlier M laws.

Concisely, the application of D's method is as follows: (*i*)
xii. 2–4 (foreign worship) are expanded upon in xii. 29–xiv.
2 (idolatry); xii. 5–28 (proper worship) are expanded upon in
xiv. 3–xvi. 17 (food laws, feasts). (*ii*) Underlying the idolatry
laws is the influence of the tradition about the Israelites'
apostasy to Baal at Peor and the related tradition about the
role of the diviner Balaam (Deut. iv. 3, 4; Num. xxii–xxiv,
xxv, xxxi). (*iii*) D also reviews a number of M laws, namely,
Ex. xxi. 2–6, xxii. 24–26, 29, 30 (*25–27, 30, 31*), xxiii. 10–12,
14–17, 19.

[28] שמור occurs three other times in D (vi. 17, xi. 22, xxvii. 1) but
only in the general sense of keeping the commandments. The M laws
on unleavened bread and on the sabbath (Ex. xiii. 3, xx. 8) have זכור,
"remember."
[29] See n. 23 above.

In the presentation of his laws, D initially works from a base that contains his ideological views, and builds upon it. His feast laws, for example, are based on the view that if Israelite society orders its ritual life aright, an atmosphere of well-being and public enjoyment will prevail. A complex relationship exists between the foundation upon which D builds and the results of the building process. On the one hand, D builds in a wide ranging, eclectic way. On the other hand, because he constantly returns to his earlier material, limits are imposed, the presentation of any one law may be molded or checked by a preceding law, and common features emerge between one part of the code and another.

5. Repetition: xvi. 18–xix. 21

The repetitive style of D is a characteristic of the entire work. But this repetitiveness is not just a style of writing. It extends to the way in which the laws are presented. Many of the laws discussed so far (xii. 29–xiv. 29, xv. 19–xvi. 17) are dependent, in terms of the order of their appearance, on preceding laws (xii. 1–28), for they repeat and expand upon this earlier material. As we shall see below, the process is now repeated; the laws in xii. 1ff. are taken up again and further expanded upon in xvi. 18–xix. 21.

The Appointment of Judges and Officers: xvi. 18–20

(18) Thou shalt appoint judges and officers in all thy towns which the Lord thy God gives thee, according to thy tribes; and they shall judge the people with righteous judgment. (19) Thou shalt not pervert justice; thou shalt not show partiality; and thou shalt not take a bribe, for a bribe blinds the eyes of the wise and subverts the cause of the righteous. (20) Justice, and only justice, thou shalt follow, that thou mayest live and inherit the land which the Lord thy God gives thee.

Another revision of xii. 1ff. begins. The opening exhortation of the code (xii. 1) is to obey all the laws about to be given. D's law on appointing judges and officers for the proper administration of justice can be considered as a particular development of this opening general exhortation. The relationship becomes clearer when the following laws (xvi. 21ff.) are seen also to connect with the material in xii. 1ff.

Another connection should also be made. The beginning of

D (i. 9–18) contains a historical account of Moses' command-ing the people to choose leaders and judges. His address to the judges there is very similar to D's law on the judges (which is also to be understood as spoken by Moses). It may be assumed that the law alludes to this narrative account, particularly since the law's motive clause promises the inheri-tance of the land and this promise recalls the historical situa-tion in i. 8, when Israel was commanded to possess the land and to appoint leaders and judges (i. 9ff.).

A similar M law (Ex. xxiii. 7, 8) is also an address to judges. The M warnings against making a false charge and slaying the innocent are not found in the D law. However, the suc-ceeding words of the M law appear verbatim in D, with the one exception that the phrase "the clear-sighted ones" is replaced by "the eyes of the wise." D's prohibition against taking a bribe is given a typical D counterpart positive com-mand, "Justice, justice thou shalt follow." [1]

Both the D narrative history (i. 16, 17) and the D law (xvi. 18–20) contain what is clearly an address to judges. Formally, the address is still directed to the people, but the words at this point are from an address to a smaller circle, namely judges. It is probable that D's instruction is directed to those who are to become judges. The literary convention of an address by the aged Moses to the people of Israel may conceal a link with education in the narrower sense of young men at school.

Aspects of Worship: Asherah, Massebah, Blemished Sacrifices: xvi. 21, 22, xvii. 1

(21) Thou shalt not plant any tree as an Asherah beside the altar of the Lord thy God which thou shalt make.

---

[1] For the same iterative use of words, *cf.* Eccles. vii. 24, "deep, very deep," and Prov. xx. 14, "it is bad, bad." J. Muilenburg, "Hebrew Rhetoric: Repetition and Style," *SVT*, 1 (1953), 97ff., refers to this iteration as an effective memory device.

(22) And thou shalt not set up a pillar, which the Lord thy God hates.

(1) Thou shalt not sacrifice to the Lord thy God an ox or a sheep in which is a blemish, any defect whatever; for that is an abomination to the Lord thy God.

These three laws provide a clear indication that the material in xii is being resurveyed for a second time. The destruction of foreign places and their relics of worship, among which are mentioned the massebah and asherah, is commanded in xii. 2–4. There, the concern with idolatry is followed (vss. 5–14) by sacrificial rules for correct worship. In xvi. 21, 22 and xvii. 1 the same sequence and the same concerns are found.

The differences can also be explained. In xii the destruction of the asherah, massebah, and other relics of foreign worship is commanded, but there is no explicit reference to the true Israelite altar that is to be built. In the transition from the rules about the destruction of idolatrous relics to the rules about sacrifice, however, the existence of the true altar is obviously assumed. In his typical fashion, D now, in his further expansion, refers to the Israelite altar and repeats the warning against any association with foreign relics. The presence of what may appear to be unnecessary repetition is explained by the lawgiver's aim to be thorough and comprehensive. The language of the laws confirms this tendency. The asherah is singled out as an example of a prohibited object of worship, but the comprehensive words "any tree" imply such other objects as are mentioned in xii. 2ff. And the phrase "any defect whatever" in reference to the blemished sacrifice is similarly comprehensive and generalizing. A law like xvii. 1 (blemished sacrifices) has already been given (xv. 19–23) in the first revision of the laws of xii; the difference is that xvii.1 applies to any blemished ox or sheep and not just to blemished firstlings.

Idolatry, the Central Tribunal: xvii. 2–13

(2) If there is found among thee, within any of thy towns which the Lord thy God gives thee, a man or woman who does what is evil in the sight of the Lord thy God, in transgressing his covenant, (3) and has gone and served other gods and worshiped them, or the sun or the moon or any of the host of heaven, which I have forbidden, (4) and it is told thee and thou hearest of it; and then thou shalt inquire diligently, and if it is true and certain that such an abominable thing has been done in Israel, (5) then thou shalt bring forth to thy gates that man or woman who has done this evil thing, and thou shalt stone that man or woman to death with stones. (6) On the evidence of two witnesses or of three witnesses he that is to die shall be put to death; a person shall not be put to death on the evidence of one witness. (7) The hand of the witnesses shall be first against him to put him to death, and afterward the hand of all the people. So thou shalt purge the evil from the midst of thee.

(8) If any case arises requiring decision between one kind of homicide and another, one kind of legal right and another, or one kind of assault and another, any case within thy towns which is too difficult for thee, then thou shalt arise and go up to the place which the Lord thy God will choose, (9) and coming to the Levitical priests, and to the judge who is in office in those days, thou shalt consult them, and they shall declare to thee the decision. (10) Then thou shalt do according to what they declare to thee from that place which the Lord will choose; and thou shalt be careful to do according to all that they direct thee; (11) according to the instructions which they give thee, and according to the decision which they pronounce to thee, thou shalt do; thou shalt not turn aside from the verdict which they declare to thee, either to the right hand or to the left. (12) The man who acts presumptuously, by not obeying the priest who stands to minister there before the Lord thy God, or the judge, that man shall die; so thou shalt purge the evil from Israel. (13) And all the people shall hear, and fear, and not act presumptuously again.

The brief laws on the asherah, massebah, and blemished sacrifices in xvi. 21–xvii. 1 stem from a resurvey of material that deals with those matters in an extensive fashion in xii.

2ff. Not so extensively treated in xii is subject matter coming under the rubric of justice. A general exhortation to keep the D laws occurs in xii. 1, but this is followed by laws on idolatry and sacrifice. The elaborate, more detailed concern with "justice" now emerges in the material of xvi. 18ff. First come the laws concerning the appointment of judges and officers and the three brief laws on idolatry and sacrifice; then D continues, not with the substance of idolatry as such, but with a procedural law for administering justice in a case of idolatry within the gates. The direction of D's concern toward matters relating to the administration of justice emerges fully in the law on the central tribunal, which concerns a case too difficult for jurisdiction within the gates.

The important formal link between xvii. 2–13 and xii is the distinction between an infraction that can be judged within the gates and one that must be judged at the central place, which is the same distinction as that which emerged in xii. 15–19 between eating flesh within the gates and eating certain sacrifices at the chosen, central place. For connections in subject matter, the laws in xiii. 2ff. (*1*ff.) must be consulted, with the knowledge that this material is itself an enlargement of material in xii. 2ff. The following points are significant. First, xiii. 2ff. (*1*ff.) concern instigation to idolatry; xvii. 2–7 concern the deed of idolatry itself. (Compare how in xii. 2ff. the asherah is to be destroyed so as not to incite imitation, while in xvi. 21 the actual planting of an asherah is in question.) Second, xiii. 2ff. (*1*ff.) give procedural directions for dealing with instigation to idolatry; xvii. 2–13 concentrate on judicial procedure in a case of idolatry and in a difficult legal case. In xiii. 2ff. (*1*ff.) there is a clear development of the procedure for dealing with the instigator to idolatry. The first law only directs that the prophet or dreamer of dreams be put to death. The next law gives more detailed directions. The hand of the person most closely associated with the instigator has to be first against him to put him to death, followed by the hand of the people. The method of execution, stoning, is also mentioned. Further, the example made of the culprit is held up as a deterrent. The third law details the need for a meticulous enquiry into the case of the idolatrous city: "Then thou shalt inquire and make search and ask diligently; and behold, if it be true and certain . . ." (xiii. 15, *14*). The directions for the systematic destruction of a guilty city are then given. In xvii. 2–13 the instruction on procedure is brought together. In xiii. 13 (*12*) a case of idolatry is reported and this report leads to a judicial enquiry. In xvii. 4 a similar report is received and a similar enquiry initiated. Hence the words of xvii. 4, "Then thou shalt inquire diligently, and if it is true and certain . . ." are almost identical to those of xiii. 15 (*14*). In xvii. 5 the culprit is to be stoned to death and, as in xiii. 10 (*9*), who is to cast the first stone is specified. The rule on witnesses in xvii. 6 is not found in xiii and is a typical D addition to his previously given instruction. Eventually, in xix. 15–21, D presents a specific law concerning witnesses. In the primarily procedural law in xvii. 8–13 (the central tribunal), the terms "to seek, inquire" and "to declare" are used, as in xiii. The evil is purged and the example of the wrongdoer is publicly heeded, again as in xiii.

A historical narrative also influences the compilation of the law on the central tribunal. It has been noted that D's narrative account (i. 9–18) of the appointment of judges and officers may be related to D's law on such appointments. In that narrative Moses directs the judges to bring any insoluble legal case to him so that he, as the chief authority, can decide it. In the law on the central tribunal, D, or rather Moses, likewise commands that if a case is too difficult for decision within the gates—presumably by the judges and officers appointed according to the law in xvi. 18–20—then it must be decided by the chief authority of the Levitical priests and judge at the central place.

There is another interesting link between D's legal and narrative material. The law mentions the man who presumptuously disobeys the decision of the central authority. The narrative, after the account of the appointment of judges and leaders, relates the incident of the presumptuous disobedience of the people when they were commanded by Moses to enter the land (i. 19ff.). On the people's advice, Moses sent out spies. After hearing from the spies, however, the people refused to enter and rebelled against the command, which is attributed to God—פי יהוה אלהיכם (i. 26). (D's law refers to the command, פי, of the torah of the Levitical priests and judge.) Because of their disobedience to a prime authority, the men of that generation were informed that they would not enter the land but would perish (i. 35). Admitting their disobedience, the people then declared their intention to enter. God, however, commanded Moses to forbid them. They again disobeyed the command of God and Moses and "were presumptuous" (זיד) and went up. In the law, the man who acts with presumption (בזדון) by not obeying the chief authority of the priest and judge will die, and the people are to hear of the example and not act presumptuously (זיד) again.

It is clear that the historical episode is responsible for part of the law. A comparison is made between the disobedience of the people to the command of God and Moses and the disobedience of a man, whose example is set before all the people, to the command of the Levitical priests and judge. In each case a severe penalty is imposed. The comparison also illuminates the reference in the law to the Levitical priests and the judge as the ones who embody the central authority. The Levitical priests in D stand in a special, intimate relationship to the deity, and it may be inferred that their authority in this law reflects the authority of the divine command in i. 26. Likewise, the judge in the law has a position corresponding to the special position of Moses, who was to hear the difficult cases of judgment (i. 17). The puzzling variation of the references to the priests (plural in xvii. 9, xix. 17) and the priest (singular in xvii. 12), to the judges (plural in xix. 17) and the judge (singular in xvii. 9), becomes more intelligible in the light of this historical background in which God and Moses have supreme authority. The use of the singular is derived from the association of the priest and the judge with the single authorities of God and Moses. For example, in xvii. 12, the priest (singular) acts as the representative of the sole divine authority. D's law on the prophet (xviii. 15–22) speaks of the prophet being like Moses. Here the judge is thought of as being like him also.

The King and the Levitical Priests: xvii. 14–20, xviii. 1–8

(14) When thou comest to the land which the Lord thy God gives thee, and thou possessest it and dwellest in it, and then sayest, "I will set a king over me, like all the nations that are round about me"; (15) thou mayest indeed set as king over thee him whom the Lord thy God will choose. One from among thy brethren thou shalt set as king over thee; thou mayest not put a foreigner over thee, who is not thy brother. (16) Only he must not multiply horses for himself, or cause the people to return to Egypt in order to multiply horses, since the Lord has said to thee, "Thou shalt never return that way again." (17) And he shall not multiply wives for himself, lest his heart turn away; nor shall he greatly multiply for himself silver and gold. (18) And when he sits on the throne of his kingdom, he shall write for himself in a book a copy of this law, from that which is in charge of the Levitical priests; (19) and it shall be with him, and he shall read in it all the days of his life, that he may learn to fear the Lord his God, by keeping all the words of this law and these statutes, and doing them; (20) that his heart may not be lifted up above his brethren, and that he may not turn aside from the commandment, either to the right hand or to the left; so that he may continue long in his kingdom, he and his children, in Israel.

(1) The Levitical priests, that is, all the tribe of Levi, shall have no portion or inheritance with Israel; they shall eat the offerings by fire to the Lord, and his rightful dues. (2) They shall have no inheritance among their brethren; the Lord is their inheritance as he promised them. (3) And this shall be the priests'

due from the people, from those offering a sacrifice, whether it be ox or sheep: they shall give to the priest the shoulder and the two cheeks and the stomach. (4) The first fruits of thy grain, of thy wine and of thy oil, and the first of the fleece of thy sheep, thou shalt give him. (5) For the Lord thy God has chosen him out of all thy tribes, to stand and minister in the name of the Lord, him and his sons for ever. (6) And if a Levite comes from any of thy towns out of all Israel, where he lives—and he may come when he desires—to the place which the Lord will choose, (7) then he may minister in the name of the Lord his God, like all his fellow-Levites who stand to minister there before the Lord. (8) They shall have equal portions to eat, besides what he receives from the sale of his patrimony.

The material of xii is again responsible for the appearance of these two laws at this point. The formal concern in xii. 15–19 with a matter (animal slaughter) permissible within the gates and a matter (sacrifices) not permissible there, but only at the chosen place, is renewed in xvii. 2–13 on the idolater within the gates and the difficult case at the chosen place. The remaining part (xii. 20–28) of D's first presentation of instruction (xii. 1–28) now exerts a similar formal influence. Like xii. 20ff., the king law uses the form of a request being made and a permission being granted for it. The request in xii. 20 specifies, "When the Lord thy God enlarges thy territory . . . and thou sayest, 'I will eat flesh,'" and the permission is granted in the words, "Thou mayest eat as much flesh as thou desirest." In the case of the king, the request is, "When thou comest to the land . . . and then sayest, 'I will set a king over me, like all the nations that are round about me'"; the permission is, "Thou mayest indeed set as king over thee him whom . . ."

Other comparisons between the king law and xii can be made. First, "to set up" is used both in reference to the king and in xii. 21 in reference to the place where Yahweh sets up his name. Also, Yahweh chooses this place, and he chooses the king. Second, the concessions to eat flesh, as much as is desired, and to set up a king have limiting conditions attached to them that are formally introduced by רק, "only": in xii. 23 the blood is not to be eaten, and in xii. 26 the holy things and the vows are to be taken to the chosen place; likewise, the king is not to multiply horses, wives, and riches.[2] The prohibitions against the blood and against multiplying horses have explanatory clauses. Third, in xii. 25, 28 and in xvii. 20 there are similar reward clauses, introduced by למען, that promise life and well-being.

The drafting of the law on the king owes much to the material in xii. 20ff. However D understandably preserves a continuity in drafting with the immediately preceding laws. In xvii. 12 the presumptuous man does not listen to the priest and judge and disregards the prohibition not to turn aside from their word to the right or left. The king is not to raise his heart above his brethren and not to turn aside from the commandment to the right or left. There is another link in the directions to the king to obey the torah and statutes which the Levitical priests have in their possession. In xvii. 9ff. the Levitical priests, along with the judge, give judgment and directions.

A law on the Levitical priests follows the law on the king and is not out of place in terms of its immediate context. Its presentation, however, is again an expansion of the material in xii concerning the holy things and votive offerings due to the chosen place and the offering of the burnt sacrifices on the altar. The new law concerns the dues to be given to the Levites: the fire offerings, the first fruits, and the first of the fleece. The permission to the Levites from the "gates" to come to the chosen place is granted with the words, "And he may come when he desires," a statement which is probably inspired by the similar one in xii. 20 about the permission to eat flesh within the gates.

[2] I refrain from puzzling over the significance of the order—horses, wives, silver, and gold—except to note that silver is put before gold.

The derivation of the two laws concerning the king and the Levites can be stated as follows. The material in xii. 20–28 has two aspects: the permission for secular slaughter of meat within the towns of Israel, and the direction about the sacred offerings due at the chosen place. The revision of this material has inspired two laws: the permission for secular royal rule in Israel, and the direction about the sacred dues for the Levites.

The role of existing traditions can be detected in the formulation of the laws permitting kingship and secular sacrifice in Israel. These two laws show a remarkable similarity in form despite the lack of common content. The most marked feature is the permissiveness of the language—for example, "And thou sayest, 'I will eat flesh,' because thou cravest flesh, thou mayest eat as much flesh as thou desirest" (xii. 20). This language of permission, with its pattern of request and concession, suggests a background where such requests could be regarded with disfavor. For each law there is such a background, which explains the similarity in language and form between the laws.

In regard to the law concerning the king, commentators point to the opposition to the request for a king in I Sam. viii. 5ff.[3] The elders of Israel asked Samuel to appoint a king to govern them after the fashion of other nations. The request met with strong disfavor; God, it was thought, considered it a rejection of himself, associating it with Israel's history of apostasy since the nation came from Egypt. It is reasonable to assume that D knew this tradition but declined to follow it. In his law, the request is granted, though with reservations, hence the law's concessive language. In view of D's general antagonism to the practices of the surrounding nations, the request that Israel like the other nations should have a

[3] S. R. Driver, *Deuteronomy*, ICC (3d ed., Edinburgh, 1902), pp. 212, 213; C. Steuernagel, *Das Deuteronomium* (2d ed., Göttingen, 1923), p. 118.

king is particularly daring, the granting of it, consequently, all the more concessive, and the expansive language—"Thou mayest indeed set as king over thee him whom"—striking.

D's law permitting the eating of meat similarly hints at a tradition in which a request to eat meat was found offensive. Such a tradition is the story of Israel's craving for meat in Num. xi.[4] There the suggestion is that the people sinned in testing and doubting God's providence, and the didactic psalms, lxxviii. 17ff. and cvi. 14, so interpret it. It is against this contrasting background that the expansive permissiveness of D's law is to be seen. The desire to eat flesh is not regarded with disfavor, as in Num. xi, but is amply indulged.

The influence that the tradition in Num. xi has on the formulation of D's law can be observed in two other specific ways. In formulating his law dealing with the secular slaughter of meat, D uses language that is peculiarly non-legal. The D lawgiver presents the matter in terms of an occasion on which a request is made in the first person: "I will eat flesh" (xii. 20). This way of putting it is accounted for by D's awareness of the incident in Num. xi. 4, 18 when the people made the request, again in the first person: "O that we had flesh to eat." The earlier story describes the people's desire for meat by the word אוה. D also uses this word, followed by נפש, in his law (xii. 15, 20, 21).

It is significant that the Deuteronomic works (II Sam. iii. 21, I Kings xi. 37) use the verb אוה followed by נפש in reference to a king desiring rule. This linguistic parallel strength-

---

[4] G. B. Gray, *Numbers*, ICC (Edinburgh, 1903), pp. 97ff., assigns the story almost entirely to JE. The place where the incident occurred, Kibrath-hattavah (Num. xi. 34, 35), is mentioned in Deut. ix. 22 as the place where the people provoked Yahweh to wrath. Deut. viii. 3 mentions bread only and not flesh in reference to God's feeding the Israelites in the desert. The expansive permission to eat flesh in Deut. xii. 20, in contrast with the anger aroused by the similar request in Num. xi (and Ex. xvi), would account for D's omission of the term "flesh" in viii. 1ff.

ens the evidence that there is a connection between D's law
on the king and his law on eating meat. It is also noteworthy
that the verb אוה and the noun תאוה occur, especially in wisdom material, in both a good sense (Prov. x. 24, xi. 23, xix.
22, Job xxiii. 13) and a bad sense (Prov. xxi. 10, 25, 26, xxiv.
1). Specifically, they are used to denote physical appetite, as
in D (Job xxxiii. 20, Ps. cvi. 14, and lxxviii. 30, in reference
to the incident in Num. xi). Prov. xxiii. 1–3 gives advice on
how to conduct oneself when eating in the presence of a
king.

Finally, the story of the people's craving for meat also contains the account of the appointment of leaders to share
with Moses the burden of ruling the people (Num. xi. 16ff.).
Attention has already been drawn (in Chapter 1) to the dependence, extending to verbal coincidence, of this account
of the appointments with D's account (i. 9–18). The contrast
between D's expansive context and the constricting situation
of the earlier Numbers story was also noted. The question of
ruling the people, which arises in Num. xi, adds significance
to D's connection between his law on the secular provision of
meat in xii. 20ff., dependent upon Num. xi, and his law on
the appointment of a king to rule the people.[5]

Abominable Practices of the Nations: xviii. 9–14

(9) When thou comest into the land which the Lord thy God
gives thee, thou shalt not learn to follow the abominable practices of those nations. (10) There shall not be found among thee
any one who burns his son or his daughter as an offering, any
one who practices divination, a soothsayer, or an augur, or a
sorcerer, (11) or a charmer, or a medium, or a wizard, or a necro-
mancer. (12) For whoever does these things is an abomination
to the Lord; and because of these abominable practices the Lord
thy God is driving them out before thee. (13) Thou shalt be
blameless before the Lord thy God. (14) For these nations, which

[5] J. R. Porter observes that the Pentateuchal traditions depict Moses
as resembling an Israelite king. See his Inaugural Lecture at the University of Exeter (1963), *Moses and Monarchy* (Oxford, 1963).

thou art about to dispossess, give heed to soothsayers and to diviners; but as for thee, the Lord thy God has not allowed thee so to do.

D's material in xii. 29–31, the warning against imitating the nations' abominable practices, is taken up again in this passage, which enumerates the practices. Only one example of the nations' abominable practices is cited in xii. 29–31, namely, the burning of children. This example is now mentioned first in a list of practices that attempts to be exhaustive.

The Prophet: xviii. 15–22

(15) The Lord thy God will raise up for thee a prophet like me from thy midst, from thy brethren—him thou shalt heed— (16) just as thou desired of the Lord thy God at Horeb on the day of the assembly, when thou said, "Let me not hear again the voice of the Lord my God, or see this great fire any more, lest I die." (17) And the Lord said to me, "They have rightly said all that they have spoken. (18) I will raise up for them a prophet like thee from among their brethren; and I will put my words in his mouth, and he shall speak to them all that I command him. (19) And whoever will not give heed to my words which he shall speak in my name, I myself will require it of him. (20) But the prophet who presumes to speak a word in my name which I have not commanded him to speak, or who speaks in the name of other gods, that same prophet shall die." (21) And if thou sayest in thy heart, "How may we know the word which the Lord has not spoken?"—(22) when a prophet speaks in the name of the Lord, if the word does not come to pass or come true, that is a word which the Lord has not spoken; the prophet has spoken it presumptuously, thou needest not be afraid of him.

This law on the prophet takes up in proper order the expansion of xiii. 1 (*xii. 32*), the dictum against adding or subtracting from the commands, and xiii. 2–6 (*1–5*), the treatment of the false prophet and dreamer of dreams. Various background materials have gone into the making of this law on the prophet. The influence of the prohibition in xiii. 1

(*xii. 32*) not to add or subtract from the commands is clear. The speaker in xiii. 1 (*xii. 32*) is Moses, and in xviii. 15 he again speaks in the first person: "A prophet like me." The prohibition in xiii. 1 (*xii. 32*) is addressed to ordinary men, not to prophets; a true prophet may add to the previous commands of Moses. This unique position of the prophet causes D to be concerned now, in xviii. 15–22, about defining the false or true word of a prophet.

The opening command in xviii. 15 to listen to the prophet as if he were Moses appears to be a response to the prohibition in xiii. 4 (*3*) not to listen to the words of the false prophet.

The law (xviii. 16) explicitly recalls a historical background: the day of the assembly at Horeb when the people desired that they no longer hear the voice of God or see the fire, lest they die (iv. 1–40). In this passage, the same prohibition as in xiii. 1 (*xii. 32*), on not adding or subtracting from the commands, occurs (iv. 2) and is followed by mention of what happened to those who had idolatrously worshiped the Baal of Peor. Then follows (iv. 10–14) a specific reference to Horeb and God speaking to the people out of the fire. The remaining section (iv. 15–40) brings out the significance of the revelation at Horeb.

Also relevant to the arrangement of D's laws is the fact that this long didactic section on Horeb (iv. 1–40) is followed by a historical notice about the appointment of the three cities of asylum beyond the Jordan (iv. 41–43). Following the law on the prophet in xviii. 15–22 comes a law concerning the cities of asylum.

The Cities of Asylum: xix. 1–13

(1) When the Lord thy God cuts off the nations whose land the Lord thy God gives thee, and thou dispossessest them and dwellest in their cities and in their houses, (2) thou shalt set apart three cities for thee in the land which the Lord thy God gives thee to possess. (3) Thou shalt prepare the roads, and divide

into three parts the area of the land which the Lord thy God gives thee as a possession, so that any manslayer can flee to them. (4) This is the provision for the manslayer, who by fleeing there may save his life. If any one kills his neighbor unintentionally without having been at enmity with him in time past—(5) as when a man goes into the forest with his neighbor to cut wood, and his hand swings the axe to cut down a tree, and the head slips from the handle and strikes his neighbor so that he dies— he may flee to one of these cities and save his life; (6) lest the avenger of blood in hot anger pursue the manslayer and overtake him, because the way is long, and wound him mortally, though the man did not deserve to die, since he was not at enmity with his neighbor in time past. (7) Therefore I command thee, Thou shalt set apart three cities. (8) And if the Lord thy God enlarges thy border, as he has sworn to thy fathers, and gives thee all the land which he promised to give to thy fathers—(9) provided thou art careful to keep all this commandment, which I command thee this day, by loving the Lord thy God and by walking ever in his ways—then thou shalt add three other cities to these three, (10) lest innocent blood be shed in thy land which the Lord thy God gives thee for an inheritance, and so the guilt of bloodshed be upon thee.

(11) But if any man hates his neighbor, and lies in wait for him, and attacks him, and wounds him mortally so that he dies, and the man flees into one of these cities, (12) then the elders of his city shall send and fetch him from there, and hand him over to the avenger of blood, so that he may die. (13) Thine eye shall not pity him, but thou shalt purge the guilt of innocent blood from Israel, so that it may be well with thee.

While the appearance of the asylum law at this point is explained by the sequence of material in iv,[6] its language and content are also influenced by xii. 29–xiii. 1ff.—as D's revision principle would lead us to expect. There is a clear connection between xii. 29 and xix. 1 in the verbal coincidence of "When the Lord thy God cuts off the nations." The text

[6] The critical question of whether or not the account in iv. 41–43 about the cities of asylum is original to iv should be answered affirmatively. Steuernagel, p. 69, suggests that a priestly redactor inserted the account in iv from xix. 1ff. in order to harmonize with Num. xxxv. 13 (P).

in xii. 29 goes on to refer to dispossessing the nations and dwelling in their land, while xix. 1 refers more specifically to dwelling in their cities and houses. This language also reflects the traditions about the conquest of the land in i–iv. A major topic there is the dispossessing of certain nations and the taking of their lands and cities (ii. 31, 34, iii. 4, 10). These notices underlie D's law. Thus the law's detailed direction about preparing the way and dividing into three the area of the land reflects the same detailed concern about the areas and divisions of the land in ii. 36, 37, iii. 12–17.

The asylum law and xii. 29–xiii. 1ff. have other language in common. The condition whereby three more cities of asylum may be added, over and above the three already established, is, "Provided thou art careful to keep all this commandment, which I command thee this day, by loving the Lord thy God and by walking ever in his ways"—which is based on the exhortations in xiii. 4–6 (3–5) about loving God, walking after him, keeping his commands, and not going aside from the way.

The M homicide law (Ex. xxi. 12–14) may also influence D's law. In M, there is the beginning of the process of limiting the power of the redeemer, or recoverer,[7] of blood by distinguishing between intentional and unintentional homicide. D carries it further through a more technical development of the place of refuge. The altar is replaced by cities where asylum is regulated by the elders.

An interesting difference between the M and D laws lies in the understanding of what constitutes absence of intent. In this respect the M law is more profound, as Daube points

---

[7] "Recoverer" is preferable to "redeemer" on the ground that the element of payment is not essential to the concept. See D. Daube, *The Exodus Pattern in the Bible*, All Souls Studies, II (London, 1963), p. 28, and *Studies in Biblical Law* (Cambridge, Eng., 1947), pp. 40ff. For discussion of the meaning of גֹּאֵל, see A. R. Johnson, "The Primary Meaning of גֹּאֵל," *SVT*, 1 (1953), 67–77.

out.[8] By ascribing to God the responsibility for the unintentional homicide, M advances a unified view of all accident; the visible agents of a killing—hand, axe, stone—are equally directed by the ultimate mover, and the matter is fundamentally equated with accident in which no human cause is discerned at all. D lacks this profound religious view of accidental homicide. Instead, the indirect cause of the accidental killing is attributed, by way of an illustration, to the head of an axe slipping off and striking a man. D's own religious attitude appears in another aspect: God's abhorrence at the sight of blood tainting the land.

The Neighbor's Landmark: xix. 14

In the inheritance which thou wilt hold in the land that the Lord thy God gives thee to possess, thou shalt not remove thy neighbor's landmark, which the men of old have set.

Without an awareness of D's method of arranging laws it would be difficult to explain why the law concerning the neighbor's landmark should follow the asylum law. Similar terms are employed in each law. One refers to dividing the territory (גבול) of the land which God is giving as an inheritance (*hiph.* נחל), while the other refers to removing the landmark (territory, גבול) which the first generation in the land set as an inheritance (נחלה). It is clear that the two laws are presented as a pair.

The reason for the conjunction is found in material given in i–iv. Moses set apart three cities of asylum east of the Jordan (iv. 41–43): Bezer, Ramoth, and Golan, for, respectively, the Reubenites, Gadites, and Manassites. The territories, divisions, and boundaries allotted to these tribes are outlined in iii. 12–17. Jair the Manassite took all the region of Argob as far as the boundary or landmark (גבול) of the

---

[8] "Direct and Indirect Causation in Biblical Law," *VT,* 11 (1961), 255.

Geshurites and Maacathites. The middle of the Arnon valley is one boundary for the Reubenites and Gadites, the Jordan another. It is these boundary lists, together with the notices about the cities of asylum in iv. 43, that account for the law forbidding the removal of the neighbor's landmark, "which the first ones [Hebrew] have set," at xix. 14, just after the law on the cities of asylum.

The reference to the "first ones" recalls the activity of the generation in i–iv. This activity provides D with a historical example of territorial boundaries being kept inviolate: Israel, when crossing the territory of certain countries, did not contend with them because land had already been allotted by God to these countries (ii. 4, 5, 9, 18, 19).

The law also reveals a close affinity with traditional wisdom teaching. Similar injunctions against removing a landmark are found in Prov. xxii. 28, xxiii. 10, and in the former there is even a reference to the antiquity of the landmark's set position—the landmark "which thy fathers have set" (compare with the "first ones" of the D law). D reflects this teaching, and his law is a fine example of a combination of law, wisdom, and history.[9]

Witnesses: xix. 15–21

(15) A single witness shall not prevail against a man for any crime or for any wrong in connection with any offense that he has committed; only on the evidence of two witnesses, or of three witnesses, shall a charge be sustained. (16) If a malicious witness rises against any man to accuse him of wrongdoing, (17) then both parties to the dispute shall appear before the Lord, before the priests and the judges who are in office in those days; (18) the judges shall inquire diligently, and if the witness is a false witness and has accused his brother falsely, (19) then you shall do to him as he had meant to do to his brother; so thou shalt purge the evil from the midst of thee. (20) And the rest shall hear, and

[9] For a more detailed discussion, see C. M. Carmichael, "Deuteronomic Laws, Wisdom, and Historical Traditions," *JSS*, 12 (1967), 198–206.

fear, and shall never again commit any such evil among thee. (21) Thine eye shall not pity; it shall be life for life, eye for eye, tooth for tooth, hand for hand, foot for foot.

This law on witnesses, like that on the cities of asylum, continues in part to revise material in xii. 29–xiii. 1ff. In xvii. 6, 7, as part of the law on idolatry arising out of xii. 29ff., there is a law on witnesses. Now xix. 15–21 concentrates on the subject. Just as xvii. 6 states that a criminal may only be put to death on the evidence of two or three witnesses, and not on that of one, so does the law in xix. 15 demand not one witness of any crime but two or three. Another affinity between xvii and xix is that the difficult legal case in xvii and the case of the false witness in xix have each to be taken to the central tribunal, to the priests and judge(s) who practise in those days. Possibly the affinity can be extended. In xvii there is a contrast between a matter (idolatry) at the gates within the cities and a matter (a difficult case) at the central place. In xix the homicide is a matter for certain cities, while the false witness is a matter for the central place.

The laws in xvii and xix are both related to the concern in xiii. 2ff. (*1*ff.) about the procedure for detecting and extirpating an instigator to idolatry. The false witness in xix is described in similar terms to the false prophet in xiii. Both rise up and speak falsely. The false witness charges a man with defection (סרה) from law and right; the prophet speaks defection (סרה) from true religion. Each law has similar procedural directions: "The judges shall inquire diligently; and behold" (xix. 18); "Then thou shalt inquire and make search and ask diligently; and behold" (xiii. 15, *14*). Each also calls for a purging of the evil and presents the case as an example to Israel.

D may have considered the M law (Ex. xxiii. 1) on false witness. There is an interesting difference in form between the two laws. M states, "Thou shalt not utter a false report.

Thou shalt not join hands with a wicked man, to be a malicious witness"; the addressee is directly warned against witnessing falsely. In D, the warning is not to pity a convicted false witness. In a sense, a distance is kept between the addressee in D and the crime of false witness. He should not be even indirectly associated with it by showing pity. The aim of this form is to enhance the heinousness of the crime, the attitude being that it is unthinkable even to raise the possibility that the addressee, a true Israelite, might be a false witness. He only hears about an example of such and fears what he hears. In Proverbs the sage holds up to his pupils some "outside" example of a senseless youth destroyed by a harlot (Prov. vii). It is not that the lawgiver or teacher thinks the person he addresses would never commit the offense in question. He fears that he will. He just does not wish to broach the subject in such a direct way.

Summary

The laws studied in this chapter can be described, in terms of D's method of presenting them, as "more of the same." The method is to return to the initial presentation of material in xii. 1–28 and to elaborate further on it. In doing this, D extends the range of his revision by returning also to material in xii. 29–xiii. 19 (*18*), which, as we have earlier noted, is itself an elaboration of the initial part of xii. In concise terms: (*i*) Deut. xii. 1–xiii. 19 (*18*) are expanded upon in xvi. 18–xix. 21. (*ii*) The role of narrative traditions is observable in the make-up of the D laws. Some of these traditions are found in D's historical retrospect, namely, the appointment of leaders and judges (i. 9–18), the obedience to the supreme authorities (i. 19ff.), the lawgiving assembly at Horeb (iv. 1–40), the appointment of cities of asylum (iv. 41–43), and the allotment of boundaries to the Reubenites, Gadites, and Manassites (iii. 12–17). Two other traditions are called upon, namely, the appointment of a king in Israel

(I Sam. viii. 5ff.) [10] and the Israelites' craving for meat in the desert (Num. xi). (*iii*) D reviews the M laws in Ex. xxi. 12–14, xxiii. 1, 7, 8.[11]

[10] D. Daube argues that the tradition in Judges viii. 29–ix. 57 about the installment of the foreigner, Abimelech, as the first "Hebrew" king is alluded to in Deut. xvii. 15, which warns against enthroning a foreigner as king over Israel. See "One from among your brethren shall you set king over you," *JBL,* 90 (1971), 480, 481.

[11] To illuminate further D's method of presenting material, a characteristic feature of Mesopotamian scribal technique may be cited. A. Leo Oppenheim, *Ancient Mesopotamia* (Chicago, 1964), p. 249, refers to the preference of the Mesopotamian scribes for additive elaboration and amplification in compiling diversified material (including laws). He states, "A formally very simple and short pattern is utilized by the scribes to render a large variety of complex and elaborate contents. In this way the form as such does not exercise any tyranny, nor does it coerce the content, but serves as vehicle; in fact, it forms a matrix for a progressive development."

6. The Idea of "Rest": xx

The peculiar laws in xx about certain individuals exempt from military service are indicative of a pervasive idea in D: the idea of "rest" (מנוחה), the notion that Israel, having conquered the land, now enters it as an inheritance, to enjoy a secure existence. This idea of rest explains, for example, the attitude of mind behind the centralization of worship in xii. The idea is expressed in other biblical material, some of which will be noted, and in D it is prominent in the context of war and peace.

The historical tradition that inspires D's thinking concerns the Reubenites and Gadites. These tribes left their wives, children, and cattle behind in the land east of the Jordan to fight for the attainment of "rest" on behalf of their brother Israelites (Deut. iii. 20, Num. xxxii). Having accomplished this, they then returned to their own rest. D's consideration of this situation raises thoughts of war and peace, victory and defeat, established security in a place and its loss and destruction. D's interest in these matters is reflected in the laws that describe exemptions from military duty and in the warnings about the disastrous loss of domestic security and the scattering of the people among enemies that will follow should the laws not be obeyed (xxviii. 15ff.). This situation of expectancy, where the question of victory or defeat is always in mind, finds an echo in the whole setting of D. Israel has not yet come to its rest (xii. 9), and the laws are given for a time in the future when obedience or dis-

obedience will lead to Israel's victory over its enemies or
defeat by them (xxviii. 7ff., 25ff.).

Four Classes of Military Exemption: xx. 1–9

(1) When thou goest forth to war against thine enemies, and
seest horses and chariots and an army larger than thine own,
thou shalt not be afraid of them; for the Lord thy God is with
thee, who brought thee out of the land of Egypt. (2) And when
you draw near to the battle, the priest shall come forward and
speak to the people, (3) and shall say to them, "Hear, O Israel,
you draw near this day to battle against your enemies: let not
your heart faint; do not fear, or tremble, or be in dread of them;
(4) for the Lord your God is he that goes with you, to fight for
you against your enemies, to give you the victory." (5) Then the
officers shall speak to the people, saying, "What man is there that
has built a new house and has not dedicated it? Let him go
back to his house, lest he die in the battle and another man
dedicate it. (6) And what man is there that has planted a vineyard and has not enjoyed its fruit? Let him go back to his house,
lest he die in the battle and another man enjoy its fruit. (7) And
what man is there that has betrothed a wife and has not taken
her? Let him go back to his house, lest he die in the battle and
another man take her." (8) And the officers shall speak further to
the people, and say, "What man is there that is fearful and
fainthearted? Let him go back to his house, lest the heart of his
fellows melt as his heart." (9) And when the officers have made an
end of speaking to the people, then commanders shall be appointed at the head of the people.

The laws relating to the cities of asylum and the boundary
mark (xix. 1–14) are influenced by the narratives of i–iv.
Some of these narratives recount how Israel took possession
of the lands and cities of the two kings, Sihon of Heshbon and
Og of Bashan. At that time, the Reubenites, Gadites, and
Manassites received territory and cities on the east side of the
Jordan (iii. 12–17). The information in iv. 41–43 about the
cities of asylum granted to these tribes is related to iii. 12–17,
which provides a background for D's law on the boundary
mark. The laws in xx about war, military exemptions, and the

capture of cities are likewise reminiscent of the accounts in i–iv of the possession of territories and cities by the Israelites. A definite connection exists between the legal material and these narratives. After the notice (which serves as a basis for the landmark law) in iii. 12–17 about the territory for the Reubenites, Gadites, and Manassites, comes an account of Moses commanding these tribes that all their men of war should pass over armed before their brothers to assist them in obtaining their rest and inheritance west of the Jordan.[1] It is this context, itself influenced by the source in Num. xxxii,[2] that explains why the laws of xx follow.

The first striking affinity between the narratives and the laws is that the subject of military exemption is explicitly raised with respect to those tribes wishing to settle east of the Jordan. The Reubenites and Gadites, having many cattle (Num. xxxii. 1; *cf.* Deut. iii. 19, "I know that you have many cattle"), requested that they be allowed to settle in the good cattle land of Jazer and Gilead. Moses rebuked them with the words, "Shall your brethren go to the war while you sit here?" (Num. xxxii. 6). According to Moses, a suspension of the war effort by the Reubenites and Gadites would have a discouraging effect on the tribes attempting to possess the land west of the Jordan. In this account he draws a parallel with the disobedience of the fathers of all the Israelite tribes when they spied out the valley of Eshcol and returned and discouraged the people from entering. D's version of this incident relates how the Israelites "melted" the hearts of their brothers with their fearful description of the enemy (i. 19–46); significantly, his law exempts from military service

[1] As S. R. Driver indicates, *Deuteronomy*, ICC (3d ed., Edinburgh, 1902), p. 59, in iii. 18, in the sentence "I command you," the "you" is said inexactly for the two and a half tribes of the Reubenites, Gadites, and Manassites.

[2] The Num. xxxii narrative has verbal parallels with the D material; *ibid.*, p. 51. Part of it is also attributed to P. See G. B. Gray, *Numbers*, ICC (Edinburgh, 1903), p. 426.

the man who is fearful and liable to "melt" the hearts of his fellows. The verb מסס, "to melt," occurs on only these two occasions in D. The notice in i. 28 about the overwhelming sight of the enemy is comparable to the note of fear expressed in the initial part of D's law in relation to the sight of horses and chariots and a people greater than the Israelites. The exhortation in i. 29, 30 not to dread the enemy because God fights for Israel is repeated almost verbatim in the law in xx.

The tribes of Reuben and Gad did in fact agree to fight for their brothers, after which they would return to enjoy their inheritance east of the Jordan. Moses informed them that they would then be free (נקי) of their obligations to Yahweh and to Israel (Num. xxxii. 22). In other words, their military obligation would be ended, and they could return to enjoy the peace and prosperity of their inheritance —their homes, flocks, children, and wives (Num. xxxii. 16, 18, 24, 26). D presents a law (xx. 7) that exempts a man from fighting if he has betrothed a wife; and in the similar law in xxiv. 5, he is exempt for a year to be free (נקי) with his new wife. Both in D and in Numbers, this freedom is from military obligation to Israel.

D pronounces four classes of individuals—each law has the same "proclamation" form [3]—exempt from military service. The strange combination of the man who is fearful with those who have built a new house, planted a vineyard, and betrothed a wife is explained by the common background in the traditions associated with the Reubenites and Gadites. One difference in emphasis between these traditions and the laws is that the traditions concern tribal inheritance, while the laws concern individuals and aspects of their inheritance.

[3] This proclamation form of address also occurs in the laws of Eshnunna. For the significance of its use see R. Yaron, "Forms in the Laws of Eshnunna," *RIDA*, 9 (1962), 150ff. The form in D should be set against the background of Moses' address to the people, for example, in Deut. i. 19ff., and his address to the Reubenites and Gadites in Num. xxxii. 6ff.

A similar shift in thought from the boundary marks of neighboring people to the individual's boundary (xix. 14) may be recalled. The singling out of the man with the new house, the man with the vineyard, and the man with the new wife does recall, however, the notices in Num. xxxii and Deut. iii. 19, 20 about the homes, flocks, children, and wives who were left behind east of the Jordan and to whom the Reubenites and Gadites would return, as to their rest and inheritance. The twin ideas of rest and personal inheritance explain the exemption laws. In order to evaluate the influence of these ideas on the exemption laws, their presence in other parts of D and in other biblical texts will be noted and explained.

In xii. 9, 10 Israel has not yet come to its rest and inheritance; but when God shall give Israel the land to inherit and rest from its enemies, Israel will go to sacrifice at the place that God has chosen and where he has made his name dwell. These verses closely relate ideas of a rest, an inheritance, and the presence or existence of a name, in this case the divine name. The name dwells in a chosen place. A similar notion appears in xxv. 5–10 regarding a childless person who dies: a dead man's name should not die out in Israel but be re-established in his estate by a male child born in the name of the dead man by his brother's intercourse with his widow. The law exempting from military service the man who has taken a new wife is founded on this same desire that a man's name should be perpetuated by the birth of a child. Further evidence that this is the motivation is found in the similar law of xxiv. 5 which permits the man to be free for one year in order to make gladness (שמח) with his wife. That this term implies the birth of a child is indicated, first, by the period of one year and, secondly and more decisively, by Jer. xx. 14, 15 where Jeremiah curses the day he was born and the man who brought news to his father, telling him a son had been born to him and making him very glad (שמח שמח). D thus grants military exemption to a man who has not ensured the continuance of his name, which also means the perpetuation of his inheritance.[4] (Note that the Reubenites and Gadites, who did go to war, already had wives and children living in their chosen place east of the Jordan.)

The ideas underlying the laws concerning the man who has built a new house but not dedicated it and the man who has planted a vineyard but not enjoyed its fruit are again those of securing one's personal possessions and establishing oneself in a place. These three exemption laws all express the fear that the man might die in battle.[5] The new house, the vineyard, and the new wife are the three things that D chooses to symbolize the establishment of an Israelite's rest and security in the land. For D this reward of security is very important, and in xxviii. 15ff. three of the appalling things Israelites will experience if they do not obey the commandments are betrothing a wife and another man lying with her, building a house and not dwelling in it, and planting a vineyard and not using its fruit (vs. 30). Among other disasters, Israel will be scattered amidst the peoples, and will find no rest (מנוח, vs. 65).

Other biblical material may also be compared with D's exemption laws. Naomi desired that each of her daughters-in-law find rest (מנוחה) as a wife in a husband's house (**Ruth i.** 9); and the same desire is expressed (מנוח is the term used) in regard to the well-being of Ruth alone (iii. 1). The felicitous conclusion of the story of Ruth is that a son is born to her by Boaz, the kinsman of Elimelech. Elimelech was the deceased father of Ruth's dead husband. Conse-

[4] "Name" in ancient Israel and surrounding cultures could be used in a broad sense—for example, to include the idea of one's property and progeny. See Th. and D. Thompson, "Some Legal Problems in the Book of Ruth," *VT*, 18 (1968), 85–87.

[5] The wisdom literature contains the idea that a man can look forward to dying in peace when he has obtained a safe house, a prosperous estate, and many offspring. This idea is well expressed in Job xxi. 8–13, even though Job is transferring it to the lot of the wicked.

quently, the name of a dead Israelite is continued in Israel. The wish is expressed that the son's name be renowned (Ruth iv. 14). The parallel here is with the law exempting a man from military service if he has betrothed a wife but not taken her, and thus not ensured the continuation of his name.

David intended to build a house of rest (מנוחה) for the ark of the covenant of the Lord and for the footstool of God (I Chron. xxviii. 2).[6] He was unable to build this house, which had God's name, because he was a man of war and had shed much blood (I Kings v. 17ff., 3ff.; I Chron. xxii. 6ff., xxviii. 2ff.). God, however, told David that a son would be born to him and that this son would be a man of peace, literally, a man of rest (איש מנוחה), to whom God would give rest from all his enemies (I Chron. xxii. 9). This son would have the name Solomon (שלמה); God would give peace (שלום) and quiet in Israel; and David's son would build a house for God's name. Solomon, then, undertook the building of this house because God had given him rest from his enemies (I Kings v. 18ff., 4ff.). This undercurrent of thought from Chronicles and Kings is reflected in D's law, in which a man has built a new house and not dedicated it (חנך). This Hebrew term is relatively uncommon and is not used elsewhere of the dedication of a private house. It is, however, used of the dedication of the house of Yahweh (I Kings viii. 63), which was preceded by a prayer, sacrifices, and a blessing in gratitude to Yahweh who has given rest to his people. It was only after this rest that Solomon could build a house for Yahweh. The account of its dedication has, "And now arise, O Lord God, and go to thy resting place" (II Chron. vi. 41).[7] A man's house is likewise his place of rest.

---

[6] Contrast Is. lxvi. 1: "Heaven is my throne and the earth is my footstool; what is the house which you would build for me, and what is the place of my rest?"

[7] The word חנך in the sense "to dedicate" occurs only in reference to the temple and the new house. There is a close relationship in thought between the building of Yahweh's house in a time of rest and the build-

David could not build Yahweh's house because he was a man of war who had spilled much blood. There is another D law that deals with the building of a new house (xxii. 8) and, as one would expect from D's revision method, it is related to the (new house) exemption law. Significantly, "setting" blood on the house is the concern of the law in xxii. 8. A parapet is put on the roof of the house to avoid this undesirable occurrence. Underlying this law, probably, is a contrast between blood shed in war and blood shed in peace, or, more specifically, in view of the idea of the rest in the land, blood shed after the land has attained rest. Such a contrast is found also in I Kings ii. 5ff. David commands Solomon to avenge the blood "set" (as in the D law) upon Joab's girdle and sandals by Joab's slaying of Abner and Amasa in peace time—a grievous fault even though Joab was avenging blood that the two commanders had shed in war.[8] The dedication of the private house in the D law symbolizes and anticipates an individual Israelite's residence in the land, in a secure place, free from the bloodshed of war.

A passage in Jeremiah illumines the law exempting the man who has planted a vineyard. Following a description of Israel's change in fortune, Jer. xxxi. 1ff. describes the well-being in prospect. Israel has been directed in search of rest (הרגיע) before in its history. The same term is used in Deut. xxviii. 65 and is paralleled there by מנוח. The virgin Israel will now be built again, vineyards will be planted, and the planters will enjoy the fruit (Jer. xxxi. 5). The term used for enjoying the fruit is *Pi.* חלל, as in D's law.

D's idea about rest coming to Israel after the defeat of its

---

ing of a new house in anticipation of the rest promised in D. Against the meaning "to dedicate" and for the translation, "Whosoever has built a house and not started to live in it," see the short note by S. C. Reif, *VT*, 22 (1972), 495–501.

[8] Some versions refer to "my loins" and "my sandals"; i.e., the blood guilt is regarded as being upon David. This is possibly what is meant, rather than the meaning of MT, which attributes the blood guilt to Joab.

enemies may be compared with the idea in the prophets
about the rest following the misfortunes and conflicts of the
latter days. In the new age the chosen people will build
houses and dwell in them; they will plant vineyards and eat
their fruit (Is. lxv. 21). Their situation then will not be the
one threatened in Deut. xxviii. 30, of one building and another inhabiting, one planting and another eating. Isaiah also
mentions the bearing of children and the blessing on them,
with which we may compare Deut. xx. 7, the betrothing of
a wife, and the supplementary law of xxiv. 5, the gladness of
producing a child. In Ezek. xxviii. 25, 26, God will gather
the house of Israel from among the peoples that they may
dwell in their own land that was given to Jacob. They
will then dwell securely (לבטח) in it, building houses and
planting vineyards. Deut. xii. 10 refers to Israel's dwelling
securely after the rest from its enemies.

Invoking some of these ideas to exempt a man from military service reflects a practice known to the Near Eastern
world. In the Ugaritic legend of King Keret, troops go forth
to war, including the exceptional case of a bridegroom:
"Even the new-wed groom goes forth. He drives [leaves?] to
mother his wife, to a stranger his well-beloved." [9]

D's exemption laws are based on ideas of rest and security:
one should have possessions in one's own place and should
establish a name there by the perpetuation of one's family.
In his usual manner, D connects these laws to a historical tradition about the Reubenites and Gadites, about their inheritance east of the Jordan and their rest there. This history
raises the question of military exemption in relation to the
notions of rest and inheritance. It also puts forward the example, which D develops into a law, of the man who was fearful and liable to discourage his fellows in battle. The military

---

[9] *ANET*, pp. 143, 144. The emendation is theirs.

exemptions granted to the man who has built a new house and the man who has acquired a new wife, although basically stemming from a traditional attitude of mind associated with attaining security in life, can also be related to the notices in Num. xxxii and Deut. iii. 19, 20, about the wives and homes left behind by the Reubenites and Gadites.

The exemption granted to the man who has not yet enjoyed the fruit of his vineyard, although not without traditional associations,[10] may owe much to D's own thinking. This is suggested by the emphasis on the fact that for the Reubenites and Gadites cattle is the prize possession and the reason they desire the pasture land east of the Jordan. For the other tribes, who seek settlement west of the Jordan, it is the fruit of these lands that is desired. Moreover, it is probably the fruit of the vine in particular that is considered the symbol of their desired possession. It was from the Valley of Eshcol ("cluster of grapes") that the land was first seen, and it was there that the spies took some of the fruit of the land, a single cluster of grapes, as a token of the land they were about to inherit.

In the symbolic ceremony in Deut. xxvi. 1ff., some of the first (ראשית) of the fruit of the new land is a token that the Israelites have entered their inheritance. Driver points out how in Deut. xxxiii. 21, which deals with Gad's seeking out a first part (ראשית) of the land, the allusion is to the narrative in Num. xxxii, according to which Gad, on condition that he assisted in the conquest of Canaan, secured an allotment in the rich pasture country east of Jordan.[11] The close association of the fruit of the land, especially the vine, with Israel's inheritance in the land west of the Jordan may also be rele-

---

[10] In the wisdom literature, possession of a place, land, vineyards, a name, a wife, and children, expresses the nature of a man's security in life; see, for example, Job xxiv. 18ff. on the wicked's portion in the land, their vineyards, their name (vs. 20), their relationship with a barren childless woman (vs. 21), their security (vs. 23).

[11] *Deuteronomy*, ICC, p. 411.

vant to the law exempting the man who has not yet enjoyed
the fruit of his vineyard.

The Idea of Rest and the Centralization of the Cult

In the light of these ideas on establishing oneself in a place
while conquering one's enemies in anticipation of a final rest
from war, it is instructive to consider again the opening laws
of the D code. Only after the destruction of the places of the
foreign gods, who are thought of as God's enemies, will
God choose a place to establish his name. The same thinking
found in the laws permitting certain men to establish their
roots in a place is transferred to the deity. Recognition of
this thinking is part of the correct explanation of the centralization of the cult in D.[12] As has been noted, in I Kings v.
17ff. (3ff.), I Chron. xxii. 6ff., xxviii. 2ff. the building of
God's house in the land and its dedication in a time of peace
and rest are thought of in the same way as the building of a
man's new house and its dedication in the exemption law.

This whole attitude of mind, expressing a basic human
drive for peace and security, prosperity and plenty, a good
name, long life and that life continued by oncoming generations, is traditional. Its conscious, literary expression is especially prominent in the wisdom literature.[13]

In D's exemption laws, a man's house, his vineyard, his
taking a wife and having the prospect of begetting a child,

[12] Orthodox discussion concentrates on, first, the political, religious
situation of the seventh century and the need then for national and
political unity, and, second, the influence of prototypes for the centralization of the cult in the religious history of Israel. See O. Eissfeldt,
The Old Testament: An Introduction (Eng. ed., Oxford, 1965), p.
232; E. W. Nicholson, *Deuteronomy and Tradition* (Oxford, 1967),
pp. 49, 94ff.

[13] *Cf.* n. 10 above. See also, M. Weinfeld, "The Book of Deuteronomy
in Its Relation to Wisdom" (in Hebrew), *Jubilee Volume for Y. Kaufmann* (Jerusalem, 1960), pp. 104ff. For general ancient Near Eastern
parallels, see R. A. Carlson, *David, the Chosen King* (Uppsala, 1964),
p. 98.

symbolize a state of security, an Israelite's rest and inheritance in the land. Many ideas applied to God in the Old
Testament are an extension of this thinking. In II Sam. vii,
for example, after God promises to appoint a place for his
people Israel that it may dwell undisturbed there, a house
will be built for his own name and he will then have a son
(the king) whose succession will continue for ever. The frequent metaphor of Israel as God's vineyard (in II Sam. vii. 10
and Ps. lxxx. 9 (*8*) God "plants" Israel in its place) may also
echo the same thinking.

The centralization of the cult in D means that God has
chosen to dwell in one place,[14] in effect to make a name for
himself there in the new land which, D underlines, must be
kept in a special state of purity and cleanness because of
God's residence. (Compare, for example, the law on the untraced murder, xxi. 1ff.) God's residence in one place ends his
own wandering and rootlessness on behalf of his people (II
Sam. vii. 6). When the occasion is celebrated by Solomon,
it is one of feasting and rejoicing, after which the people turn
to their "tents" as to their own places of rest (I Kings viii. 62–
66). Likewise, in D's laws for sacrificing at the new central
place, the emphasis is on feasting and rejoicing.

The Capture of Cities: xx. 10–18

(10) When thou drawest near to a city to fight against it, offer
terms of peace to it. (11) And if its answer to thee is peace and
it opens to thee, then all the people who are found in it shall do
forced labor for thee and shall serve thee. (12) But if it makes no
peace with thee, but makes war against thee, then thou shalt
besiege it; (13) and when the Lord thy God gives it into thine
hand thou shalt put all its males to the sword, (14) but the
women and the little ones, the cattle, and everything else in the
city, all its spoil, thou shalt take as booty for thyself; and thou

[14] The chosen place is understood to be Jerusalem, yet this is never
stated. A factor in D's avoidance of geographical explicitness could be
the proverbial character of the thinking that is transferred to the deity;
as a man has his "place" in the land, so too has God.

shalt enjoy the spoil of thine enemies, which the Lord thy God has given thee. (15) Thus thou shalt do to all the cities which are very far from thee, which are not cities of the nations here. (16) But in the cities of these peoples that the Lord thy God gives thee for an inheritance, thou shalt save alive nothing that breathes, (17) but thou shalt utterly destroy them, the Hittites and the Amorites, the Canaanites and the Perizzites, the Hivites and the Jebusites, as the Lord thy God has commanded; (18) that they may not teach you to do according to all their abominable practices which they have done in the service of their gods, and so to sin against the Lord thy God.

The military exemption laws in xx. 1–9 are related to the notice in iii. 18–22 about the words of Moses to the Reubenites and Gadites. For the laws in xx. 10–18, the historical narrative in i–iv is again an influencing factor—in particular, the notices about the capture of the cities of the kings, Sihon and Og (ii. 26–iii. 11). The Israelites sent words of peace to Sihon, were rebuffed, and proceeded to put all the inhabitants to the ban, withholding the cattle and the spoil for themselves. Og was similarly eliminated.

The laws describe three situations of military conquest. The first is one in which terms of peace are offered to a city; if they are accepted, the inhabitants are put to forced labor. In the second, if terms of peace are not accepted, but war is made, the males are slain but the women, children, cattle, and spoil are taken by the Israelites. In both these cases the cities are far off from Israel. In the third situation, concerning the cities that belong to Israel's inheritance, "nothing that breathes" is saved from the ban. The procedures in these laws differ from the procedures adopted in the narratives. For example, terms of peace were offered to Sihon but were refused, and all the inhabitants were exterminated. This example does not conform to the law stating that if terms are refused only the males should be slain. Sihon, however, was an Amorite, and xx. 17 commands the total destruction of the Amorites; yet if this is the reason for the severe treatment of Sihon in ii, peace terms should not have been offered.

The explanation for the discrepancy is that the laws attempt to be systematic in their treatment of such military conquests and represent, not an extraction of rules based upon tradition,[15] but a reflection on them informed by certain criteria. The chief criterion introduced is the geographical location of cities, the reasoning behind the criterion being that cities nearby are liable to infect Israel with idolatry, while those that are distant will not. This criterion can be traced to the law in xiii. 13–19 (*12–18*) on instigation to idolatry within an Israelite city. This is precisely the law which, in the revision pattern, can now be expected to contribute to further laws. (The material in xiii. 2–12; *1–11*, on convicting an instigator to idolatry, contributes to the law in xix. 15–21 on the false witness.) The cities that God gives the Israelites as an inheritance, "the cities of the nations here," have to undergo a total destruction—exactly as does the city in xiii which God has given the Israelites but which has been infected by idolatry. There are no details in the law in xx about how the "ban" is to be carried out. It may be assumed that the procedure is to be understood from the detailed directions in xiii. The reason for the destruction of these cities is the same as in the case of the apostate city—infection of the Israelites by the abominations done in the service of foreign gods.

Fruit Trees of the Enemy: xx. 19, 20

(19) When thou besiegest a city for a long time, making war against it in order to take it, thou shalt not destroy its trees by wielding an axe against them; for thou mayest eat of them, but thou shalt not cut them down. Are the trees in the field men that

[15] These traditions are regarded as conforming to patterns already established before D's use of them. See W. A. Sumner, "Israel's Encounters with Edom, Moab, Ammon, Sihon, and Og According to the Deuteronomist," *VT*, 18 (1968), 216–28.

they should be besieged by thee? (20) Only the trees which thou knowest are not trees for food thou mayest destroy and cut down that thou mayest build siegeworks against the city that makes war with thee, until it falls.

Driver suggests that the destruction by invading armies of the fruit trees of the besieged enemy was a common practice.[16] For example, at Elisha's instigation, the Israelites invading Moab "felled all the good trees" (II Kings iii. 19, 25). D's law on the capture of cities that precedes the law on the fruit trees also deals with the subject of enjoying an enemy's spoil (xx. 14). A number of notices in the historical narratives are likewise concerned with food for the conquering Israelites (ii. 6, 28, 29). It is puzzling, however, that there is a special law for the trees. No previous notice mentions the destruction of enemies' fruit trees. Adding to the puzzle is the, for a law, strange statement, "For are the trees in the field men that they should be besieged by thee?" [17] Such language implies that the practice existed, may even have been enjoined, but that common sense and practical counsel call for its cessation. In xx. 16, 17, and in its influencing law, xiii. 13ff. (*12*ff.), all of an enemy's spoil, including by implication his fruit trees, must be totally destroyed. Possibly D is thinking back to this policy of total extermination, as expounded in his earlier laws, and decides that the fruit trees, exceptionally, are to be exempted. A contrast would then exist: practical good sense in one case balancing the religious zeal (literally destructive in its practical aspect) in the other.

Summary

An analysis of the laws on military exemptions reveals the rich texture of the thought that has gone into the composi-

---

[16] *Deuteronomy*, ICC, p. 240.

[17] This rendering implies the alteration of a point, הָאָדֶם for הָאָדָם, in the Masoretic vocalization, which, as Driver, p. 240, points out, yields no appropriate sense.

tion of D's legal material. In the case of the exemption laws, D's thinking, which reflects upon the substance of a man's lot in life, is motivated by a desire for rest from enemies and for the establishment of roots in a permanent place.

The background material upon which D works in present-ing the laws in xx is again detectable. It consists largely of the historical traditions recounted by D in i–iv (the fearsome sight of the enemy in i. 28ff., the military conscription of the Reubenites and Gadites in iii. 18ff., which is drawn from the account in Num. xxxii, and the capture of the Amorite cities in ii. 26–iii. 11). As we have come to expect, the legal material previously presented by D also exercises an influence, in this case the law dealing with the extirpation of idolatry in an Israelite city (xiii. 13–19; *12–18*).

7. Artificiality in the Laws: xxi. 1–xxii. 5

Many D laws are "made up." This characteristic means, among other things, that these laws are not designed for practical application, although as an ultimate aim this possibility is not ruled out. The artificial aspect of the laws is readily apparent when the influences affecting any one law are studied. The reasons for such a synthesis of influences are many. One concerns the making of a fiction: laws are presented which can be recognized as ancient in character because they incorporate elements found in early traditions. Another is related to the didactic setting of D. By combining in a law not only earlier legal and historical traditions but also matters arising out of previously presented laws, D reveals a method that, in its comprehensiveness, argues for a classroom setting. A teacher refers his pupils to what has previously been taught. He then shows how what is taught or alluded to in another law or historical narrative can be expanded to impart further instruction. In this way he builds up in his pupils a body of knowledge in law, religion, morality, national obligations, social duties, and other matters. A third reason for the eclectic, contrived character of the laws is illustrated in the activity of the sages when compiling the book of Proverbs. This work also has a strong eclectic stamp. For example, Prov. x. 19–21 combine three pieces of instruction concerned with the tongue and the lips. Statements like "There are six things" (Prov. vi. 16) and "Have I not written for thee thirty things" (Prov. xxii. 20) indicate a feeling that the sum of a number of things is a forceful way of imparting instruction. The cumulative effect of many wise sayings is wisdom (Eccles. xii. 11). D's system of combining many strands of tradition and putting them together in one law preserves and imparts the traditions with economy and authority. The following law on the untraced homicide is a striking example of a made up law.

Untraced Homicide: xxi. 1–9

(1) If in the land which the Lord thy God gives thee to possess, any one is found slain, lying in the open country, and it is not known who killed him, (2) then thy elders and thy judges shall come forth, and they shall measure the distance to the cities which are around him that is slain; (3) and the elders of the city which is nearest to the slain man shall take a heifer which has never been worked and which has not pulled in the yoke. (4) And the elders of that city shall bring the heifer down to a valley with running water, which is neither plowed nor sown, and shall break the heifer's neck there in the valley. (5) And the priests the sons of Levi shall come forward, for the Lord thy God has chosen them to minister to him and to bless in the name of the Lord, and by their word every dispute and every assault shall be settled. (6) And all the elders of that city nearest to the slain man shall wash their hands over the heifer whose neck was broken in the valley; (7) and they shall testify, "Our hands did not shed this blood, neither did our eyes see it shed. (8) Forgive, O Lord, thy people Israel, whom thou hast redeemed, and set not the guilt of innocent blood in the midst of thy people Israel; but let the guilt of blood be forgiven them." (9) So thou shalt purge the guilt of innocent blood from thy midst, when thou doest what is right in the sight of the Lord.

The laws in xix and xx concerning cities of refuge, neighbor's landmark, false witness, exemption from military service, and capture of cities form a set. All of them, except that on false witness, allude in one way or another to historical traditions connected with the conquest of the land east and west of the Jordan. One concern of these traditions is the

capture of cities and their future use by the Israelites as
cities of refuge. This concern with the inheritance of cities
is carried over into the untraced homicide law.

There is an obvious affinity between this law in xxi and
the laws in xix on homicide. In the drafting of a law code,
it might be expected to appear after the homicide laws in
xix. The reasons why other laws intervene have been discussed. D's method of instruction is digressive. Where a subject under consideration is related to a historical background,
and where matters of interest to D arise in that history, D
treats the historical matters before returning to the original
subject. A process like this is observable for the homicide
law in xix. The untraced homicide law in xxi returns to the
subject of homicide, which in xix. 1ff. initiated an excursion
into matters other than homicide. In addition to the common factor of homicide, the elders have a similar role in both
laws. In xix, the elders of the city of the murderer send to a
city of refuge for him. In xxi, the elders of the city nearest
the slain victim, and hence, one may infer, regarded as the
murderer's city, are responsible for expiating the crime. The
command to purge the blood of the innocent occurs in each
law.

The matter of the made up character of the untraced
homicide law may now be considered. The murder takes
place in the open country, not in a city. It is possible that
this situation is chosen for the law because the law originally
resulted from just such a case. However, given the peculiar
character of other D laws and of D's method, another analysis is possible. Following the homicide law in xix is the law
on the boundary mark. The untraced homicide law in xxi
describes how the distance to the cities in the proximity of
the slain man is to be measured. There is, therefore, a formal
similarity between the laws on the untraced homicide and
the boundary mark in that a standard of measurement respecting territorial limits is to be reckoned with in each case.

In other words, it is the influence of the boundary law that accounts for the instruction being applied to the case of a man slain in the open country rather than within a city. By citing an offense in the open country D is able to demonstrate further the importance of proper boundary marks in the land—in this instance, so that the elders and judges could, by measurement from the territories of the surrounding cities, decide on the city responsible for the crime.

Two other laws also contribute to the untraced homicide law. One is the law on false witness, which follows the boundary law. In that law, the matter is dealt with by the priests and the judges. Similarly, in the present case, where no witnesses to the crime exist, the priests and the judges, along with the elders, deal with the matter. D's law is conceived largely on the basis of his previous thinking. D recalls how, in the similar case in xix involving a question of witnesses, the priests and judges participated; and now in xxi he brings them in to function along with the elders. Part of his reason for doing so may reflect the fact that the untraced homicide case involves neither the central place in the land, where the priests and (sometimes) the judges function, nor a town, where the elders and judges function. It is probable that legislation proper would dispense with such procedural directions about priests, judges, and elders.

The second law that contributes to xxi. 1–9 is xiv. 1, 2, the prohibition against mourning a slain idolater. Two factors indicate a connection. First, this mourning law is, under D's scheme of development of the laws at the beginning of the code, now due for revision (see Chapter 6). Second, the untraced homicide law shows a peculiar concern with the offense to the land caused by a slain man.[1] The land is regarded as being polluted by the corpse, and an elaborate ritual ceremony is prescribed to remove the taint. It is significant that the law in xiv is concerned with the *infection* of

[1] For the shame-cultural factor in D, see pp. 181ff.

idolatry. Sympathetic mourning means contact with this infection and is therefore proscribed. Each law then deals with ceremonial rites for the dead. In one case the rites are prohibited, but the reason for the prohibition is to avoid the infection of idolatry. In the other the rites are necessary, and the reason for their prescription is also to avoid an undesirable infection.[2]

Captive Maid, Son of Unloved Wife, Rebellious Son:
xxi. 10–14, 15–17, 18–21 (for a statement of these laws, see pp. 57, 58, 44.)

These three D laws represent a reworking of the M laws Ex. xxi. 7–11 (slave concubine) and Ex. xxi. 15, 17 (striking, cursing of parents). D treats these M laws at this point (xxi. 10–21) as part of his comprehensive revision of both the earlier Mishpatim and his own preceding laws. The specific reason for this part of the revision is that D's homicide laws in xix. 1–13 and xxi. 1–9 represent a reworking of Ex. xxi. 12–14, concerning intentional and unintentional homicide. D wishes, therefore, to complete the reworking of the section in M, Ex. xxi. 2–17, with the exception of Ex. xxi. 16 (on the theft of a man) which is left over for a particular application in xxiv. 7. If one imagines D turning to M at this point, his position is that he has reworked Ex. xxi. 2–6 in his law on the release of slaves (xv. 12–18), and Ex. xxi. 12–14 in his laws on homicide (xix. 1–13, xxi. 1–9). There is a gap, therefore, in that Ex. xxi. 7–11, on the slave concubine, has not yet been dealt with. Two of the three laws in xxi. 10–21 are interested in these early rules relating to slave concubines. The three laws will be considered in turn.

[2] G. von Rad's view of the untraced homicide law is that in its present shape it is woven together out of ancient customs and more recent ones to form a unified whole. He also finds the references to the priests and the judges additional, even unnecessary. He thus implies the same eclectic character for the law as noted in the above discussion, but attributes it to different historical layers. See *Deuteronomy* (Eng. ed., London, 1966), pp. 135, 136.

It has been argued that the two M rules in Ex. xxi. 8, 11 contribute to D's law on the foreign captive maid (see Chapter 3). Both M and D relate the case of a slave woman who, because she displeases her master, is released by him. In both Ex. xxi. 11 and in D the release of the woman must not involve payment of money to the master/husband. D's revision principle accounts for the special character of his subject matter, with its references to such things as war and mourning. His preceding law on the untraced homicide (xxi. 1–9) reflects, in part, the role of the priests and judges in the law concerning a case of false witness in xix. 15–21. Following this law on false witness is one that concerns going forth to war (xx. 1ff.), in which there is reference to the sight of the horses and chariots of the enemies. The law on the captive maid in xxi. 10–14 has the same opening words as xx. 1 ("When thou goest forth to war against thine enemies") but changes the reference to the sight of the beautiful woman captive instead of the horses and chariots. The indication is that the law on the captive maid is partly related to xx. 1 and the material that follows it. For example, xx. 7 concerns the case of a man betrothing a wife and being exempted from war service. In xxi. 10–14 the subject is an Israelite's marriage to a woman captured during war service.

D's revision method also involves a return to the initial laws of his code. The influence of the mourning law of xiv. 1, 2 on the untraced homicide law of xxi. 1–9 has already been noted. In xxi. 10–14 the continuing influence of this earlier law explains why D chooses to mention that the captive maid must mourn her father and mother for a month.

Turning to the law on the inheritance rights of the first born son by the unloved wife, it has already been noted how this law reflects the Genesis tradition about Jacob and his two wives, Leah and Rachel, and the first born son, Reuben (see Chapter 3). D uses this tradition to provide a historical example for the reworking of the M rule on the

slave concubine. This M rule (see Chapter 3) upholds the
rights of a concubine whose position might be prejudiced
when her master takes a second concubine.

One other point worthy of notice in relation to this law
on the unloved and the loved wife is that it concerns the
division of an inheritance—a divergence from the influencing M law. This concern is consistent with D's overall interest
in the inheritance of the land and with his particular interest
in the exemption laws (xx. 5–7), which deal with an individual's possession of a place in the land.

The third law in this group, that on the rebellious son, is a
reworking of Ex. xxi. 15, on striking parents, and Ex. xxi.
17, on cursing parents. It is clear why the law appears at this
point in D. These two M laws immediately follow the M
laws in Ex. xxi. 2–14, and D has just completed his treatment of this material. D's special subject matter, however, has
still to be accounted for. One contribution to it is D's interest
in traditional wisdom teaching, in this case concerning a
son's honoring his parents. Affinities between the law and
Proverbs are twofold. The parental chastening of the son may
be compared with Prov. xix. 18, xxix. 17 and also, since
bodily correction is probably meant in D, with Prov. xiii. 24,
"He who spares the rod hates his son" (*cf.* Prov. xxii. 15). In
addition, the same combination of words, "a glutton and a
drunkard," is found in D and in Prov. xxiii. 21.

D's systematic practice of returning to his previously given
laws may also account for his special bias in respect to this
son who, besides being stubborn and rebellious and failing
to obey his parents, is also a glutton and a drunkard. Immediately after the mourning law in xiv. 1, 2, which contributes to the laws in xxi on the untraced homicide and the
captive maid, come the food laws (xiv. 3–21). These laws
prohibit eating certain abominable things and list clean and
unclean foods. It is tempting to suggest that the description
of the rebellious son as a glutton and a drunkard stems from

D's renewed reflection on these food laws. An obvious association exists between the food laws and a concern with gluttony. In Prov. xxiii. 20, preceding the mention of the glutton and the drunkard, there is a warning about not being among those who drink wine or those who are gluttonous eaters of meat.

The Hanged Man: xxi. 22, 23

(22) And if a man has committed a crime incurring a judgment of death and he is put to death, and thou hangest him on a tree, (23) his body shall not remain all night upon the tree, but thou shalt bury him the same day, for a hanged man is accursed by God; thou shalt not defile thy land which the Lord thy God gives thee for an inheritance.

Unlike the laws that precede it, the law concerning the hanged man has no specific link with any one M law. It is a law that reflects on the death penalties prescribed in the M laws that D has just been considering, namely, Ex. xxi. 12–17 (Ex. xxi. 16 on the stolen person is held over for treatment in xxiv. 7 but may be included here). In each of the four M laws, sentence of death is passed. The reference in the law on the hanged man to the crime that incurs a judgment of death may result from D's thinking of the death penalties in Ex. xxi. 12–17. The same expression, "a judgment of death," occurs in D's homicide law (xix. 6), which is dependent on Ex. xxi. 12–14. This law on the hanged man is, in a sense, the culmination of D's treatment of the M laws in Ex. xxi. 2–17—certainly of the four prescribing the death sentence. It is noteworthy that only at this point in the M code is there a concentration of capital cases (the sole exceptions are the rather special laws concerning sorcery, bestiality, and idolatry in Ex. xxii. 17–19; *18–20*).

The subject of defilement by a corpse provides a link between the law on the hanged man and the earlier food laws. The food laws regarding unclean meat (xiv. 8, 21a) treat this subject; and the influence of these food laws on the law on the gluttonous son, which precedes the law on the hanged man, has already been suggested. It may be coincidence, but given D's artificial, allusive way of presenting laws, it might be suggested that the question of defilement by an animal corpse led, by an association of ideas, to concern with the defilement of the land by the corpse of a hanged man. The main connection is not so much the association between a human corpse and an animal corpse [3] as D's sensitivity about the pollution of the land.

Straying Animals: xxii. 1–4

(1) Thou shalt not see thy brother's ox or his sheep go astray, and hide thyself from them; thou shalt take them back to thy brother. (2) And if he is not near thee, or if thou dost not know him, thou shalt bring it home to thine house, and it shall be with thee until thy brother seeks it; then thou shalt restore it to him. (3) And so thou shalt do with his ass; so thou shalt do with his garment; so thou shalt do with any lost thing of thy brother's, which he loses and thou findest; thou mayest not hide thyself. (4) Thou shalt not see thy brother's ass or his ox fallen down by the way, and hide thyself from them; thou shalt help him to lift them up again.

This law on straying animals, and the two laws that follow it, provide excellent material for a study of the allusive nature of the D laws. Such a study will indicate how the laws draw on a rich background of meaning. A similar M law on straying animals exists in Ex. xxiii. 4, 5. There are differences between the M and D laws, which, though minor, demand explanation. For example, the M law refers to the "ox of thine enemy or his ass," while D has, "thy brother's ox or his sheep." There is a difference in form: M says, "If thou meetest . . . thou shalt take it back to him," while D says,

[3] It is nonetheless noteworthy that D uses the term נבלה for both human and animal corpses whereas P restricts נבלה to animals and uses פגר for humans.

"Thou shalt not see . . . and hide thyself from them; thou shalt take them back to thy brother." Again, the context in which D places his law is different from that of M, and this difference raises the question as to why D reworks this M law at this point in the code. D's renewed reflection on his previously given laws explains these differences and reveals the lines along which this D version of the law should be interpreted.

The law on the untraced homicide (xxi. 1–9) reflects the influence of the three laws contained in xix. The next law, on the captive maid (xxi. 10–14), has the same opening form as the statement in xx. 1 about going forth to war and seeing certain objects of the enemy. There is also a similarity of content, in that the marriage to a captive maid after war could be compared with the marriage to a new wife and the consequent exemption from war service in xx. 7. The following three laws in xxi (vss. 15–23) are related to M laws, from which they are partly derived. With the straying animals law (xxii. 1–4), also related to an M law, D returns to the connection, established by the law on the captive maid, with the military material in xx. 1ff.; and the following laws (xxii. 5ff.) can also be seen in relationship to this material.

There is, first, an interesting connection in form between xx. 1, xxi. 10, and xxii. 1. The openings of the first two laws (xx. 1, xxi. 10) are almost identical in form: "When thou goest forth to war against thine enemies . . . and *seest.*" The straying animals law (xxii. 1) has, "Thou shalt not *see* thy brother's ox." This formulation is in contrast to M's: "If thou meetest thine enemy's ox." Why D changes the "enemy" of M for the "brother" is a genuine puzzle. (The problem begins with the M law. I shall not, however, go into the question of the nature of the M law's concern with the animals of an enemy.[4] D must have given the matter his attention.)

---

[4] I give a solution to the problem in the Festschrift for David Daube. See C. M. Carmichael, "A Time for War and a Time for Peace: The

The M reference to the "enemy" suggests to D a revision of the M law in the context of his interest in warfare, the situation of going forth to meet the enemy. The form of D's law is some indication of this. The context brought to mind is typically a historical one.

D's warfare laws in xx have as background the traditions about the Reubenites and Gadites. It is they, brothers to the Israelites, who have many cattle (as both Deut. iii. 19 and Num. xxxii. 1 emphasize), who raise for D the question of exemption from military duty, and who go forth to war with their fellow Israelites and leave behind their wives, children, and cattle. It is this historical tradition, the example of certain brothers of the Israelites who leave their cattle unattended, that, in D's allusive way, explains the "brother" of the D law and is the background out of which D refashions the M law on straying animals.

The movement of thought in D's mind as he formulates the straying animals law is similar to what occurs in the case of the landmark law. The law on individual boundary marks is suggested by the historical account in i–iv about the boundary marks of neighboring peoples. In the law on straying animals D is influenced by the historical account concerning the obligation of the Reubenites and Gadites to their brother Israelites that was fulfilled when they helped the latter to conquer the land west of the Jordan. To meet this obligation the Reubenites and Gadites left behind, east of the Jordan, their wives, children, and cattle. What has caught D's attention is the situation of the unattended cattle. That was potentially a situation in which animals were liable to stray, in which brothers were helping out their brothers, and in which mutual help could be rendered. D's law is about such a situation but, doubtless, with regard to an individual's

---

Influence of the Distinction upon Some Legal and Literary Material," in B. S. Jackson, ed., *Studies in Jewish Legal History* (London, 1974), pp. 56ff.

cattle. However the statement that, if one's brother is not near or is not known, the straying animals should be kept until such time as their owners seek them does point to D's historical "model." The Reubenites and Gadites were living east of the Jordan at a distance from their fellow Israelites on the west side. Moreover the term "brother" in the D law has a wide meaning, as in its application to the tribes, the Reubenites and Gadites, who are "brothers" to their fellow Israelites.

The allusive nature of the law on straying animals, with its specific background and idealistic coloring, lessens the legal problem that it poses. The problem lies in the fact that a man who has taken a straying animal into his care is in a vulnerable position and could be accused of the animal's theft. The code of Hammurabi punishes with death the person who receives for safekeeping an ox, sheep, or ass without witnesses and contracts.[5] In formulating his law, D is apparently unaware of any legal complication because his thoughts are taken up with nonlegal matters.

The two laws in xxi. 18–23 that precede the law on straying animals are influenced by laws in the initial part of D's code, namely, the food laws in xiv. 3–21. These same laws appear to influence the law on straying animals, but only in regard to an unnecessary detail. If this observation is correct, it is strong proof of D's artificial method of drafting laws. The law refers to "thy brother's ox or his sheep," or, more accurately, "thy brother's ox or one of his flock of sheep and goats" (the word שׂה means a sheep or a goat).[6] M, on the other hand, has, "thine enemy's ox or his ass." It is puzzling that D does not repeat the ox and the ass in this order, especially as he eventually refers to the ass when he generalizes the meaning of the law. Such a difference seems at first be-

---

[5] *ANET*, p. 166, no. 7. *Cf.* G. R. Driver and J. Miles, *The Assyrian Laws* (Oxford, 1935), pp. 331–33.

[6] BDB, p. 961.

yond explanation, but if D has before him the list of animals
in xiv. 3ff. then it is explained. That list has the order: the
ox, the שה of the sheep, and the שה of the goats.

This process of returning to a previous law, even in such a
detail, also suggests a classroom setting for the presentation of
the D laws. A writing exercise is indicated. The command
(vi. 9, xi. 20) to write the laws on the doorposts and gates
assumes the literacy of the addressee. In xxii. 1–4 it seems
that he is made to return to the list of domestic animals with
which the food laws open, and which he has already written
out. That list sets down comprehensively, in school fashion,
a large number of animals, domestic and game. In the law
on straying animals D is limited to domestic animals, and the
use of the generic term שה to include the two animals, the
שה of the sheep and the שה of the goats, is an abbreviation
of the full reference in xiv. 4.

The expansive language of the law suggests a broader
meaning. The gathering (אסף) of the animals that have been
driven away (נדח) and their return to their rightful owners
recall prophetic texts employing an implied analogy between
people and straying animals. In future days, nations will come
and seek the house of the God of Jacob (Mic. iv. 2). God will
judge between peoples, war will be over, swords will become
ploughshares, and each man will sit under his vine and fig
tree. God will gather (אסף) the lame and those driven away
(נדח)—Mic. iv. 6, cf. Deut. xxx. 4, Zeph. iii. 19. The same
language and theme are found in Is. xi, where the simile of
animals living in harmony is also used to portray the future
security. D later describes a situation contrary to this security
which will follow should Israel fail to obey the laws. A betrothed wife will be taken by another man, a man building
his house will not dwell in it, the fruit of a planted vineyard
will not be enjoyed, a man's ox will be slain before his eyes,
his ass will be torn from him and not returned, and his flock
will be given to his enemies (xxviii. 30, 31). The notion of a

rest emerges in all of the preceding material. The same notion is explicit in the traditions relating to the Reubenites and Gadites. The rich meaning associated with this rest influences the composition of D's law on straying animals.

Transvestite Practices: xxii. 5

A woman shall not wear anything that pertains to a man, nor shall a man put on a woman's garment; for whoever does these things is an abomination to the Lord thy God.

This law is also inspired by the material in xx. 1ff. The background is that of going forth to war, and the topic, the prohibiting of women from entering the army by dressing as men and the prohibiting of men from dressing as women in the army for homosexual purposes. A literal translation is: "There shall not be the weapon of a man upon a woman and a man shall not put on a woman's garment."

The word כלי means in general an article or object made of any material. One of its most common meanings, and it is the meaning in xxii. 5, is an "implement of war." The word גבר is paraphrased in BDB as, "a man as strong, distinguished from women, children and non-combatants whom he is to defend." [7] It has a decidedly military connotation. The adjective גבור is used most of a strong man of war. C. Gordon also suggests this translation.[8] He implies that D sets down this prohibition because such a transvestite practice was found among the Canaanites and points out that in Ugaritic literature an honored place is given to the wearing of clothes of the opposite sex. The heroine Pughat disguised herself as a man and wielded a sword to exact revenge.[9]

[7] *Ibid.*, pp. 149, 150.

[8] "A Note on the 10th Commandment," *JBR,* 31 (1963), 208, 209. Josephus, *Antiquities of the Jews,* trans. W. Whiston (London, n.d.), p. 281, also understood the law in this way. Recall that he was a military commander.

[9] See G. R. Driver, *Canaanite Myths and Legends* (Edinburgh, 1956), pp. 8, 65–67.

While this general parallel with ancient Near Eastern literature is interesting, the tradition that inspires this law is more usefully illumined by considering the situation of the Reubenites and the Gadites. Their situation offers D two suggestive features: the preparation for war, and the explicit reference in the tradition to the women being left behind while the men went to war (iii. 18ff., Num. xxxii). Given D's associative method, it is not an improbable step from reflections upon these features to the transvestite law's concern with women being smuggled into an army. Similarly, when the law prohibits a man's wearing a woman's garment, the situation contemplated is that of men deprived of women during war service.[10]

One other contributory factor should be noted. The laws in xiv influence laws that precede the transvestite law. The next chapter will deal with D's reasons for presenting laws concerned with unnatural or undesirable mixtures at this point in his code. The influencing law is xiv. 21b, which prohibits the mixture of a kid boiled in its mother's milk. This subject of unnatural mixtures plays its part in determining D to consider unnatural, transvestite practices in xxii. 5.

Summary

The "made up" character of the D laws has been noted. D knits together, in a single law, various elements of previous laws, wisdom, and history. In working out the constituent parts of any single law, one has to pay attention to subtle clues, to go backwards and forwards between legal provisions, wisdom ideas, and historical narratives. Nonetheless, a coherent picture of D's artificial method emerges. The analysis is aided by the fact that D is systematic in looking again at

---

[10] Uriah the Hittite would not go to his wife because, it is implied, of a custom that ruled out conjugal relations while a man was engaged in war service (II Sam. xi. 11). *Cf.* U. Simon, "The Poor Man's Ewe-Lamb," *Biblica,* 48 (1967), 214.

laws that he has previously presented. Sometimes, too, he works through the earlier M laws with some measure of coherence.

D deals with a variety of material in the systematic revision of his own laws and the reworking of M laws. The striking feature is that he is able to work with this diverse material and mold it according to his aims. This ability reveals the not uncommon attitude of treating "text" as laden with meaning. That is, a sentence, or even a word (recall the word "corpse"), implies matters other than that contained in the context under discussion. One statement of law carries implications for another law. If this feature is recognized in D, then the fact that the code has many gaps and has, in general, a haphazard appearance can be viewed in a different light. D would not have thought in terms of gaps. Rather, he would have considered that what was written in his code could be filled out. Other subjects could be covered by applying associative methods.

In general summary: (*i*) D reviews a number of M laws, namely, Ex. xxi. 7–15, 17, xxiii. 4, 5. (*ii*) The chief guide to the arrangement of these laws is the material on military conquest in xix and xx. (*iii*) D continues to look back to laws in the initial part of his code, namely, xiv. 1–21. (*iv*) Narrative traditions again influence the presentation of some D laws: the tradition about Jacob, his two wives, and his first-born son (Gen. xxix, xlix) and the tradition about the women and cattle of the Reubenites and Gadites in a war situation (Deut. iii. 19, Num. xxxii).

8. Legal Drafting:
xxii. 6–xxiii. 9 (*8*)

An interesting observation can be made about the laws in xxii. 5–12: they share a concern with mixtures or combinations of one kind or another. Among these concerns are the unnatural practice of transvestism, the undesirability of taking the mother bird with the young, and the unwanted mixture of blood cleaving to a house. Three unnatural combinations are: two kinds of seed in a vineyard, an ox and an ass plowing together, and wool and linen worn together. The culminating law of the series differs from the prohibitions that precede it in that a positive duty is commanded: the insertion of tassels in the corners of a man's cloak. The interest in pairs of things throughout the series serves to introduce the laws on sexual commerce that follow. These laws in turn culminate in the prohibition of an unnatural union—a man must not take his father's wife (xxiii. 1; *xxii. 30*).

An interest in incompatible or undesirable pairs is found in many proverbs:

Like snow in summer or rain in harvest, so honor is not fitting for a fool (Prov. xxvi. 1).

Under three things the earth trembles; under four it cannot bear up: a slave when he becomes king, and a fool when he is filled with food; an unloved woman when she gets a husband, and a maid when she succeeds her mistress (Prov. xxx. 21–23).

I have seen slaves on horses, and princes walking on foot like slaves (Eccles. x. 7).

If a man is burdened with the blood of another, let him be a fugitive until death; let no one help him (Prov. xxviii. 17).

The latter proverb recalls the D law concerning blood on a house and also I Kings ii. 5, concerning blood on a man's loins and sandals. The peculiar attitude of mind that produces such pairings is related, if by contrast, to D's general method of constructing law. That method is characterized by combinations of different strands of material, where the chief criterion is the association or compatibility of ideas between one strand and another.

The Bird's Nest: xxii. 6, 7

(6) If thou chancest to come upon a bird's nest, in any tree or on the ground, with young ones or eggs and the mother sitting upon the young or upon the eggs, thou shalt not take the mother with the young; (7) thou shalt let the mother go, but the young thou mayest take to thyself; that it may go well with thee, and that thou mayest live long.

There is a specific explanation as to why D is prompted to list laws on undesirable combinations at this point in the code. It has been noted that D's return to laws in xiv. 3–21 influences his drafting of the laws preceding the transvestite law. It may now be noted that the law in xiv. 21b, concerning the kid in its mother's milk, influences, in typical D fashion, the law on the bird's nest. The substance of the two laws is similar. One law prohibits cooking a kid in its mother's milk; the other prohibits taking a mother bird with its young. It is permissible to take the young, but the mother bird must be sent off; so too is it permissible, it is implied, to cook a kid for eating but not in its mother's milk. One law is about birds and the other about animals, but it may be noted that part of the food laws in xiv. 3–21 concerns birds. It is the kid law that provides D with an example of a prohibited mixture and that explains D's concern with undesirable mixtures in xxii. 5ff.

By D's time, the kid law was very old and probably obsolete. As such, D would have considered it useful for his own purposes, for example, to suggest other laws on unnatural or undesirable mixtures. An indication that the kid law has been taken over without knowledge of its original meaning— a good example of D's preservation of old material—is that, whereas in M the law is a sacrificial one, in D it is a food law. The implication is that by D's time the law, as a sacrificial one, had become obsolete [1] and was understood by D in another way. The law on the bird's nest is generally accepted as being based on humane motives and as respecting the parental relationship in animals. The reward clause, "That it may go well with thee," is the same as in the command to honor human parents (v. 16). In view of the connection between the bird law and the kid law, it is conceivable that D understood the kid law to have the same humane basis. In Lev. xxii. 27, 28, attention is also apparently directed to the parental relationship in animals; the young have to remain seven days with their mother, and it is prohibited to kill both on the same day.

Despite the plausible attempt to explain these laws in humane terms, a note of scepticism must be expressed. Since each law concerns the taking or killing of the young, the humanenes supposedly present is of an odd kind. One begins to doubt its presence at all. In regard to the law that prohibits a kid being cooked in its mother's milk, it seems more likely that D was especially, possibly solely, interested in the fact that it contained an example of an unnatural mixture— cooking the dead kid in the very milk that was its life and sustenance.[2] It is interesting to recall that a somewhat similar

[1] For two different interpretations of the original meaning of the law, see H. Kosmala, "The So-called Ritual Decalogue," *Swedish Theological Institute Annual,* 1 (1962), 50ff., and D. Daube, "A Note on a Jewish Dietary Law," *JTS,* 37 (1936), 289–91.

[2] Philo stressed the humane nature of the law, but he also noted the

abhorrence underlies the prohibition in xii. 23; the blood of a slaughtered animal is not to be eaten, "for the blood is the life." The dead animal and the blood do not go together, just as the dead kid and the milk do not.

The bird law, no matter how one looks at it, reads strangely. It is ostensibly concerned with honor to a parent bird. But such a concern is strange and should make the interpreter wary. In fact, the law becomes intelligible only when D's typical background thinking is traced.

The laws on straying animals and transvestism, which precede the bird law, issue from D's reflections upon warfare. The bird law, its pastoral setting notwithstanding, also issues from such a background. The law is prompted by the same consideration as leads to D's law on the fruit trees of the enemy (xx. 19, 20). The law on the fruit trees deals with a city under siege and prohibits cutting down the trees for the purpose of building siege works. The reason is that these trees provide food. The author adds that they are not human enemies, to be placed in a state of siege. Just so, when a man encounters (the verb קרה usually refers to an adverse encounter) a bird's nest (the noun קן is sometimes used figuratively of a state of siege) on the way, he is not to destroy the mother with the young (the proverbial phrase אם על-הבנים occurs two more times in the Old Testament in reference to atrocities in war). That is, he is not to treat the birds as if they were human enemies. Rather, he has come upon a source of food; therefore the young or eggs may be taken, but the mother is to be sent off. Like the fruit trees, she will eventually produce more eggs, more young—that is, more food. To destroy the mother, as to destroy the fruit trees, is wasteful. The law, brilliantly allusive, even fanciful, is soberly practical.

---

juxtaposition of the opposites, life and death; *De Virtutibus,* The Loeb Classical Library, VIII (Cambridge, Mass., 1939), pp. 248–51, ll. 140–44.

Daube points out that the verb (א)קרה is used in the Old
Testament predominantly of adverse meetings, but that in
this law it implies a welcome rather than an unwelcome
meeting.[3] While this is apparently so, there is in fact an allusion to a human hostile encounter in war. In the law concerning the fruit trees an explicit comparison is made between a tree and a man (of war). In the more allusive law on
the bird's nest there is an implied comparison between the
bird and a human enemy: the bird is not an enemy to be
encountered in battle. The clear parallel between the two
laws and the comparison in one of the tree to a man in
battle underline the significance of קרה used in reference to
encountering a bird's nest. The word has a double reference,
plainly, to a chance happening that occurs "on the way"—
allusively, to an encounter in battle.[4]

The word "nest" figures elsewhere in contexts of military
siege, conquest, and the like. The king of Assyria plunders
as from a nest the wealth of the nations (Is. x. 14). The
Moabites resemble the fluttering to and fro of birds that have
been driven out of their nests (Is. xvi. 2). God will attack the
Edomites even though they make their nest as high as the
eagle's (Jer. xlix. 16, *cf.* Ob. 4).

The expression in the law, "the mother(s) with the children," is proverbial in character. It occurs in two other con-

[3] *Suddenness and Awe in Scripture,* Robert Waley Cohen Memorial
Lecture (London, 1963), p. 6.

[4] Daube states (*ibid.,* pp. 17, 18), "Curiously, both in form and substance the opening of Deut. xxii. 6, the provision concerning a bird's
nest, is closer to the laws in Exodus—particularly to Ex. xxiii. 4, 'If
thou meet' (פגע)—than are Deut. xxii. 1–4, concerning straying and
broken-down beasts. The latter provisions begin: 'Thou shalt not see.' "
The reason for this curious similarity between the opening of D's
law about encountering the bird's nest and M's law about meeting the
ox of the enemy is this last reference to the enemy. Just as M refers
to the ox of the enemy, so D, for the purpose of dismissing the idea,
allusively refers to the mother bird and its young as if they were "of
the enemy." It may also be noted that the conditional form of D's law
is an imitation of Ex. xxiii. 4.

texts in the Old Testament, each time in reference to what happens or might happen in war. Messengers come to Jacob and tell him how Esau is coming to meet him with four hundred men (Gen. xxxii). The verb "to meet" in Gen. xxxii. 7 (6) is קרה, in the sense of a hostile encounter. When Jacob hears of his impending meeting with Esau he prays for deliverance, for he fears he will be slain and likewise "mother(s) with children" (Gen. xxxii. 12, *11*). Hosea (x. 14) refers to the fearful incident when Shalman destroyed Betharbel on the day of the battle and "mother(s) with children" were dashed in pieces.

It is conceivable that the D law about the birds has a double meaning, the second meaning stemming from the implied contrast between the mother and young of the birds, and mothers and children in a war situation. The law, in passing, *may* be pointing to a humane concern. Unquestionably it alludes to the slaying of "mother(s) with children" in war. D is saying that the mother bird with her children should not be attacked as if they were enemies. Since, like the fruit trees, the birds are not enemies, and therefore a war situation does not prevail, the young may be taken. The question is whether D, mindful of the occasions on which human mothers and children are slain in war, is condemning such slayings. This is a difficult issue. It is true that some laws in xx can be interpreted as enjoining forbearance in war. For example, the law concerning an attack on an enemy city (xx. 10, 11) opens with rules for peace negotiations; only after the offer is refused may the Israelites attack; and if the city is captured all the males are to be slain but the women and children are to be spared. Driver underlines the leniency of the treatment: "The law implies no sanction or excuse for such atrocities [the slaying of pregnant women and children] as are alluded to in Am. i. 13, Hos. xiv. 1 [*xiii. 16*], II Kings viii. 12." [5] On the other hand, in xx. 16–18, ideological com-

[5] *Deuteronomy*, ICC (3d ed., Edinburgh, 1902), p. 239.

mitment requires the slaying of all that breathes. It is to be
doubted that the bird law reveals any humane consideration.

The New House: xxii. 8

When thou buildest a new house, thou shalt make a parapet
for thy roof, that thou mayest not bring the guilt of blood upon
thine house, if any one fall from it.

D's law on building a new house and the two that follow
it, on planting a vineyard and on not plowing with an ox
and an ass together, are related to the subjects treated in xx.
5–7: building a new house, planting a vineyard, and betrothing a wife. The law concerning the ox and the ass is one of
those D laws that cleverly alludes to human affairs.

The notices in Kings and Chronicles in which the building
of God's house is only possible in the rest of Solomon's time
has been compared with D's law in xx. 5 concerning the new
house (see Chapter 6). Because David had shed blood he
could not build God's house (I Chron. xxviii. 3). In D's law
on the new house in xxii. 8, his concern is with setting blood
upon a house; he commands that a parapet be put on the
roof to prevent such a possibility. The lawgiver has in mind
the undesirable prospect of blood being shed in Israel after
its enemies are defeated and rest is attained. The author of
I Kings ii. 5ff. also thinks in this way by contrasting blood
shed in war with blood shed in peace; David commands
Solomon to avenge the blood set upon Joab's girdle and
sandals by Joab's slaying of Abner and Amasa in peacetime.
Joab's sin is considered to be great, even though he was
avenging blood which the two commanders had shed in war.[6]

---

[6] The setting of David's counsel to Solomon has parallels with the
D setting: David, like Moses in D, gives counsel just before his death.
In I Kings ii. 3 there is reference to the law of Moses, and vs. 4, about
the royal succession, may be compared with D's king law. One might
also compare vss. 8ff., in which Shimei's curse must be avenged, with
Deut. xxiii. 4ff. (3ff.), in which the Ammonites and Moabites are never
to enter the assembly of Yahweh because they cursed the Israelites.

The subject of this law on the new house comes from the law on the new house in xx. 5. Its substance is suggested by the law on the untraced homicide (xxi. 1–9), which is in line for revision. The bird law, we have seen, is close in substance to the law concerning the enemies' fruit trees. The new house law, which follows the bird law, is related in substance to the untraced homicide law, which follows the fruit trees law. A major concern of the law on the untraced homicide is that innocent blood shed by an unknown murderer be not set in the midst of the newly inherited land of Israel (xxi. 8). This same concern, taken over from the earlier law, underlies D's law on the new house.

The common interest in a war situation that runs through the four laws of xxii. 1–8 may be summarized as follows. D recalls an occasion when the Reubenites and Gadites were engaged in war service, and this situation, reminding him of the large quantities of cattle possessed by these brother Israelites, raises the problem of unattended, straying animals. This reflection underlies the presentation of the law on straying animals. In the law on transvestism D is similarly thinking of circumstances in a time of war, in this instance, of men deprived of women while on war service—a situation offering the most likely occasion for men dressing as women and women being smuggled into the army dressed as men. In both the law of the bird's nest and that of the parapet for the new house D is ensuring that in a time of peace situations will prevail that are far removed from a time of war. Blood and war are virtually synonymous and hence the permitted slaying of even a bird is to be carried out in as nonhostile a manner as possible; only the young, when some blood will be shed, or the eggs are to be taken. Likewise, a parapet is to be placed on the roof of a house in order to guard against blood being shed in peacetime by someone falling from the roof.

The Vineyard: xxii. 9

Thou shalt not sow thy vineyard with two kinds of seed, lest the whole yield become holy, the crop which thou hast sown and the yield of the vineyard.

In a pattern parallel to that of the previous law, the subject of this vineyard law comes from xx. 6, on planting a vineyard, but its substance, once again, from the law on the untraced homicide (xxi. 1–9). In the ceremony to expiate the homicide, a heifer that has never worked or borne the yoke is taken to a valley that has never been plowed or sown. The untouched character of the animal and the place serves to stress their sanctity. The priests, the sons of Levi, participate in the ceremony.

The vineyard law implies that a certain sanctity is attached to the land used for planting vines, and it further implies that this sanctity is compromised if two kinds of seed are planted. Should this happen, the full produce of the vineyard will be forfeited (קדש). Driver indicates that the Hebrew term means "to become holy" and interprets the law as meaning that the mixture will be forfeited to the sanctuary.[7] It may be added that in this case the mixture will go to the priests at the sanctuary, the sons of Levi. As Driver also points out, the word קדש in D is a synonym of היה קדש,[8] which is used in Lev. xxvii. 21 about a field that is holy to Yahweh and thus becomes a priest's possession. It is the notices about the unplowed, unsown land and about the priests, the sons of Levi, which suggest the substance of D's vineyard law.

The law in xx. 6 exempting a man from military service because he has planted a vineyard is not unrelated in substance to the vineyard law in xxii. 9. Underlying the exemption law is the idea that a man should establish his personal possession in the land by cultivating his own vineyard. In the vineyard law, a man who plants a mixture of seeds in his

---

[7] *Deuteronomy*, ICC, p. 252.   [8] *Ibid.*

vineyard now forfeits the fruit of his possession in Israel, and the fruit becomes the possession of the Levites. In D the Levites have no secular possessions in Israel. Instead, they have the sacred things (קדשים, xii. 26) due to them, and the forfeited mixture would come into this category.

The Ox and the Ass: xxii. 10

Thou shalt not plow with an ox and an ass together.

This law is perhaps the most fascinating in the D code. It is not to be understood literally. For one thing, oxen and asses are known to plow together;[9] and for another, it is difficult to understand how a taboo is thought to exist in the "mixing" or harnessing together of an ox and an ass to a plow. "To plow" in Greek and Rabbinic literature is used figuratively of sexual intercourse.[10] The sense in D's law is similar, as a comparison between the prohibitions in xxii. 9–11 and the similar ones in Leviticus indicates:

Deut. xxii. 9–11: Thou shalt not sow thy vineyard with two kinds of seed. . . . Thou shalt not plow with an ox and an ass together. Thou shalt not wear a mingled stuff, wool and linen together.

Lev. xix. 19: Thou shalt not let thy cattle breed with a different kind; thou shalt not sow thy field with two kinds of seed; nor shall there come upon thee a garment of cloth made of two kinds of stuff.

The prohibition against breeding (רבע) two kinds of cattle together, which involves real mixing, suggests a similar mean-

[9] *Ibid.,* p. 253. That the practice was nonetheless regarded as an odd one in antiquity is indicated by the action of Odysseus. He yoked an ox and a horse, or an ass, to the plow in order to suggest madness. See J. G. Frazer, *Apollodorus,* The Loeb Classical Library, II (London and New York, 1921), p. 177.

[10] See Liddell and Scott's *Greek Lexicon* (9th ed., 1968), p. 245, for ἀρόω and similar terms; and M. Jastrow, *Dictionary of the Targumim, the Talmud Babli and Yerushalmi, and the Midrashic Literature* (New York, 1950), p. 507, for חרש.

ing for the "plowing" in reference to the ox and the ass. And a further indication can be found in D's method of arranging laws. He is concerned with the subject matter of the laws on military exemption in xx. 5–7. The order there is the new house, the vineyard, and the new wife. Here it is the new house, the vineyard, and "plowing." [11] D associates the "plowing" with taking a wife. The source of this association is the Genesis tradition concerning Shechem's attempt to take Dinah for his wife (Gen. xxxiv). D uses this tradition in writing the law on the ox and the ass.

Shechem was the son of Hamor, the Hivite or Canaanite. Hamor is Hebrew for ass. Shechem, the son of an ass, humbled Dinah by lying with her. In other words, he "plowed" her by having intercourse with her.[12] Dinah was the daughter of Jacob-Israel, the ox. The proof that Jacob-Israel is compared to an ox in this particular incident lies in Jacob's comments on it in Gen. xlix. 6. He complains about Simeon and Levi's action against the Hivites. They had slain the Hivite men because of the moral outrage done to Dinah by Shechem. They had slain a "man," says Jacob in Gen. xlix. 6, and hamstrung an "ox." The slain man is Hamor, the ass, the representative head of all the Hivites. The animal com-

---

[11] The difference in D's order (mixed seeds, plowing, mixed stuff) from that in Lev. xix. 19 (breeding, mixed seeds, mixed stuff) is therefore explained by D's dependence upon the order in xx. This dependence also explains D's reference to the vineyard rather than the field, as in Leviticus.

[12] Samson told the Philistines that they would not have solved his riddle, "If you had not plowed with my heifer" (Jud. xiv. 18). The heifer is Samson's bride. "To plow" is figurative but in this case means "to devise a plan, to scheme" and indicates the Philistine men's scheming with Samson's wife. This sense of "to plow"—discussed by S. E. Loewenstamm, "The Hebrew Root חרשׁ in the Light of the Ugaritic Texts," *JJS*, 10 (1959), 63–65—is close to the sense of sexual seduction of a woman. In Jud. xiv. 15 the Philistine men request (with a threat) that Samson's wife entice her husband to explain the riddle. "To entice" in Jud. xiv. 15 is פתה with the sense of persuasion and is used of sexual seduction in Ex. xxii. 15 (*16*).

parison implicit in his name has inspired the use of the animal, the ox, to indicate the effect of this slaying upon Jacob's own house. That effect has already been described by Jacob. By their action Simeon and Levi had placed Jacob and his house in a vulnerable position in relation to the surrounding enemies, the other Canaanites. The Canaanites would hear about the fate of the Hivites and would take vengeance on Jacob and his men, who were few in number. Simeon and Levi's action in slaying Hamor and his house had, in effect, "hamstrung" their own house, the house of Israel, the ox. Hamstringing animals took place in warfare (II Sam. viii. 4, Josh. xi. 6, 9) and resulted in the weakening of an enemy's strength. The use of "to hamstring" (עָקַר) with regard to the ox in Gen. xlix. 6 is a good example of the fondness for wordplays displayed throughout all these Genesis sayings. The word is a deliberate echo of עָכַר in the story (Gen. xxxiv. 30), the word used in reference to the trouble brought upon the house of Jacob by Simeon and Levi's action.[13]

By a clever use of figurative language,[14] a use partly exemplified in the Genesis material, D's law takes up the matter raised by Shechem's treatment of Dinah. In fact the law is best understood as thinking of, and in a sense addressed to, the original Israel. A noteworthy feature in Genesis is that Jacob (Israel) is opposed to the action of Simeon and Levi. Moreover his attitude to Shechem's seduction of Dinah appears not to be one of especial concern.[15] It is reasonable to

[13] For a discussion of this saying see C. M. Carmichael, "Some Sayings in Gen. 49," *JBL,* 88 (1969), 435–44.

[14] The ox and ass law is not alone in its use of figurative language. Compare the following examples: "Are the trees in the field men that they should be besieged by thee" (xx. 19); "The first-fruits of his strength" (xxi. 17); "To uncover his father's skirt" (xxiii. 1; *xxii. 30*); "The wages of a dog" (xxiii. 19, *18*).

[15] Shechem probably did not force Dinah. His fault was that he failed to obtain her father's consent. Dinah was possibly willing to meet Shechem's desire. He had spoken tenderly to her (Gen. xxxiv. 3). In

infer that D would be opposed to the seduction and would favor the high moral attitude of Simeon and Levi. Later in D (xxxiii), Levi is praised for his moral stature. The ox and ass law is critical of the original Israel and may be freely paraphrased as, "Thou, Israel, should not approve of an ox and an ass plowing together." It would be wrong to establish an exact meaning for such a figurative law. The law's allusive background must be kept in mind. It is conceivable that a broader reference to certain foreign marriages is intended. Pertinent in this respect is the fact that D explicitly rules out marriages with, among others, the Hivites (Hamor, Shechem, and their tribe, vii. 1, 3, *cf.* xx. 17).

An indication that D uses the Genesis traditions is seen in their common vocabulary. Shechem, in lying with Dinah, humbled her (עִנָּה, Gen. xxxiv. 2). Jacob's sons were angry because disgrace or folly (נבלה, vs. 7) had been perpetrated in Israel. The humbling of a woman in this way, and this kind of folly, are mentioned in the Pentateuch only in this Genesis story and in the D laws concerning men's humiliating treatment of women (xxi. 14, xxii. 24, 29) and the folly of an Israelite woman's harlotry (xxii. 21).[16] The verb חשק, in the figurative sense of loving a woman, occurs in the Old Testament only in Gen. xxxiv. 8, in reference to Shechem's loving Dinah, and in Deut. xxi. 11, concerning an Israelite's love for a foreign maid. D's figurative use of the ox and the ass is drawn from Jacob's reference to the ox and implied reference to the ass, Hamor, in his words to Simeon and Levi in Gen. xlix. 6. The use of Genesis traditions in the D laws increases from this point in the code. The vocabulary

---

Deut, xxii. 24 the humiliation of the woman has again nothing to do with the man's compulsion for she is assumed to have consented. See D. Daube, *The Exodus Pattern in the Bible,* All Souls Studies, II (London, 1963), pp. 65ff.

[16] עִנָּה occurs elsewhere in: Jud. xix. 24, xx. 5; II Sam. xiii. 12, 14, 22, 32; Ezek. xxii. 10, 11; Lam. v. 11. נבלה occurs elsewhere in: Jud. xix. 23, 24, xx. 6; II Sam. xiii. 12; Jer. xxix. 23.

common to the law on the inheritance rights of the first-born son (xxi. 15–17) and the Genesis traditions about Jacob's first-born son, Reuben (Gen. xxix. 31, xlix. 3), has already been noted.

Mixed Stuff: xxii. 11

Thou shalt not wear a mingled stuff, wool and linen together.

The laws on the house, the vineyard, and the new wife in xx. 5–7 are revised in xxii. 8–10: the house, the vineyard, and the ox and the ass. The revisions are made, in typical D fashion, by association with the law in xxi. 1–9, concerning the untraced homicide, and by appeal to a Genesis tradition. In the homicide law, there is reference to a heifer that has never worked or plowed, and this reference is probably the connecting link that suggests a law about animals plowing. The other association is with the new wife of xx. 7. The two lines of association suggest to D a figurative meaning, and this he cleverly achieves by a cryptic allusion to the Genesis tradition about Shechem's "plowing" of Dinah. The law following that of the untraced homicide concerns marriage to a foreign captive maid (xxi. 10–14), and this captive maid law suggests an explanation for the law concerning mixed stuff. The captive maid must shave her head, pare her nails, and remove the raiment of her captivity. The law on mixed stuff takes up this concern with the kind of clothes a foreign maid should wear as the wife of an Israelite.

D reflects on this question of clothing in conjunction with that part of the Genesis tradition that follows the Shechem incident. Being thoroughly acquainted with the Genesis traditions, he probably writes the law concerning the captive maid with the aftermath of the Shechem incident in mind. There are linguistic contacts: the humbling of Dinah and the humbling of the captive maid, and the use of חשק, loving a woman, on only these two occasions in the Old Testament.

Furthermore, following the Shechem incident, Jacob commanded his household and all who were with him to put
away (סור, as with the maid's garment) the foreign gods
among them, to purify themselves, and to change their garments (Gen. xxxv. 2). "All who were with him," that is,
those over and above Jacob's household, must refer to the
wives and children who remained after the slaughter of the
male Shechemites. Their position would be similar to that
of the captive maid in D's law, and Jacob's command is necessary because he and his household had contact with them.

D's interest in clothing is, therefore, also to be related to
this Genesis background. His particular concern is that an
Israelite's clothing must not suggest harlotry. The question
of harlotry arose in the case of Dinah, and D's ox and ass
law addresses itself particularly to this aspect of the story.
The question probably arises again in connection with the
purification required of the Israelites because of their association with the Shechemite women and the foreign Shechemite gods. Association with foreign gods is commonly conceived of in terms of harlotry (Num. xxv. 1, 2, Deut. xxxi.
16). Another factor suggesting that the law on mixed stuff is
concerned with the relationship between clothing and harlotry is that the next law, concerning the tassels on an
Israelite's garment, shows the same concern.

There are indications that wool and linen worn together
specifically suggest the trade of the harlot. In Hos. ii. 7 (5),
Israel, the harlot, is supplied by lovers with her wool and
linen. In Is. i. 18b, in a context (vs. 21) that refers to Jerusalem as a harlot, it is said of Israel's sins, "Though they are
red like crimson [scarlet stuff or robes, שנים, parallel to תולע]
they shall become like wool." Linen or brightly colored material apparently made up the harlot's alluring garment, and
this thought may be reflected in the Isaiah metaphor. In
Lam. iv. 5, תולע is a token of luxury. In Josh. ii. 6, Rahab,
the harlot, hid the spies with stalks of flax or linen (פשתים, as

in D's law). The adulteress in Prov. vii, who is dressed as a harlot (vs. 10), covers her couch with Egyptian linen (vs. 16). These examples imply that wool is a token of purity, while linen is a token of wanton luxury. Worn together, as they sometimes were by harlots, they represent an incompatible mixture.

D is not thinking specifically of a harlot's dress in his law, but, as Jacob was in issuing his command in Gen. xxxv. 2, of Israelite clothing in general. An Israelite is prohibited from wearing wool and linen together because no sign of harlotry should be seen in Israel. The law is a good example of D's concern with outward appearances.

Tassels: xxii. 12

Thou shalt make thyself tassels on the four corners of thy cloak with which thou coverest thyself.

Like the law on mixed stuff, its successor may also be related to the law on the captive maid (xxi. 10–14) and its concern with clothing. The positive duty enjoined in this law can be interpreted to mean that the Israelites outwardly and symbolically show themselves free from harlotry by wearing tassels. The similar law in Num. xv. 37ff. explains that the tassels are for looking upon and remembering the commandments, so that the Israelites may not wantonly follow (זנה, "to commit fornication") their hearts and eyes.

The terms in the law, "cover, cloak" (כסות) and "corner of a garment" (כנף), may also carry overtones that suggest a concern with harlotry. Abraham was paid by Abimelech for his wife, or rather sister, Sarah, after she had been taken into his house (Gen. xx. 16). The payment was a "covering [כסות] of the eyes" to all who were with Sarah, that is, it was a token of her virtue and honor. כנף can be linked with the idea of legitimate intercourse in Ezek. xvi. 8 and Ruth iii. 9 ("spreading the skirt"), and with illegitimate intercourse in

Deut. xxiii. 1 (*xxii. 30*), xxvii. 20 ("uncovering the father's skirt"). In the law that follows the tassels law, a garment is evidence of an Israelite woman's innocence of harlotry.

G. von Rad believes that the laws against mixing dissimilar things have been handed down without their original significance being known.[17] He argues that the tassels law is retained because it can be reinterpreted in a didactic sense— as is made clear in the reference to wanton looks in Num. xv. 37–41. (He is unaware of the sense D appears to be giving to the other laws.) The prohibition, however, against plowing (in the literal sense) with an ox and an ass did not exist as on old law before D's time. Possibly there existed such a law as Lev. xix. 19 against breeding with two kinds of cattle. D gives the three laws in xxii. 10–12 (the ox and the ass, the mixed stuff, the tassels) a sexual connotation and places them at the beginning of a series of laws (xxii. 10–xxiii. 3, 2) concerned with sexual matters.[18]

The Israelite Wife, Adultery, Seduction: xxii. 13–29

(13) If any man takes a wife, and goes in to her, and then spurns her, (14) and lays charges against her, and brings an evil name upon her, saying, "I took this woman, and when I came near her, I did not find in her the tokens of virginity," (15) then the father of the young woman and her mother shall take and bring out the tokens of her virginity to the elders of the city in the gate; (16) and the father of the young woman shall say to

[17] *Deuteronomy* (Eng. ed., London, 1966), p. 141.

[18] The prohibition against mixed sowing in the Hittite laws probably indicates that the mixture laws in D contain ancient vestiges. See sections 166–67 in E. Neufeld, *The Hittite Laws* (London, 1951).

Old laws that lose their original meaning may, of course, be reinterpreted later and given a quite different meaning. Agricultural phenomena are readily given figurative meanings, as the Egyptian instruction of Ptah-hotep illustrates when it refers to a man's wife as a profitable field for her lord (*ANET*, p. 413). The allusion is to the birth of children. *Cf.* the reference in Sirach xxvi. 20 to a man's wife and the birth of children: "Seek a fertile field within the whole plain and sow it with thine own seed, trusting in thy fine stock."

the elders, "I gave my daughter to this man to wife, and he spurns her; (17) and lo, he has made charges against her, saying, 'I did not find in thy daughter the tokens of virginity.' And yet these are the tokens of my daughter's virginity." And they shall spread the garment before the elders of the city. (18) Then the elders of that city shall take the man and chastise him; (19) and they shall fine him a hundred shekels of silver, and give them to the father of the young woman, because he has brought an evil name upon a virgin of Israel; and she shall be his wife; he may not put her away all his days. (20) But if the thing is true, that the tokens of virginity were not found in the young woman, (21) then they shall bring out the young woman to the door of her father's house, and the men of her city shall stone her to death with stones, because she has wrought folly in Israel by playing the harlot in her father's house; so thou shalt purge the evil from thy midst.

(22) If a man is found lying with the wife of another man, both of them shall die, the man who lay with the woman, and the woman; so thou shalt purge the evil from Israel.

(23) If there is a betrothed virgin, and a man meets her in the city and lies with her, (24) then you shall bring them both out to the gate of that city, and you shall stone them to death with stones, the young woman because she did not cry for help though she was in the city, and the man because he violated his neighbor's wife; so thou shalt purge the evil from thy midst.

(25) But if in the open country a man meet a young woman who is betrothed, and the man seizes her and lies with her, then only the man who lay with her shall die. (26) But to the young woman thou shalt do nothing; in the young woman there is no offense punishable by death, for this case is like that of a man attacking and murdering his neighbor; (27) because he came upon her in the open country, and though the betrothed young woman cried for help there was no one to rescue her.

(28) If a man meets a virgin who is not betrothed, and seizes her and lies with her, and they are found, (29) then the man who lay with her shall give to the father of the young woman fifty shekels of silver, and she shall be his wife, because he has violated her; he may not put her away all his days.

D's method of presenting his laws illumines the lines of thought that contribute to the laws in xxii. 13–29. The two laws on clothing that precede them are related to the law on an Israelite's marriage to a foreign captive maid (xxi. 10–14), and the clothing signifies an Israelite's innocence of harlotry. The law in xxii. 13–21 on the Israelite wife is more explicit: the "tokens of virginity" (clothing) are proof of an Israelite woman's innocence.

The law deals with an accusation of harlotry against a new wife who is an Israelite. The situation here can be compared with that in which an Israelite marries a foreign captive maid (xxi. 10–14). It was argued above that the law on the foreign maid and the law on the first-born son of the un-loved wife that follows it (xxi. 15–17) are related to the rules in Ex. xxi. 7–11 on the slave concubine (see Chapter 3). One intention of both the M rules and the two D laws is to up-hold the rights of the woman should she lose favor with her husband. In the xxii. 13–21 law, one concern is the protec-tion of a wife who is hated by her husband and who is, by his allegation, not a virgin. If it is a false allegation, the parents bring proof that she is a virgin, and the elders chastise the husband and fine him a hundred shekels.

The law on the Israelite wife is a typically eclectic one, en-compassing strands from what has been taught, or alluded to, in certain preceding laws. First, there is the link with the law on the foreign maid in xxi. 10–14. Second, that part of the law regarding the woman's guilt when she was a daughter in her father's house complements the law on the wicked son in xxi. 18–21.[19] He too is stoned to death; and in each law both the father and the mother play a part: they bring the son before the elders, and they are involved in bringing the matter of the daughter's virginity before the elders. Third, the law may also complement the material relating to Shechem. D upholds Simeon and Levi's attitude in con-

[19] L. M. Epstein, *Sex Laws and Customs in Judaism* (New York, 1948), p. 165, suggested that this law might be the female counterpart to the law concerning the rebellious son. For a similar law to Deut. xxii. 13–21 in the laws of Lipit-Ishtar, see J. J. Finkelstein, "Sex Offenses in Sumerian Laws," *JAOS*, 86 (1966), 367.

demning Shechem for humbling their sister, for doing folly
in Israel, and for treating her as a harlot (Gen. xxxiv. 2, 7,
31). D's law concentrates on the harlotry of an Israelite sister,
as D would think of her. An evil name is not to be brought
upon a virgin of Israel by a false accusation of harlotry. But
if harlotry is proved, death is to be the punishment; for, as
in the case of Shechem, so now in the complementary case of
a daughter of Israel, folly has been done in Israel.

The laws on adultery and seduction follow naturally at
this point in the code.[20] The law concerning the seduction of
an unbetrothed virgin is related to the M law of Ex. xxii. 15,
16 (*16, 17*): "If a man seduces a virgin who is not betrothed,
and lies with her, he shall give the marriage present for her,
and make her his wife. If her father utterly refuses to give
her to him, he shall pay money equivalent to the marriage
present for virgins." The D law is of a later date and is designed to improve upon M's law. This improvement takes
two forms. First, in M the seducer could evade the law by
divorcing the woman soon after marriage. D rules that out.
Second, in M the bride-price is not fixed, while in D it is
fixed at fifty silver pieces so that there can be official supervision of the transaction.[21]

A Forbidden Degree of Affinity: xxiii. 1 (*xxii. 30*)

A man shall not take his father's wife, nor shall he uncover
his father's skirt.

Unlike the priestly legislation's extensive lists of forbidden
degrees of affinity (Lev. xviii. 6ff., xx. 11ff.), this is the only

[20] A concern with marriage laws and the related subjects of adultery,
seduction, divorce, etc., is a significant feature of D. In some respects,
and especially in his high-minded attitude, D reflects the wisdom concern with strict sexual morality.

[21] For a discussion of this law see G. R. Driver and J. Miles, *The
Assyrian Laws* (Oxford, 1935), p. 62, and D. Daube, Book List of Society for Old Testament Study, 1950, p. 54. M. Weinfeld suggests that,
in contrast to the M law, D shows sensitivity to the maiden's dishonor.
See *Deuteronomy and the Deuteronomic School* (Oxford, 1972), p. 285.

law of its kind in the D code (although the list of curses in xxvii. 15ff. mentions two other forbidden degrees). In M, there is a law against bestiality (Ex. xxii. 18, *19*); but this law does not correspond to it, and D has a curse against bestiality in xxvii. 21. It is D's method of presenting material that causes him to mention only this particular forbidden degree of marriage with a father's wife.

The laws preceding D's affinity law are presented as revisions, or expansions, of the law on marriage to a captive maid. Following the captive maid law is one concerning the inheritance rights of the first-born son of the unloved wife (xxi. 15–17); and this inheritance law leads D to present his affinity law. In the inheritance law the father has two wives (the unloved and the loved). S. R. Driver points out that in ancient Arabia a man's wives passed to his heir.[22] Driver and Miles suggest that the stories of Absalom and his father's concubines (II Sam. xvi. 20–23) and Adonijah and Abishag, whom Solomon seems to have inherited (I Kings ii. 13–25), indicate that in Israel too a son at one time inherited his father's concubines. They also claim that the later provision in Lev. xviii. 7, 8 prohibiting relations between a man and his father's wives, whether his own mother or a stepmother, proves the previous existence of the custom.[23] The possibility of a son's inheriting his father's wife, the one who is not his mother, could arise from D's reflection on the inheritance law, which is in line for expansion.

A more decisive link exists, however, between the affinity and inheritance laws; each shows an interest in the Genesis traditions about Reuben. Reuben is acknowledged by Jacob as his first-born son, as the first-fruits of his strength (Gen. xlix. 3). The D law on inheritance upholds the rights of the first-born who, like Reuben, is the son of an unloved wife

[22] *Deuteronomy*, ICC, p. 259. For the position in Assyria, see G. R. Driver and J. Miles, *The Assyrian Laws* (Oxford, 1935), pp. 182, 236.
[23] *The Assyrian Laws*, p. 239.

because he is the first-fruits of his father's strength, exactly as with Reuben in Gen. xlix. 3. In Gen. xlix. 4 Jacob reminds Reuben of how he went up to his father's bed and defiled it. This is an allusion to the notice in Gen. xxxv. 22 about Reuben's intercourse with Bilhah, his father's concubine. The D affinity law is inspired by this Genesis tradition, which explains why D sets down the particular forbidden degree of a man taking his father's wife.

The Assembly of Yahweh and the Deuteronomic Setting

In the laws following the affinity law, certain classes are excluded from, and others are admitted into, the "assembly of Yahweh." [24] The source of D's idea of such an assembly has already been discussed (see Chapter 1). The tradition in Gen. xlix about the assembly of the sons of Jacob-Israel inspires D's conception of Israel as an ideal brotherhood, to which he gives the name "the assembly of Yahweh." Brotherly ties are constantly emphasized in D, and often confirmed by reference to Israel's sons. Traditions associated with Reuben, Gad, and Levi play an important part in the presentation of many laws. Connections, extending to language, are made between certain laws and Jacob's words to Reuben, and to Simeon and Levi, in Gen. xlix. 3–7. The law prohibiting relations with a father's wife, which precedes the first mention of the assembly of Yahweh, is, as we have seen, related to Jacob's words of censure to Reuben in Gen. xlix. 4.

The Genesis setting of the aged and dying Jacob with his

[24] M. Noth, *The Laws in the Pentateuch* (Eng. ed., Edinburgh, 1966), pp. 21ff., 46, thinks that the "assembly of Yahweh" was an actual institution and readily identifies it with his constructed sacred confederacy of the twelve tribes of Israel. He is unaware of the influence the tradition in Gen. xlix, with its assembly of Jacob and his sons, had on D. Similarly, K. Galling, "Das Gemeindegesetz in Deuteronomium 23," *Festschrift A. Bertholet* (Tübingen, 1950), pp. 176–91, attempts to relate the laws about the assembly to different historical periods.

sons has a wider parallel in D. The setting of the entire D work is an address to Israel by Moses just before his death. In xxxiii, the aged Moses gathers the sons of Israel and blesses them before his death; and there is reference to the law as a "possession" for the assembly of Jacob (vs. 4), a reference that seems to acknowledge the tradition about Jacob's assembly in Gen. xlix. Jacob called his sons to assemble, and in his words to Simeon and Levi he excluded himself from their type of assembly. The term used is the same as in the D laws about entering the assembly of Yahweh.

The narrower parallel that exists between the ideas of assembly in the D laws in xxiii and in Gen. xlix is strong confirmation that the entire setting of the book of Deuteronomy is modeled on the setting of Gen. xlix. An interesting question is why the expression, "the assembly of Yahweh," is used in D and not "the assembly of Israel." Apart from the possibility that "the assembly of Yahweh" may have been used before D's time in connection with Israel and his household,[25] another pertinent factor is that D adopts a critical stand in regard to the Genesis tradition. D's attitude toward Simeon and Levi is the opposite of Jacob's. Jacob excluded them from his assembly. D would certainly admit them. Jacob, although critical of Reuben's conduct, does not dismiss him entirely. D probably would dismiss him. Such considerations, inspired by D's ideal standards, would account for D's using the name, "the assembly of Yahweh."

In sum, the "assembly of Yahweh" in D is not a definable political or religious institution. The "assembly" refers to the nation, Israel, and its high moral worthiness. It came into being with Jacob (Israel) when, just before his death, he assembled his sons and considered their ways, and it had existed from that time. It is a loose, imprecise way of referring to the nation that is called by the name, Israel. Associa-

---

[25] Mic. ii. 5, which seems to be the earliest use of the expression "the assembly of Yahweh," refers in vs. 7 to the house of Jacob.

tion with that name is a matter of high moral seriousness, and D therefore properly refers to Israel's assembly as the "assembly of Yahweh."

The Eunuch: xxiii. 2 (1)

He whose testicles are crushed or whose male member is cut off shall not enter the assembly of Yahweh.

D's affinity law is based on the tradition about Reuben and his father's concubine. The material that leads D to this concern with consanguinity is the law on the first-born son and the words of Jacob to Reuben in Gen. xlix, both of which refer to the first-born son as the first fruits of the father's strength. D continues to dwell on the significance of a man's "first-fruits" in his law on the eunuch. A eunuch can have no strength of this kind. This vigor is important to D; his justification for upholding the special rights of a first-born son is that he is a father's "first-fruits." D therefore excludes a eunuch from the assembly of Yahweh because a eunuch can have no offspring. D regards this sonless situation as contrary to the model—which is at the heart of his thinking about the assembly—of the patriarch, Jacob, surrounded by his sons.

The Bastard: xxiii. 3 (2)

No bastard shall enter the assembly of Yahweh; even to the tenth generation none of his descendants shall enter the assembly of Yahweh.

D's concern with the permanent exclusion from the assembly of the "bastard," and, in the following law, of Ammon and Moab, is due to the influence of the tradition in Gen. xix. 30ff. concerning the first-born daughter of Lot and her younger sister who sinned by lying with their father and getting offspring incestuously. The offspring were Moab and Ammon, the sons of Lot (acknowledged as such in Deut. ii. 9, 19). The theme of D's laws at this point (xxiii. 1ff.;

*xxii. 30*ff.) in his code can be stated as follows. Reuben, the first-born son of Jacob, lay with his father's wife; D's reflection on this ancient tradition leads to the law on a forbidden degree of affinity in xxiii. 1 (*xxii. 30*). The first-born daughter of Lot, and afterwards her sister, lay with their father; consideration of this ancient tradition prompts the law on the bastard, and then the law on Ammon and Moab in xxiii. 3–7 (*2–6*).[26]

Ammon and Moab: xxiii. 4–7 (*3–6*)

(4) No Ammonite or Moabite shall enter the assembly of Yahweh; even to the tenth generation none belonging to them shall enter the assembly of Yahweh for ever; (5) because they did not meet you with bread and with water on the way, when you came forth out of Egypt, and because he hired against thee Balaam the son of Beor from Pethor of Mesopotamia, to curse thee. (6) Nevertheless the Lord thy God would not hearken to Balaam; but the Lord thy God turned the curse into a blessing for thee, because the Lord thy God loved thee. (7) Thou shalt not seek their peace or their prosperity all thy days for ever.

The Ammonites and Moabites are permanently excluded from the assembly on account of their behavior to Israel at the time of the exodus from Egypt. It might be expected, on the basis of the argument that D's concern with bastardy arises from his interest in the incestuous origins of Ammon and Moab, that this disgrace of incest would be cited as the reason for their exclusion from Israel's assembly. The explanation for the lack of an explicit reference to their origins supplies evidence both of D's digressive, eclectic method and of his doctrinaire beliefs.

The Genesis tradition recounts the incestuous origins of Ammon and Moab, and for D this "bastardy" rules out relations between them and Israel. Rather than refer ex-

---

[26] The "bastard" in the D law is therefore one born, not out of wedlock, but of an incestuous union. Rabbinic tradition, e.g., Yebamoth iv. 13, interprets the term in this way.

plicitly to these origins, however, D shows that the later generations of Ammonites and Moabites are equally unfit for the assembly of Yahweh. An interest in "the generations," in their education and past history, is marked throughout D. In the laws of xxiii. 3–7 (2–6), the stain of a bastard's birth clings to him and stays with his descendants for ten generations, that is, for all time. In the same way, the stain of their birth clings to Ammon and Moab, even to ten generations, and D believes that no generation of the Ammonites and Moabites will ever prove themselves worthy of ties with the assembly. D claims that the generations of Ammonites and Moabites were unworthy at the time of Israel's exodus from Egypt.

Against the Ammonites and Moabites it is charged that they did not meet Israel with bread and water on the way from Egypt and that the king of Moab ("he" in the text) [27] hired Balaam to curse Israel. Nothing is said in ii. 19ff. about the conduct of the Ammonites; and the Moabites, it is implied, sold the Israelites bread and water for money. There are discrepancies in D, and a plain reading of the various texts does not remove them. W. A. Sumner may well be right in arguing that, in effect, D's ideological interests create or erase past events and actions.[28] D's intention in his law on the Ammonites and Moabites is to prove that their generations at the time of the exodus must have manifested the "fault" of their ancestry. In doing so, he has been persuaded more by his doctrinaire beliefs in the effects of heredity than by tradition.

The high-minded thinking of this law reflects the wisdom tradition. D implies that the failure to provide bread and

[27] The fact that the king of Moab is not explicitly referred to in the text is an indication that the D laws allude to certain traditions, in this instance to the tradition in Num. xxii.

[28] "Israel's Encounters with Edom, Moab, Ammon, Sihon, and Og According to the Deuteronomist," *VT*, 18 (1968), 216–28.

water was a considerable crime. The provision of bread to those in need is a concern in Job xxxi. 31, where the gravity of failure to do so is underlined. Interestingly, Job, like D, mentions together the "crimes" of cursing a person (vs. 30) and withholding food.[29]

Edom and Egypt: xxiii. 8, 9 (7, 8)

(8) Thou shalt not abhor an Edomite, for he is thy brother; thou shalt not abhor an Egyptian, because thou wast a sojourner in his land. (9) The children of the third generation that are born to them may enter the assembly of Yahweh.

D's historical reflections explain the bias of these two laws. Israel's time of sojourn in Egypt was initially one of expansion and well-being, as xxvi. 5 states, and D's willingness to have relations with the Egyptians rests on this consideration. The law also bears in mind, however, the slavery to which Israel was subjected in Egypt. This fault in Egypt's historical relations with Israel explains D's unenthusiastic statement that the Egyptians are not to be abhorred because Israel was a sojourner in Egypt, in contrast to the more enthusiastic statement of x. 19, which commands that the sojourner be loved. Egypt's lapse also explains the delayed admission of the Egyptians into the assembly; only after three generations may they enter.

D applies similar considerations to the Edomites. His positive attitude to Edom is based on the fact that Esau (Edom) received Jacob (Israel) with brotherly affection after Jacob's flight from Laban (Gen. xxxiii). His statement imposing a condition on Edom's entrance into the assembly, and thereby implying a negative judgment, is explained by another historical consideration, however. The Edomites, who lived at the

---

[29] *Cf.* Job xxxi. 16, 17, xxii. 7; Prov. xxii. 9, xxv. 21. The story of Moab's attempt to curse Israel is in Num. xxii. There is reference to Israel as an assembly (vs. 4) and frequent mention of Israel as Jacob (Num. xxiii. 7, 10, 21).

time of the exodus, refused to permit Israel transit through Edomite territory, and this fault detracts from Edom's record (Num. xx. 18–21).[30] This lapse explains the delayed admission of the Edomites into the assembly; like the Egyptians, only offspring of the third generation may enter.[31]

Summary

Apart from the eclectic, which is constantly used throughout the code, two other interesting methods by which D arranges material are observable in the laws considered in this chapter. One is dependent upon the concept of incompatible, unnatural, or undesirable mixtures. The other is dependent upon the concept of acceptability for admission into Israel's assembly of Yahweh. In some ways these two concepts overlap: certain groups manifest faults that render them incompatible with Israel. If these three methods of arranging laws are recognized, one may discern the movement of thought that links one law to the next with a degree of coherence which appearances would not suggest.

D's eclectic method for the laws in xxii. 6–xxiii. 9 (8) embraces the following material: (*i*) The last law in the list of food laws in xiv, namely, seething a kid in its mother's milk, inspires D's interest in incompatible mixtures at this point (xxii. 5ff.) in the code. (*ii*) The three laws in xx. 5–7 (house, vineyard, new wife) are expanded by relating their subjects to matters raised by the law concerning the untraced homicide (xxi. 1–9) and the two following laws concerning wives (xxi. 10–17). (*iii*) Narrative traditions also exert their influence on the laws, specifically: the traditions about Israel and

---

[30] For the complex relationship between the historical notices in ii. 2–8, 29 about Edom's reception of Israel and those in Num. xx. 18–21 about Edom's rebuff, see Sumner, p. 221, and C. M. Carmichael, "A New View of the Origin of the Deuteronomic Credo," *VT*, 19 (1969), 279, n. 2.

[31] See Chapter 9 (the law on a neighbor's crops) for further discussion of Edom's entry into the assembly.

his sons (Gen. xlix), about Israel's sons, Reuben and Gad
(their women and children in a war situation, Deut. iii. 19,
Num. xxxii), about Reuben himself (Gen. xxxv, xlix), and
about Simeon, Levi, and Israel's daughter, Dinah (Gen.
xxxiv, xxxv); a tradition about Lot's daughters (Gen. xix);
traditions about the Ammonites and the Moabites (Deut. ii,
Num. xxii) and about the Edomites (Gen. xxxiii, Num. xx)
and the Egyptians (Gen. xlv–Ex. iff.). (*iv*) The M law in Ex.
xxii. 15, 16 (*16, 17*) is revised.

9. The Edomite Series:
xxiii. 10–26 (9–25)

M contains a double series of laws, Ex. xxii. 20–30 (*21–31*), xxiii. 9–19 (see Chapter 3). Each series begins with a law on the oppression of the sojourner and embodies an appeal to remember Israel's sojourn in Egypt. D was aware of this pattern of arrangement, as a number of factors indicate. First, since he combines laws from the double series in two of his own laws—namely, in xiv. 21, which links torn animal flesh and the kid in its mother's milk, and in xv. 1–11, concerning the seventh year release of debts—it is clear that D recognizes the correspondence. Second, D's own method of arranging laws, whereby correspondences are sought between one law and another, resembles the M method. Third, D imitates M by presenting his own double series of laws (in xxiii and xxiv), each series being prompted by the two similar laws of xxiii. 8 (7), on not abhorring an Edomite, for he is a brother, and not abhorring an Egyptian, for Israel was a sojourner in Egypt. Fourth, that D's double series is the equivalent of M's is indicated by the fact that laws in the M series also appear in the D series. For example, there is a law about lending at interest in Ex. xxii. 24 (*25*) and Deut. xxiii. 20, 21 (*19*, *20*); a law about pledges in Ex. xxii. 25 (*26*) and Deut. xxiv. 10–13; a law about justice for the sojourner, widow, and orphan in Ex. xxii. 20–23 (*21–24*), xxiii. 9 and Deut. xxiv. 17ff.

The correspondence factor in the M double series is often the general concern with justice for the poor. D's series are more complex. His two lists of laws show only a slight degree of intercorrespondence. However, for each list, the method by which the laws are set down is similar to the procedure adopted for the second list in M. If in M a law in the second list is suggested by a particular concern in the first list—for example, the rights of the poor and oppressed—so in D laws may be suggested by a particular concern in an earlier law in the code. In D this method of arrangement takes precedence throughout the code, and it causes the dissimilarity of correspondence between the M double series and the D double series.

An additional factor, the eclectic one, also influences the nature of the D series. The first series is prompted by the law about Israel's recognition of the Edomites. Consequently, the laws in the series are influenced by historical traditions about the relations of Israel, sometimes in the person of Jacob, with Edom, sometimes in the person of Esau. Likewise, for the laws in the second series traditions about Israel and Egypt play a part, because this series is prompted by the law concerning Israel's relations with Egypt.

A glance at the laws in xxiii and xxiv reveals some characteristics of a double series. The first law in each series uses the phrase "the nakedness of a thing" in two quite different contexts—uncleanness in the camp, and uncleanness in a woman. There is a law concerning loans at interest in one series and a law concerning loans on pledge in the other; a law concerning the slave in one, the hired servant in the other; a law concerning the plucking of crops in one, gleanings in the other. The resemblance to a double series is inconspicuous, however, because of the complex, eclectic method used by D in compiling any one law.

Many laws, in both series, reveal a concern that revolves around the concept of refusal or permission to enter a place and the related concept of removal or nonremoval from a place. If one remembers that the two series are inspired by the laws that admit some Edomites and some Egyptians into Israel's assembly while refusing entrance to some others, then it is clear why D continued to be influenced by these concepts. An examination of the concern common to both sets of laws provides further evidence that they are intended to be a double series. In characterizing the nature of D's concern in his assembly laws, Daube points to D's interest in matters of honor and disgrace.[1] To be excluded from the assembly is manifestly degrading; to be admitted is a mark of honor. This shame-cultural aspect—concern with appearances, outward form, public repute—can be traced in both series of laws.

In xxiii these examples may be noted:

To avoid an unclean occurrence in Israel's camp, a man "shall go outside the camp, he shall not come within the camp" (vs. 11, *10*). The reason for his exclusion is that God may not see a shameful, unseemly thing.

A runaway slave is not to be sent back to his master but is to be admitted into the midst of Israel. The implications are that exclusion is humiliating and generosity is the outward mark of a civilized society.

The hire of a harlot or the price of a sodomite has not to be brought into the house of the Lord. To bring such gains of prostitution into the house of God patently disgraces the place.

In xxiv the following examples illustrate D's combined concern with admittance into and exclusion from a place and with honor and disgrace:

[1] "The Culture of Deuteronomy," *Orita* (Ibadan), 3 (1969), 31.

If a woman who is divorced by her husband and sent out of his house because he finds "an unseemly thing" (vs. 1) in her marries another man and that union is dissolved, she cannot be taken back by her first husband.

A man who takes a new wife "shall not go out with the army and nothing shall pass over upon him," (vs. 5) because he is free for a year to be at home in order to give joy to his wife. This joy consists in their producing a child. They thereby honor themselves, perpetuate their name, and establish themselves in a place. As Daube points out,[2] in a society sensitive to honor and public appearance, one's name, in a broad sense, plays an important role.

One of two laws about pledging in xxiv states, "Thou shalt not go into his [the debtor's] house to fetch his pledge" (vs. 10). The creditor must wait outside for the debtor to bring the pledge to him. As Daube says, "To have the creditor inside the house . . . would be the most down-putting, dishonouring experience for the debtor and his family. The handing over outside preserves appearances, the worst of the visible, formal disgrace is avoided."[3] In this law the implication emerges, as it often does in the wisdom literature,[4] that a man is sensitive about his "place." The interrelated ideas of privacy and dignity are associated with one's place in the land. The other, more proverbial pledge law states that to take a millstone in pledge is to take a life in pledge. Removal of the millstone makes a family destitute and degrades it.

Finally, the leprosy law, which cites the case of Miriam, who was excluded for seven days from Israel's camp, exhibits a clear concern with exclusion from a place because of shame-

---

[2] *Ibid.,* pp. 30, 41.   [3] *Ibid.,* p. 34.
[4] *Cf.* Job xviii. 5–21, xix. 13ff., xxix.

cultural considerations. It is the notion of leprosy as a mark of disfavor inflicted by God that is uppermost in the lawgiver's mind, and for this reason he recalls Miriam's shameful exclusion from Israel's camp.

D's allusiveness makes it difficult to assess the influence of an earlier law on a later one. Allusiveness, by its nature, involves subtlety and makes the task of interpretation less easy. It is certain that D returns to material treated before and revises, reflects on, and expands upon it, often by means of an association of ideas. In regard to the law concerning the Moabites and Ammonites (xxiii. 4–7; 3–6), the degree of influence is less clear. D wishes to show how the stain of their incestuous origin clings to later generations, and accordingly he relates their despicable behavior at the exodus. The question is whether the law next in line for revision, that concerning the wicked son (xxi. 18–21), is influential in any way. Influence from this source can be regarded as a possibility only because of the general parallel that the "crime" in each law is one of outrageous moral behavior. The son curses his parents and is gluttonous. Ammon and Moab fail to provide Israel with bread and water and attempt to curse Israel. The parallel also applies to the law concerning Edom and Egypt. There is an implied stricture on the behavior of Edom and Egypt toward Israel, and only sons of the third generation are to be admitted into Israel's assembly.

The next law in line for revision is xxi. 22, 23, concerning the hanged man, and again it is not possible to state definitely whether an aspect of it contributes to the law on the camp (xxiii. 10–15; 9–14). The corpse of the hanged man makes the land unclean if it is left unburied overnight; and the faeces, the uncleanness by night, must be buried. The affinity appears coincidental until the allusive way in which D draws different elements together in any one law is recalled.

Cleanliness in the Camp: xxiii. 10–15 *(9–14)*

(10, *9*) When thou goest forth against thine enemies and are in camp, then thou shalt keep thyself from every evil thing. (11, *10*) If there is among thee any man who is not clean by reason of what chances to him by night, then he shall go outside the camp, he shall not come within the camp; (12, *11*) but when evening comes on, he shall bathe himself in water, and when the sun is down, he may come within the camp. (13, *12*) Thou shalt have a place outside the camp and thou shalt go out to it; (14, *13*) and thou shalt have a stick with thy weapons; and when thou sittest down outside, thou shalt dig a hole with it, and turn back and cover up thine excrement. (15, *16*) Because the Lord thy God walks in the midst of thy camp, to save thee and to give up thine enemies before thee, therefore thy camp must be holy, that he may not see anything indecent among thee, and turn away from thee.

The affinity between the hanged man's corpse and nocturnal uncleanness reveals nothing about why D places here a law concerning the army camp. The reasons, however, can be readily determined. D has just noted Israel's encounters with the Ammonites and Moabites and Israel's relations with Edom and Egypt. The army camp law pursues an interest in Edom. D has kept in mind his historical accounts relating to the time of the land's military conquest, when Israel encountered Edom (ii. 1–8), Moab (ii. 9ff.), and Ammon (ii. 19ff.). At that time Israel was not to contend with any of these peoples. For example, in regard to Edom, it is said that these brothers of Israel, the sons of Esau living in Seir, were afraid of Israel, and Israel was "to take good heed" not to contend with them (ii. 4). The warning uses the *niph.* perfect form of "to keep," the same form that is used in the army camp law, in the warning that Israel is to keep itself from every evil thing. (The form only occurs once more in D, in the warning in iv. 15 against making images.) In the army camp law Israel's military situation is again under discussion and D is recalling Israel's rather special encounters with Edom, not primarily that of ii. 1ff. but the initial one, described in Gen. xxxii, xxxiii.

In Genesis, Jacob, on his way after his flight from Laban, with whom he has served twenty years, meets the angels of God. He refers to them as God's "army" or "camp" and calls the place "Mahanaim" (two camps). He then sends messengers to Esau in preparation for what is expected to be a fearful encounter. The messengers return and relate how Esau is coming with four hundred men. Jacob, afraid of this hostile approach to himself and his family, asks God for deliverance from his enemy, from the hand of his brother Esau, for he fears Esau will come and slay them all, including mothers with children. Jacob is left alone in the camp, and a mysterious man who comes and wrestles with him puts his thigh out of joint. Before dawn the antagonist blesses Jacob and Jacob's name is changed to Israel. Jacob-Israel calls the place where he has lodged overnight "Peniel" because he has seen God face to face and his life has been delivered. Esau comes, but he unexpectedly receives Jacob affectionately. Jacob acknowledges this deliverance from a potential antagonist by saying that to see Esau's face is like seeing God's.

In the xxiii. 10–15 (9–14) law, Israel, as a military camp, is to avoid uncleanness by night in the camp. In the Genesis story, Jacob is in a camp with the members of his household, but the situation is one of preparation to meet a hostile enemy. In the army camp law, an unclean happening at night is envisaged. In the Genesis story, Jacob encounters by night an unknown antagonist who puts his thigh out of joint. Because of this incident the Israelites regard the sinew of the hip upon the hollow of the thigh as unclean for eating (Gen. xxxii. 33, 32). D's law is based on this tradition, and his explanation of the need for cleanliness in the camp —that God walks in the midst of the camp to deliver Israel (hiph. נצל) from its enemies—is illuminated by the Genesis narrative. When Jacob hears of Esau's hostile approach he asks God to deliver him (*hiph.* נצל) from his enemy. After his encounter with the antagonist during the night, he says that his life has been delivered. That antagonist proves to be, at least figuratively, God himself. When Jacob sees that Esau's face is welcoming, and not hostile, he says that it is like seeing God's face, the implication being that his life has been delivered once more (Gen. xxxiii. 10). In other words, as D notes for the writing up of his law, God is present in the midst of Jacob's camp in order that Jacob, who there becomes Israel, be delivered from his enemy. Striking confirmation of the connections between D and this Genesis tradition is found in the following law on the fugitive slave.

The Fugitive Slave: xxiii. 16, 17 (*15, 16*)

(16, *15*) Thou shalt not give up to his master a slave who has escaped from his master to thee; (17, *16*) he shall dwell with thee, in thy midst, in the place which he shall choose within one of thy towns, where it pleases him best; thou shalt not oppress him.

This law, as is often pointed out, stands in sharp contrast to similar laws on escaped slaves in other ancient Near Eastern legal codes.[5] The law can be explained as a D creation based on the Genesis tradition about Esau's reception of Jacob. Jacob fled from Laban, whom he served for twenty years (Gen. xxxi. 22, 41). What Jacob's exact status was under Laban is difficult to determine. In D's view, however, Jacob was a slave, and much in the Laban story supports

[5] See G. R. Driver and J. Miles, *The Babylonian Laws: Legal Commentary*, I (Oxford, 1952), 107, on fugitive slaves in Babylonia. The taker of the slave is bound to return him to his owner. If the slave is appropriated the penalty is death. Driver and Miles think D's slave law refers to an Israelite slave who has fled to Palestine (sic) from a heathen master. They do not raise the pressing question of why, if the law is a serious, practical piece of legislation, this situation is not spelled out. They suggest that normally slaves running away from Israelite masters were restored to them.

such a view. The fugitive slave law is a remarkably expansive one. The slave who delivers himself to someone is not to be restored to his former master but to be well received; indeed, he is to dwell in whatever place he chooses, in any town he wishes.

Underlying this unique law is Jacob's flight from Laban and his favorable reception by his brother Esau. When Jacob prepares to meet Esau, he thinks of himself as a servant going to a master. He instructs his messengers to address Esau: "Thus you shall say to my lord, to Esau, thus says thy servant, Jacob" (Gen. xxxii. 5, *4 cf.* vs. 19, *18,* xxxiii. 5, 14). The terms used are אדון and עבד, as in the D law. Jacob's "lord" or "master" receives him well. Moreover, in the ensuing conversation, Esau is well disposed to Jacob's wish to choose a place in which to dwell (Gen. xxxiii. 12–17). In the law, the fugitive slave is to dwell where he wishes, and this direction seems puzzling because it implies that he will not dwell with a new master. The influence of the Genesis story solves the puzzle. The fugitive slave, Jacob, does not become a servant to his new master, Esau, but goes where he pleases.

There is linguistic evidence of a connection between the D legal material and the Genesis story, evidence indicating that both the fugitive slave law and the preceding army camp law arise jointly from the story. In the law concerning the camp, God is in its midst to deliver Israel from its enemies, and the *hiph.* form of נצל is used. In the next law, concerning the fugitive slave, the *niph.* form of נצל is used in reference to the slave who leaves his master and delivers himself to someone else. The Genesis tradition accounts for this use of נצל. Jacob asks God to deliver him from his enemy (Gen. xxxii. 12, *11, hiph.*). After his encounter with the antagonist, he claims that he has seen God's face but his life has been delivered (Gen. xxxii. 31, *30, niph.*). This encounter in some ways anticipates Jacob's meeting with Esau, when his life is again delivered (Gen. xxxiii. 10).

D's laws concerning the camp and the fugitive slave issue from reflection upon a Genesis tradition. D turns to this tradition about the first ancestors of the Israelites and Edomites because of his interest in the generations and their history. He recounts in ii. 1ff. Israel's association with the Edomites at the time of the exodus. In the law code, the Edomites of the third generation after the exodus are to be allowed to have relations with Israel (xxiii. 9, 8). The law concerning the camp, which follows this permission, returns to Israel's relations with the first generation of Edomites, and the next law, on the fugitive slave, is likewise concerned with this tradition. The position is similar for the Ammonites and Moabites. Israel's relations with them at the exodus are recounted in ii, and a law explicitly recalling relations at that time is presented. But D also returns to the first generation of the Ammonites and Moabites and to the tradition about their incestuous origin (Gen. xix). The law on the bastard is the result.

In some laws historical traditions are explicitly cited, while in others they are latent. Traditions about the exodus are cited, while those about the patriarchal period are not. A factor in explaining D's reasons for stating a historical tradition in one law and not stating it in another is the D setting, in the historical period toward the end of the exodus and before the entrance into the new land. Moses speaks to Israel out of his own experience and therefore cites what occurred within that experience. The earlier history of his people is a formative aspect only in his experience, but it is nonetheless a means by which to make judgments about his present experience. For example, the first generations of the Ammonites and Moabites were without worth and so the generations encountered by him in his time must be viewed similarly.

In regard to the Edomites, their first generation behaved ambivalently. There was hostility initially, but this disposition changed to a welcoming one. In regard to the Edomites of the time of Moses, hostility certainly existed. The account of this hostility in Num. xx. 14ff. is probably more accurate than the tradition recounted in Deut. ii. 1–8, 29, which tells of Edom's favorable reception of Israel. Some scholars argue that these two traditions may be related to different incidents.[6] The correct assessment, however, may be that D represents Moses as seeing a contemporary generation in the light of the example of the first one. The behavior of the Edomites in their reception of Israel at the time of the exodus parallels the behavior of Esau in his reception of Jacob after the flight from Laban.

The laws in xxiii. 10ff. (9ff.) form a series initiated by the law concerning the Edomites (xxiii. 8, 9; 7, 8), and the idea of a series is inspired by the M double series. Connections with aspects of Israel's relations with Edom are manifest in the law on the camp and the law on the fugitive slave. A connection probably also exists between D's fugitive slave law and one of the laws in the first of the M series, namely, Ex. xxii. 20 (21), concerning the oppression of the sojourner. These two laws are similar in intent, in that one is concerned with the sojourner's welfare and the other with the fugitive slaves's. Moreover, each uses the uncommon verb ינה, "to oppress." It is noteworthy that the D law has no motive clause referring to the time in Egypt, while the M law does have such a clause. The reason for the absence in D is that D returns to the earlier patriarchal time for his inspiration to commend a slave's well-being.

There is a possible link between the law on straying ani-

[6] For example, S. R. Driver, *Deuteronomy*, ICC (3d ed., Edinburgh, 1902), p. 34. Von Rad thinks there must be a correspondence between the two traditions; *Deuteronomy* (Eng. ed., London, 1966), p. 41. W. A. Sumner, "Israel's Encounters with Edom, Moab, Ammon, Sihon, and Og According to the Deuteronomist," *VT*, 18 (1968), 221, argues that D deliberately discounts the tradition in Num. xx. 14–21 and retells it in line with his own interests and intentions.

mals (xxii. 1–4), which is due for revision in xxiii, and the law on the fugitive slave. In one case straying animals are to be returned to their owners; in the other, by contrast, a fugitive slave is not to be returned to his owner. Each law is expansive in character. Straying animals are to be taken within a man's house and to remain there until the owner comes for them. The slave is to dwell wherever he pleases. This amplitude reflects Esau's reception of Jacob and his acceding to Jacob's request to make his own way.

Cultic Prostitution: xxiii. 18, 19 (*17, 18*)

(18, *17*) There shall be no cult prostitute of the daughters of Israel, neither shall there be a cult prostitute of the sons of Israel. (19, *18*) Thou shalt not bring the hire of a harlot, or the wages of a dog, into the house of the Lord thy God in payment for any vow; for both of these are an abomination to the Lord thy God.

The subject of the fugitive slave law may have been suggested to D by the Genesis tradition about Jacob's flight from Laban, the M law on the oppression of the sojourner, or the law on straying animals. In the following law (concerning cultic prostitution), however, it is clear that the subject is directly suggested by a return to an earlier law in D. After the law on straying animals comes one on transvestism (xxii. 5). The female deviation is mentioned first; a woman is not to put on a man's clothing in order to be smuggled into the army for men's pleasure. The male deviation is then mentioned; men are not to wear women's clothes for homosexual purposes. The law of xxiii. 18, 19 (*17, 18*) first mentions cultic prostitution of the daughters of Israel and then cultic (homosexual) prostitution of the sons of Israel. The connection between the laws is apparent and accounts for what is a recurring phenomenon in D, namely, the often puzzling appearance of a law at one point in the code rather than another.

The cultic bias of the prostitution law may be explained in terms of the continuing influence of the Genesis traditions concerning Jacob and Esau. The laws on the army camp and the fugitive slave, which precede the prostitution law, are influenced by the story of Jacob's association with Esau. If one assumes that D's thinking continues in the same vein, it seems probable that the history of Jacob after his meeting with Esau, involving Jacob's fulfillment of a vow made after his earlier flight from Esau, determines the prostitution law's cultic nature. The law is an excellent example of D's eclecticism.

The law prohibits bringing the hire of a harlot and the price of a dog (the male prostitute) [7] into the house of the "Lord thy God" in payment of any vow. Reference to God's "house" occurs only once in D, in the prostitution law. (It also occurs in the M law [Ex. xxiii. 19] about the first-fruits, but there is no connection with D's law.) [8] Following Jacob's meeting with Esau comes the incident of Shechem's treatment of Dinah as a harlot (Gen. xxxiv. 31), and following this the account of how God tells Jacob to go to Bethel—the house of God—and to make an altar to the God who appeared to him when he fled from Esau (Gen. xxxv. 1ff.). Jacob instructs his household and those with him, that is, the female and younger inhabitants of Shechem, to put away their foreign gods, purify themselves, and change their garments. He then goes to Bethel.

If D is following these traditions, it may be observed that

---

[7] D. W. Thomas, "*Kelebh* 'dog': Its Origin and Some Usages of It in the O.T." *VT*, 10 (1960), 410ff., suggests that the term "dog" for a male prostitute can refer nonpejoratively to a devoted follower of a god. No such reference is implied in D's law.

[8] The M law closest in spirit to D's cultic prostitution law is Ex. xxii. 19 (*20*), which prohibits sacrifices to other gods and states (possibly an addition, the Samaritan text deletes) that only sacrifices to Yahweh are permitted. Cultic prostitution was practised in the name of foreign gods (II Kings xxiii. 7).

the subject of the harlotry of a daughter of Israel arises in this context, and that it is a concern in the prostitution law. It may then be assumed that for D part of the meaning of the Bethel narrative is that no impurities are to desecrate the place, God's house, where Jacob worships his God. D would readily relate this aspect of the narrative to the preceding aspect concerning harlotry—the more so since he has already shown particular interest in this harlotry (see pp. 160ff.). The prostitution law refers to the impure worship involved in bringing the gains of prostitution into God's house. Specifically, the law refers to these gains in terms of payment of a vow. It is significant, therefore, that Jacob's worship at Bethel is in fulfillment of the vow made at Bethel on the earlier occasion of his flight from Esau (Gen. xxviii). The account of Jacob's worship in Gen. xxxv. 1, 7 recalls that occasion. The cultic terms of the prostitution law are inspired by these Genesis traditions. Moreover, Jacob's relationship with Esau is again a background factor. Jacob's vow related to his safe deliverance from Esau. That deliverance is the vital background factor in the two laws (army camp, fugitive slave) that precede the law on cultic prostitution.

Lending at Interest: xxiii. 20, 21 *(19, 20)*

(20, *19*) Thou shalt not lend upon interest to thy brother, interest on money, interest on victuals, interest on anything that is lent for interest. (21, *20*) To a foreigner thou mayest lend upon interest, but to thy brother thou shalt not lend upon interest; that the Lord thy God may bless thee in all that thou undertakest in the land which thou art entering to take possession of it.

The three concluding laws in xxiii continue the allusion to Israel's relations with Edom, taking up the historical notices on the Edomites in ii. 1ff.

A law on lending appears at this point because D is reworking the similar law in the M double series (Ex. xxii. 24, 25) and at the same time weaving in an allusion to Israel's trading relationship with Edom, which he has mentioned earlier in ii. 6. The law prohibits lending money or goods at interest to a brother, but permits lending at interest to a foreigner. When Israel passed through their brother Edomites' territory, God commanded Moses to have the Israelites purchase food and water with money from the Edomites (ii. 6). Although this purchase only involved a straight commercial transaction, D's lending law, which is revising an earlier M law specifically concerned with the subject of lending at interest, has this historical incident in mind. This is why D's law, unlike the M law, is more interested in trading relations than in relations with poor people in need. The law mentions interest on money, interest on food, anything lent at interest, and reflects an awareness of the episode of trade with the brother nation, Edom, in matters of money, food and water. It is a typical D presentation. A historical example is sought out and brought into conjunction with a common legal concern. Edom serves as an example of a brother country with whom Israel has traded. The "foreigner" refers to the distant nations (*cf.* xx. 15); with them, Israel may engage in trading practices that involve lending at interest.

A more explicit indication that D appeals to this particular tradition is to be found in the promise contained in the law: Yahweh will bless Israel in all that its hand undertakes in the land it is about to possess. The setting is the time described in the historical notice in ii. Immediately following the notice in ii. 6 about Israel's trade with Edom at a time prior to entering the land occurs an almost identical statement to that in the law about Yahweh's blessing Israel in all the work of its hand (ii. 7). Driver points to this parallel in language,[9] but draws no conclusion. He also argues that this law is like the ones in Ex. xxii. 24 (25) and Lev. xxv. 36ff., in that it concerns loans directed to the relief of distress. This concern,

[9] *Deuteronomy,* ICC, p. 265.

however, is not the primary one. The fact that D alone mentions lending at interest to the foreigner indicates that he is thinking more of commercial trading relations.

In addition to continuing the theme of relations with Edom, the lending law, as we might expect, also takes up an earlier law in D, that concerning the seventh year release of the money debt (xv. 1ff.).[10] There are a number of parallels to be noted. In both laws there is the same contrast between the brother, who is equated with the neighbor (xv. 2), and the foreigner. There are similar statements about Israel lending to many nations but borrowing from none. There are similar promises about God's blessing on all that will be undertaken in the land that is being entered. This conscious use of the language of a preceding law in no way precludes D's eclectic use of the historical material in ii; rather it underlines the interwoven unity of the entire D material.

Vows: xxiii. 22–24 (21–23)

(22, 21) When thou makest a vow to the Lord thy God, thou shalt not be slack to pay it; for the Lord thy God will surely require it of thee, and it would be sin in thee. (23, 22) But if thou refrainest from vowing, it shall be no sin in thee. (24, 23) Thou shalt be careful to perform what has passed thy lips, for thou hast voluntarily vowed to the Lord thy God what thou hast promised with thy mouth.

Possible delay in the payment of a vow is the major concern of this law. The law might represent a reworking of the law (Ex. xxii. 28, 29) in the M double series about delay in offering from one's harvest and press. The payment of a vow is mentioned in D's law on cultic prostitution, but there is nothing to suggest a concern about delay in paying it. Appeal

---

[10] D does not return to the laws in xxii but, not unreasonably, to a law similar in substance in xv. Thus begins a revision and expansion of material in xv. 1ff., a process that is continued through the remaining laws in xxiii, suspended for the initial laws in xxiv, and taken up again in the remaining laws of xxiv.

to D's manner of presenting laws proves more fruitful in accounting for the particular interest of this law. D has just returned (in his law on lending at interest) to a revision of earlier material in xv. 1ff. The law on vows also returns to this material. The expression, "And it would be sin in thee," used in regard to the failure to pay a vow promptly, is taken from xv. 9, where it is applied to the Israelite who holds off giving a loan to his brother because the year of the remission of debts is but a short time away. The subject of delay in making a payment, in one case a loan, in the other a vow, is prominent.

Sometimes D presents a law that combines a proverbial concern with a historical illustration; the law concerning the neighbor's boundary mark is of this kind (see Chapter 5) as is the law concerning weights and measures (see Chapter 11). The law on delay in paying a vow is probably similar. In Prov. xx. 25 and Eccles. v. 1–5 (2–6) there are warnings against making precipitate vows, and the words of Eccles. v. 3 (4) about not postponing payment of a vow, if one is made, are very similar to D's. The reference in D's law to what comes from the lips also recalls traditional wisdom concern.[11] Since D presents a series of laws which echoes Israel's historical associations with Edom, he may be thinking of a historical tradition that illustrates the need for prompt payment of a vow.

The law on lending, which precedes the law on vowing, is based on the tradition about Israel's trade in Edom's territory. It is likely that the vow law is influenced by the tradition about the vow made by Israel at the time of the nation's wandering in and around Edomite territory. This tradition is associated with the place Hormah. The Canaanite king of Arad took some Israelites captive, and they vowed that if God gave this Canaanite people into their hand they would destroy them (Num. xxi. 1ff.). The vow was promptly fulfilled,

11 There are numerous proverbs on the subject, e.g., Prov. v. 2, 3.

and Israel then set out to go around the land of Edom (vs. 4). This incident is a historical example of an Israelite vow made and fulfilled. D makes no mention of this episode but records only an earlier incident at Hormah when Israel delayed the attack on the Canaanites, regretted the delay, and, ignoring the divine prohibition not to proceed, was defeated at Seir in the land of Edom (i. 41–45). After this defeat Israel dwelt "many days" at Kadesh, then turned to go around the mountains of Seir, and prepared to pass through Edom's territory (ii. 1ff.). This first incident at Hormah, common to Deut. i and Num. xiv, when Israel suffered defeat, occurred at the beginning of the forty year period in the desert. The second incident, when Israel fulfilled its vow, occurred at the end of this period (Num. xxi. 1ff.).[12]

It is difficult to assess D's relationship to these traditions. Hence it can only be suggested that D's law on vowing reflects upon the nature and history of both incidents at Hormah. In its concern with delay in paying a vow, the law may be contrasting the later episode at Hormah, when Israel did not delay in fulfilling a vow, with the earlier occasion, when Israel's delay in carrying out its expressed intention brought punishment. D's account of the latter incident mentions no vow as such. However, unlike the corresponding account in Num. xiii. 1ff., D indicates that it is the people who take the initiative in preparing to overcome the enemy (i. 22).[13] That initiative, similar to a vow, breaks down, despite the assurance that God will deliver the enemy to Israel (i. 30).

There is a puzzle inherent in D's account in i of the defeat at Hormah: why did God not respond to the people's renewed faith, expressed in their decision to proceed to battle with the enemy? D's assessment of the situation may stem from his belief that a promise must be fulfilled promptly.

[12] This is Driver's view (*ibid.*, p. 32). G. B. Gray, *Numbers,* ICC (Edinburgh, 1903), p. 272, is less sure of the time difference.

[13] See p. 28f.

The people of Israel freely volunteered to conquer the enemy, but, and this was their fault, their subsequent action did not immediately follow their words of promise. The law stresses that the event of the promise—what comes out of the mouth—should result, without hesitation, in the corresponding event of the action indicated. A promise in these terms can be a weightier matter than an action. The law makes the seemingly obvious point that if no promise is made, nothing is required.

The Neighbor's Crops: xxiii. 25, 26 (24, 25)

(25, 24) When thou goest into thy neighbor's vineyard, thou mayest eat thy fill of grapes, as many as thou wishest, but thou shalt not put any in thy vessel. (26, 25) When thou goest into thy neighbor's standing grain, thou mayest pluck the ears with thine hand, but thou shalt not put a sickle to thy neighbor's standing grain.

This law is an expansive one. It permits eating as many grapes as desired from a neighbor's vineyard and plucking as many ears of corn as desired from his standing grain. But the law is also peculiar. The prohibitions that are added, that the grapes may not be put in a vessel and a sickle may not be put to the grain, although they might appear to constitute a reasonable limitation on the expansiveness, have an odd tone. The law is bizarre in the situations it envisages. In normal circumstances it is unrealistic to imagine that a person will confuse casual eating of a neighbor's crops with wholesale garnering by means of implements. Plucking grapes or grain is one thing, a matter of people's habits controlled by notions of social conduct; using a vessel or sickle is quite another, a different area of conduct, namely, thieving. Yet the law is not dealing with a punishable offense. It moves in a different realm of thought. The law in fact is prompted by D's reflections on the historical situation when Israel, seeking transit through Edomite territory, stood armed before Edom's fields and vineyards. The law puts into terms of the individual living in a time of peace D's judgment on what a people's behavior should be in this exceptional situation in a time of war.

Israel asked permission to cross Edom's land, saying that they would neither pass through field or vineyard nor drink water from a well (Num. xx. 14ff.). Edom refused this request, as well as permission for Israel to pass through on foot and to pay for any water they might use. The law on the neighbor's crops reflects D's reaction to this incident. The expansive permission to eat as much as desired of a neighbor's grapes and grain, on entering his vineyard or cornfield, indicates D's disapproval of Edom's inhospitable refusal of Israel's request.

Specifically, underlying the law is D's reflection on Israel's words of assurance that they would not pass through Edom's fields or vineyards with the implication that they would not eat anything there. D's attention remains on this subject of entering a field or vineyard and focuses on Edom's attitude, which is found wholly wrong. This attitude is like that of the Moabites and Ammonites, who did not meet Israel with bread and water (xxiii. 4–6; *3–5*). D thinks that Edom should have granted Israel permission to eat of their fields and vineyards. This moralizing on past history lies behind D's law on the neighbor's crops. Israel's assurance that they would not turn aside into the Edomite fields or vineyards indicated their readiness to behave correctly if Edom responded positively to their request to cross Edomite territory. The same moral sensibility exists in the law. Permission is granted in the law to eat freely of a neighbor's field and vineyard, but no advantage is to be taken of the liberty given. Correct behavior demands that no vessel be used for the grapes and no sickle for the standing grain. D's reasons for considering such possibilities lie in the model of the historical episode involving Israel and Edom. Israel should have been permitted to eat; but, had permission been forthcoming, it would have been incumbent on them not to use their weapons in taking the food.

The generous provision of food is a subject touched on in xv. 14 with regard to the departure of a released slave. We have seen that the two laws that precede the law on the neighbor's crops are written up in relation to the material in xv. 1ff., and hence it is likely that the subject of generosity in matters of food in xxiii. 25, 26 (*24, 25*) is suggested to D by his reversion to this material.

Having considered the background of D's law on the neighbor's crops, we can see why this incident involving Edom, as reported in Num. xx, is recounted quite differently in D's historical retrospect in ii. To have repeated the story and yet to have permitted Edom to enter Israel's assembly would have been inconsistent. The Moabites and Ammonites, after all, are excluded from the assembly because they did not meet Israel with bread and water, and this lapse, it must be noted, is a less serious offense than Edom's refusal either to permit Israel transit through their land or to give them water in return for payment (Num. xx. 18, 19). D admits Edom to the assembly because the country is Israel's brother nation. Since D wants this positive relationship, and since he considers the failure of Moab and Ammon to provide bread and water as a "crime," [14] he discounts the fault in Edom's record, or rationalizes it away. Probably he chooses to rationalize it by seeing a parallel between Edom's behavior at the exodus and Esau's in regard to Jacob. Esau first showed hostility toward Jacob and then changed his attitude; D, noting Edom's hostility to Israel in the tradition of Num. xx, partly discounts it and concentrates instead (ii. 6, 28, 29) on a later, more favorable attitude.[15] Edom's fault is not entirely forgotten, however, as is implied by the limiting condition that only

[14] D's view reflects wisdom belief (see p. 175f.).
[15] See the similar discussion above on the fugitive slave law.

Edomites of the third generation may enter Israel's assembly (xxiii. 9, *8*).

It is interesting to note other indications of D's suppression of Edom's bad behavior. As Driver points out, there is a curious feature in D's record of Israel's treatment by Sihon. In the account of Num. xxi. 21ff., Sihon, exactly like Edom in Num. xx. 14ff., refused Israel passage through his territory, despite assurances that Israel would not turn aside into field or vineyard. D takes over this account, using many of the same words, in ii. 26ff.[16] However, D substitutes a phrase about not turning aside to the right or left for the words in Numbers about the field and vineyard. Moreover, the phrase is taken from the Edom account in Numbers, except that D uses a different word for "to turn." This is a curious phenomenon. The writing up of one event through association with another, similar one is common enough in all historical writing. D's associative thinking is especially marked. The curious thing in ii. 27 is the absence of reference to the field and vineyard and the substitution of the more general wording from the earlier Edom account. It is, perhaps, another indication that D is anxious to discount any record of Edom's failure in the elementary duty of providing food and drink. Yet another indication may lie in the use of the term "neighbor" rather than "brother" in the law on the neighbor's crops. In the law concerning loans at interest (xxiii. 20, 21; *19, 20*), the term "brother" is used because of the historical model of Israel's trade with the brother nation, Edom. The law on the neighbor's crops avoids the term "brother" even though the law has been prompted by another Edomite situation. The reason appears to be that, although the law stands in condemnation of Edom, no attention must be given to this aspect.

[16] Driver, *Deuteronomy*, ICC, p. 43.

Summary

In referring to the laws studied in this chapter as the Edomite series, we must remember that the reference is only to a background feature used by the lawgiver in composing his laws. No law makes this feature explicit. D is again working on a broad canvas and bringing other elements into his laws. The law admitting the Edomites into Israel's assembly exercises a pervasive influence throughout the laws in the series, inspiring the interest in Edom (Esau) which lies behind all the laws. It also contributes to the concern in most of the laws with exclusion and removal from, or admittance and reception into, a place.

The Edomite traditions underlying the laws are as follows: (*i*) Jacob's advance to meet Esau and his reception by him (Gen. xxxii, xxxiii); (*ii*) Jacob's vow at Bethel regarding his safe deliverance from Esau (Gen. xxviii, xxxv); (*iii*) Israel's commercial transactions with Edom (Deut. ii. 1ff.); (*iv*) The vow associated with Israel's imminent transit through Edom's territory (Num. xxi. 1ff.); and (*v*) Israel's transit through Edom's territory (Num. xx. 14ff.).

D is also influenced in writing this series of laws by preceding material in his own code (xxi. 22–xxii. 5 and xv. 1ff.) and by earlier laws from M's double series (Ex. xxii. 20–30; *21–31* and Ex. xxiii. 9–19).

10. The Egyptian Series: xxiv

The law in xxiii. 8a (7a) about the Edomites, Israel's brothers, prompts the presentation of a list of laws all of which are inspired by D's reflections on traditions concerning the relations of Israel, sometimes in the person of Jacob, with Edom, sometimes in the person of Esau. The law in xxiii. 8b (7b) turns to the Egyptians, who are to be permitted into the assembly of Yahweh because Israel was at one time a sojourner in Egypt. As with the Edomites, only Egyptians of the third generation are to be admitted. The restriction is made in this case because the Egyptians changed their favorable attitude to the Israelites during Israel's sojourn in Egypt and enslaved them (Ex. i). In xxiv D presents a list of laws touching on aspects of Israel's contacts with the Egyptians, both during the patriarchal period described in Genesis and in the later period of the enslavement in Egypt and the exodus from Egypt.[1]

It will be recalled that the D double series of laws is inspired by the model of the M double series and that some laws in the M series are reworked in the D series. Each series in M begins with a law recalling the sojourn in Egypt. D's second series (xxiv) contains explicit mention of Egypt in three laws as well as allusion to the sojourner in three laws. That these references are not haphazard, but attributable to D's scheme of presenting an Egyptian series, may be better

[1] See the opening of Chapter 9 for discussion of the D double (Egyptian and Edomite) series.

understood by noting that no law in the Edomite series contains any reference to Egypt, despite the fact that certain laws in the Edomite series (for example, that on the fugitive slave) might have been expected to make such allusion.

The "Egyptian" character of the laws in xxiv may also be appreciated by considering the concentration of interest on the oppression of the poor and needy. This emphasis on oppression is in marked contrast to the expansive character of the "Edomite" laws in xxiii. Five of the ten laws in xxiv concern victimization of the poor. The reason for this emphasis is clear. Israel's oppression in Egypt is a prominent background factor. D's sensitivity to the humiliation involved would make him dwell on the experience.

It has to be borne in mind, in speaking of an Egyptian series, that the Egyptian element is only one of a number of contributions to any law in the series. D's associative method of linking legal, proverbial, and historical elements means that the laws are diverse by nature, and therefore no obvious thread connects one law with the next. The task is to unravel D's eclectic process and trace his background thinking.

The Renovation of a Marriage: xxiv. 1–4

(1) When a man takes a wife and marries her, if then she finds no favor in his eyes because he has found some indecency in her, and he writes her a bill of divorce and puts it in her hand and sends her out of his house, and she departs out of his house, (2) and if she goes and becomes another man's wife, (3) and the latter husband dislikes her and writes her a bill of divorce and puts it in her hand and sends her out of his house; or if the latter husband dies, who took her to be his wife, (4) then her former husband, who sent her away, may not take her again to be his wife, after she has been defiled; for that is an abomination before the Lord, and thou shalt not bring guilt upon the land which the Lord thy God gives thee for an inheritance.

This law forbidding the renovation of a marriage is a prohibition without parallel in any legal material in the ancient world.[2] A man marries a woman, dislikes her, and divorces her. She marries another man but again is released, either by divorce or by the second husband's death. The law prohibits the first husband's taking her again as his wife. The reason for the prohibition is puzzling. If the law were the result of a specific case it would be less puzzling, but there is little evidence in D to suggest that laws are formulated on the basis of practical problems known to D in his own time. Yaron effectively dismisses two interpretations frequently offered: [3] one, that the law is designed to deter hasty divorce; and the other, that it treats the offense in question as somehow tantamount to adultery. Yaron introduces the surprising argument that the law is explicable in terms of the considerations that lead to the formulation of incest rules. Incest rules protect approved existing relationships within a family. Yaron thinks D extends the principle of protection to approved marriage relationships. The law protects the second marriage—the one contracted by the woman divorced by her first husband—from the possibility of breakdown because the first husband regrets divorcing the woman, she responds to his regret, and both wish to renew the original marriage. In a closeknit community this kind of strain is a real possibility, and the lawgiver considers it intolerable.

Yaron's argument is unconvincing. As he admits, rules of incest ordinarily apply within a family group. If the protection of the second marriage is the law's intention, it is obscure in this respect. After all, the law considers the cases of the second husband's divorcing the woman for reasons of his own and his death. It seems unnecessary that the law should mention these possibilities if it is designed "to ensure the stability and continuation of the second marriage." [4] If the second husband disappears from the scene, the woman is

[2] See R. Yaron, "The Restoration of a Marriage," *JJS*, 17 (1966), 1–11.

[3] *Ibid.*, 5–8.   [4] *Ibid.*, 9.

then free to marry again—only she is not free to renew marriage with the first husband. It is the possibility of a renewed relationship between the former husband and wife that concerns the lawgiver, not, as Yaron argues, the woman's second marriage. It would be remarkable in any case for a law to go to such lengths to prohibit what would surely be a rare occurrence. Moreover, Yaron does not consider the law in its Deuteronomic context and states that no considerations other than legal ones apply to the text. Even the term "defiled," used in reference to the woman, expresses for Yaron only a straight legal fact (the second marriage puts the woman beyond the reach of her first husband).[5] But D's interests encompass more than legal matters. The uniqueness of the law suggests this. So does the language: a renovated marriage after the woman has been with another man causes the land to sin.

D's method of presenting laws discloses the considerations that have led to the formulation of this peculiar law. There are two accounts, in Gen. xii, xx, of situations in which a man is married to a woman, her status is changed, another man takes her, and eventually she is restored to her first husband. (The similar tradition in Gen. xxvi can be discounted because the situation of Isaac and Rebekah recounted there does not develop.) In Gen. xii. 10ff. Abram goes down to Egypt to sojourn. (The law under discussion is the first of the Egypt/sojourning laws.) Sarai is his wife, but reasons of expediency cause him to give the impression that she is his sister. He therefore does not prevent Sarai from being taken by the Egyptian Pharaoh. Only after divine intervention does the Pharaoh learn that the woman is in fact a man's wife. She is then restored to Abram. The story in Gen. xx again concerns Abraham and Sarah (their names are changed by this time) and involves a sojourning in Gerar. This story reveals a remarkable moral sensibility. It recounts how a

[5] *Ibid.,* 8.

situation almost identical to the one in Egypt is *not* allowed
to develop to the point where Abraham's wife is actually
taken (sexually) by another man, in this case Abimelech,
before being restored to Abraham. There is clearly an attempt to preserve Sarah's virtue as the wife of Abraham.
Abimelech almost takes her, but God intervenes in time to
warn him that Sarah is a man's wife.[6]

It is these two traditions that furnish the model for D's
thinking and inspire his law prohibiting the renovation of a
marriage. D, like the author of Gen. xx, is reacting against a
situation such as that described in Gen. xii, where Sarah
actually is taken by Pharaoh. D shows the same moral sensibility as the story in xx. Both D and this narrator find it
offensive that Sarah could be taken by another man and
then restored to Abraham. That would be a defilement of
Sarah. Abimelech, a righteous man, says that by letting
Sarah be taken into Abimelech's palace Abraham brings, not
just on himself but also on his kingdom, a great sin (Gen. xx.
9). The D laws speaks not just of the woman's being defiled
but of causing the land to sin. In the story, the sin is against
God himself (Gen. xx. 6). Likewise, in the renovation law,
the woman's defilement is an abomination before God.

It is readily understandable why D discusses the problem
of renovating a marriage in terms of divorce. The situation
in Genesis is peculiar. Formally (we have to remember that
we are dealing with a story), Abraham does not divorce
Sarah, but he interferes with her status as his wife to the
point of disavowing it, and in reality he lets her go from
him. For D, the institutional use of divorce, which is taken
for granted in the law, affords the most likely example of a
comparable, if nonetheless rare, occurrence in normal life.

Considered from one viewpoint—a viewpoint unacceptable
to D—the change in Sarah's status from wife to sister means
that Pharaoh's taking her did not constitute adultery. Con-

---

[6] The phrase used is literally "married to a husband" and occurs
only in this story and in the adultery law in Deut. xxii. 22.

sidered from the viewpoint of the deity in the Genesis story, however,—a viewpoint shared by D—adultery did take place since Sarah's true status as a wife was unaffected by Abraham's action. Notwithstanding this background tradition, it is still misleading to interpret the law as dealing with a matter that is regarded as tantamount to adultery.

The renovation law begins a series that reflects upon traditions about the experiences of Israel's ancestors when associated with Egypt. This fact provides the explanation for the much debated expression "the nakedness of a thing," "some indecency" in the RSV (עֶרְוַת דָּבָר). The use of the expression in this law is determined by its use in the law concerning uncleanness in the army camp. For the army camp law opens the Edomite series. In other words, D's formal arrangement of material is the key factor in explaining the appearance of the expression in xxiv. 1. In regard to its meaning there, if D has in mind the situation of Sarai and Abram in Egypt, he is thinking in their case of Abram's defenseless position because his wife's beauty is exposed to foreign eyes. We can infer that for the purposes of his divorce law D is thinking of the embarrassment caused to a husband by his wife's public behavior.[7]

The New Wife: xxiv. 5

When a man is newly married, he shall not go out with the army or be charged with any business: he shall be free at home one year, to be happy with his wife whom he has taken.

This law is an example of D's returning to a previously given law. The law in xx. 7 exempting a man from military service if he has taken a new wife immediately comes to mind. However, while D certainly has that law in mind, other evidence indicates that he returns to it by way of the law of

[7] The (male) concern with the public behavior of women in Mesopotamian society emerges clearly in the law codes. Cf., for example, the Hammurabi law, no. 143, "If she was not careful, but was a gadabout, thus neglecting her house (and) humiliating her husband," *ANET*, p. 172.

xxi. 10–14, the captive maid taken as a new wife. This captive maid law is itself related to the law in xx. 7 (see p. 139). The reason D is again interested in the captive maid law is that the subject of divorce arises in the law concerning renovation of a marriage (xxiv. 1–4), and it has arisen previously in regard to the captive maid. Either the association works in this direction or else the issue of the dissolution of a marriage in xxi. 10–14 prompts D's thinking about the problem of renovating a marriage in xxiv. 1–4. In any case, the law concerning the captive maid is in the background of the law on the new wife, and also of the two following laws concerning the cruel pledge and the theft of a man.

The one striking addition in the law on the new wife to the provisions of the law that exempts a man from military service if he has just taken a wife is that the husband is to remain at home for a year to give joy to his wife. (What a remarkable statement of law.) The meaning of this joy is the birth of a child and the perpetuation of the man's name (see p. 122). The period of one year, which gives time for the birth of a child, suggests this interpretation; Jeremiah's exclamation about the giving of joy at the birth of a child helps to confirm it (Jer. xx. 15). D's allusiveness is responsible for his dealing with the matter at all, and for the expansive way in which it is handled. In the law on renovating a marriage, which precedes the law on the new wife, the influence of the Genesis traditions about Abraham and Sarah's marriage is observable. One of these traditions tells of Sarah's childlessness and the birth of a son in her old age. Indeed, the story of the birth is told immediately after the account in Gen. xx of Sarah's restoration to Abraham, the healing of Abimelech, and the healing of his wife and female slaves so that they could bear children again. (God had closed the wombs of Abimlech's house because of Sarah, Abraham's wife.) The topic of marriage in both the law on the renovation of a marriage and the law on the new wife is the only obvious indication of any connection between them. However, once their common source of inspiration is seen to be these traditions involving Sarah, the connection becomes clearer.

The giving of joy to a newly married wife is suggested by the peculiar situation of Sarah's giving birth in her old age. In the law, the man gives joy to the wife. The birth of a child is joyful for him too, yet the concentration is on the wife. This emphasis in the law reflects the emphasis given to Sarah's situation in the tradition. Her pregnancy and delivery evoked laughter that included a little ribaldry and certainly great joy because of her long, sad history of childlessness.[8] (Sarah laughed at the prospect of giving birth in her old age, having delight, as she expressed it—Gen. xviii. 12). The son's name, Isaac, is said to reflect the laughter surrounding the odd event (Gen. xxi. 3, 6).

The D law is thus a typically eclectic one. A previously given law, on taking a new wife and being free from military duty, is expanded along a line suggested by the earlier Genesis tradition about the birth of Sarah's son.

A Life in Pledge: xxiv. 6

No man shall take a mill or an upper millstone in pledge, for he would be taking a life in pledge.

This law, expressed in a brief, pithy form, is proverbial in character. Such extreme, oppressive pledging is mentioned in Prov. xxii. 27, Job xxii. 6, xxiv. 9. Moreover the millstone

---

[8] J. Skinner, *Genesis,* ICC (2d ed., Edinburgh, 1930), p. 321, takes the laugher in xxi. 6a and 6b as an expression of joy, whereas von Rad, *Genesis* (Eng. ed., London, 1961), p. 226, sees only 6a in this sense and 6b as laughter of embarrassment among Sarah's acquantances; but both commentators underline the aspect of joy in the birth of the child. R. A. Carlson, *David, the Chosen King* (Uppsala, 1964), p. 122, *cf.* p. 118, suggests that the D group of writers link the tradition about the birth of Isaac in Gen. xv. 1–6 to the statement in II Sam. vii. 12 about David's offspring.

has an attested literary use as a symbol. This proverbial usage indicates the nature and meaning of both the pledge law in xxiv. 6 and the new wife law in xxiv. 5. Jeremiah inveighs against the people of Josiah's time and warns that they will be denied the voice of mirth and the voice of rejoicing, the voice of the bridegroom and the voice of the bride, the sound of the millstone and the light of the lamp (Jer. xxv. 10). Isaiah, referring to the virgin daughter of Babylon, describes her humiliation in terms of a millstone. No more will she be called "tender and delicate," but she will take the millstone and grind meal (Is. xlvii. 1ff.). In other words, her grinding with the millstone makes her a slave. Job xxxi. 10 says, "Let my wife grind for another," that is, serve as a slave.[9] Working the handmill, as Driver points out,[10] is associated with female slaves (Ex. xi. 5).

D presents a law on taking a life in pledge at this point in his code because, as in the preceding law on the new wife, he is returning to the law concerning the captive maid (xxi. 10–14). If the Israelite husband of a captive maid dismisses her from his house, he must not treat her harshly by selling her and making her an article of trade—she is not to be treated as a slave. D combines a renewed interest in this concern about the oppressive treatment of a person as an object in a transaction with a reflection on the events that followed the birth of Isaac to Sarah. The Genesis tradition tells how Isaac grew up and how Ishmael, Abraham's son by Hagar, the Egyptian slave girl, displeased Sarah who did

[9] The context suggests that the Hebrew טָחַן, "to grind," is to be understood metaphorically in a sexual sense. The translation of the LXX and the Vulgate is explicitly sexual. The Qumran Targum and the Targum of the Rabbinic Bibles simply take over the Hebrew. The Peshiṭta tends toward a literal sense.

[10] *Deuteronomy*, ICC (3d ed., Edinburgh, 1902), p. 274. *Cf.* "Good speech is more hidden than the emerald, but it may be found with maidservants at the grindstones," *ANET*, p. 412.

not wish the son of the slavegirl to be coheir with her son, Isaac (Gen. xxi. 8ff.). On his wife's instigation, Abraham dismissed Hagar with her child. Hagar wandered with Ishmael in the wilderness, and when her water was finished she put the child away that she might not look upon its death. The cries of the child, however, were heard by God, and both child and mother were miraculously rescued.

D's law on taking a life in pledge is not an instance of an artificial combination of elements from a preceding law and a narrative tradition. Rather, the common factor of the dismissal of the captive maid in the xxi. 10–14 law and the dismissal of Hagar in the Genesis story suggests to D a proverbial kind of law about taking a mill or millstone in pledge. A handmill is especially associated with the lot of the female slave. Taking a millstone in pledge constitutes a harsh action against the owner of the mill and his family, but the slavegirl who works the mill is affected even more harshly. A family under such pressure would have to dismiss her. The law states that the millstone's removal would be tantamount to taking a life in pledge.

The pledge law concerns the oppressive dismissal of a slavegirl, and there is thus a connection in substance with the oppressive dismissal of the captive maid in xxi. 10–14 and the oppressive dismissal of Hagar, the Egyptian slavegirl. As do preceding laws in xxiv, D's law on taking a life in pledge reveals background consideration of the relations of Israel's ancestors with Egypt, in this case, Abraham and Sarah's relations with Hagar, the Egyptian. The theft law that follows the pledge law has an implicit interest in Israel's relations with the descendants of Ishmael, Hagar's son. The narrative about Abraham's dismissal of Hagar contains the divine promise to make a nation of Ishmael (Gen. xxi. 13, 18). As a first step, Hagar takes a wife for Ishmael from the land of Egypt (vs. 21).

Man-stealing: xxiv. 7

If a man is found stealing one of his brethren, the people of Israel, and if he treats him as a slave or sells him, then that thief shall die; so thou shalt purge the evil from thy midst.

This law further demonstrates D's eclectic method of utilizing different sources to present a new law. It is a particularly clear example of D's method and illustrates well the allusive, comprehensive character of the laws. Three different sources are involved.

First, the law clearly represents a reworking of the M law against man-stealing (Ex. xxi. 16): "Whoever steals a man, whether he sells him or is found in possession of him, shall be put to death." It was pointed out above that D does not deal with this M law in xxi, where M laws in Ex. xxi. 2–17 are reworked, but leaves it for later treatment (see p. 138). Daube argues that the D law is confined to the early form of the M law on theft, which states that theft of a person is proved only if the stolen person is sold by the thief.[11] The M law, if translated literally, has a manifest interpolation in its reference to a man's being found in the thief's hand; the kidnapped man cannot both be sold by the thief and found in his hand. The significance of the interpolation is that it relaxes the conditions of proof; even a thief who has not sold the stolen person may be convicted of his theft. Although probably aware of the additional legal statement in the M law, D ignores it.

D's version varies in another respect from M's. D refers to treating the stolen person as an article of trade and selling him. This is his own language, used earlier in his treatment of an Israelite's oppression of the captive maid he has taken as his wife (xxi. 10–14). This captive maid law, which, as we have seen, also influences the two laws of xxiv. 5, 6, is D's second source for his law on man-stealing. In this case, the

[11] *Studies in Biblical Law* (Cambridge, Eng., 1947), p. 95.

influence on D's language is clear, and the connection between the two laws is a good illustration of how D simply
writes up laws by thinking back in a systematic, if often artificial, way to laws he has previously set down.

The third source is the Genesis tradition about the sale of
Joseph, a son of Israel, by his brothers. The influence of this
source accounts for the two main differences between the D
and (amended) M laws. M refers to the stealing of a man,
but D refers to the stealing of a brother, one of the sons of
Israel. And D's law, because of its association with the Genesis story relating the sale of Joseph, confines itself to this
aspect, even though by D's time the law on man-stealing encompassed more, as the M interpolation in Ex. xxi. 16 indicates.

The law in xxiv. 6 against taking a millstone in pledge is
related to the story of Hagar, the Egyptian slave-girl, and
Ishmael, her son by Abraham. The law on man-stealing in
xxiv. 7 (which is the male complement to xxiv. 6 in the same
way that the law on the wicked son in xxi. 18–21 is related to
the law on the wicked daughter in xxii. 20, 21) also has an
Ishmaelite tradition in mind, and this background explains
why the law is set down at this point. D is adding to his series
of laws on aspects of Israel's historical experience of events
and sojournings associated with Egypt. It was to Ishmaelite
traders on their way down to Egypt that Joseph was sold
(Gen. xxxvii. 25ff.). This common background of traditions
about Ishmael and his descendants accounts for D's use of the
term "life" (נפשׁ) in the two laws concerning the life in
pledge and man-stealing. A life is not to be taken in pledge,
and the life of one of the brothers of the children of Israel
is not to be stolen. In the Joseph story, Reuben explicitly
requested his brothers not to take Joseph's life (נפשׁ, Gen.
xxxvii. 21).

Many D laws are characterized not just by their background of ancient tradition but also by their proverbial na-

ture. Consequently much in them reflects the proverbial wisdom of the generations. This is why the D laws appear to be idealizations and often removed from practical legal needs. The law against taking a millstone in pledge hardly issues from a need to combat a common practice but reflects traditional wisdom teaching against the oppression of persons of inferior status. It is doubtful, too, that in D's time there was any special need to stop the theft and sale of Israelites. This D law shows little concern with the legal problem of theft— the earlier M law is more advanced in that respect. Rather, it reflects traditional wisdom teaching. Job refers to those who snatch (גזל) the fatherless child from the breast and take in pledge the infant of the poor (Job xxiv. 9). Similarly, in Ezek. xviii. 16, xxxiii. 15, oppressive pledging and committing robbery (גזל) are mentioned together. In the two D laws on pledging and man-stealing the same close association between pledging and theft exists. The D law uses גנב, "to steal," rather than גזל, but this is because of the use of גנב in the earlier M law.[12]

Authority and Leprosy: xxiv. 8, 9

(8) Take heed, in an attack of leprosy, to be very careful to do according to all that the Levitical priests shall direct you; as I commanded them, so you shall be careful to do. (9) Remember what the Lord thy God did to Miriam on the way as you came forth out of Egypt.

The appearance of such a law at this point would be difficult to account for if one were unaware that D is presenting a series of laws touching on traditions about Israel's historical relations with Egypt. The laws in xxiv. 1–7 are based on experiences before the time of Israel's slavery in Egypt. Now the leprosy law explicitly refers to the Miriam incident,

[12] For an important difference sometimes found between the terms גנב and גזל, see B. S. Jackson, *Theft in Early Jewish Law* (Oxford, 1972), pp. 1–19.

which occurred as Israel was "coming forth from Egypt." Why is this particular incident chosen? There are, after all, many others relating to Israel's exodus from Egypt.

It is just possible that another quasi-Egyptian element in the story is relevant. Miriam's leprosy breaks out because she and her brother Aaron question the authority of Moses. This questioning is initially, and somewhat obscurely, prompted by the complaint about the Cushite woman Moses has married (Num. xii. 1). Cush in the Old Testament refers, rather imprecisely, to the land and people of the Nile valley south of Egypt.[13] The complaint appears to be against the Cushite woman's foreignness. Given D's interest in Israel's relations with Egypt, this connection, involving Cush which is probably considered as geographically proximate to Egypt, might explain D's turning to the Miriam story at this particular point in the code.

A more likely explanation, however, follows from noting D's method of presenting material. Earlier laws in xxiv review the law concerning the foreign captive maid (xxi. 10–14), part of which refers to the humiliation of the woman honorably taken (in marriage) into an Israelite home and then wrongfully dismissed from it. The laws in the two D series of xxiii and xxiv show a continuing interest in the notion of honorable admittance into, and humiliating exclusion from, relationship with Israel. The example of Miriam contrasts with the example of the foreign woman who is dismissed in humiliating fashion from the house of her Israelite husband. Miriam is rightfully dismissed in disgrace from the Israelite camp (Num. xii. 14) for speaking against Moses' marriage to the foreign Cushite woman. D is often interested in contrasting cases, and the contrast between the captive maid's dismissal and Miriam's explains his reference to the Miriam story.

The question remains as to why the main point of the law

[13] See E. Ullendorff, *Ethiopia and the Bible* (Oxford, 1968), pp. 5–9.

is obedience to authority. This concern with authority is observable in two, not quite complementary, respects. First,
obedience to the Levitical priests in an outbreak of leprosy
is enjoined. Second, the Miriam incident is cited, presumably
in support of such an injunction. In that incident, however,
Miriam's leprosy was the consequence of her questioning
Moses' unique authority. There is no mention of her obedience after her leprosy. One is led to the interesting reflection that D understands Miriam's readmission into Israel's
camp to be dependent upon her obedience to Moses in her
leprous state. In other words, just as her questioning of
Moses' authority led to her leprous infliction, so will her
acceptance of his authority remove it.

In setting down his leprosy law, D may also have in mind
two parallel laws in the M double series, those of Ex. xxii.
27 (28) against reviling God and cursing a ruler of the people,
and Ex. xxiii. 13, on heeding all that God says and not men-
tioning the names of other gods. A consideration of these laws
in relation to the Miriam incident does raise the topic of
obedience to authority, which is the chief concern of the D
law. In the Miriam incident a ruler of the people is spoken
against. Such presumption arouses God's anger; Miriam and
Aaron have treated lightly God's delegation of authority over
the people to Moses (Num. xii. 7). To speak against Moses is
a serious offense, being tantamount, it is implied, to speaking
against God.[14] For D, the obedience due to the Levitical
priests is a comparable matter, for Mosaic authority is in-
vested in them and they are the rulers of certain areas of the
people's life.[15] To speak against God or a person in high
authority might be considered a degree less heinous than
cursing God or that person. For D, however, the crimes

[14] *Cf.* Ex. vii. 1, "And the Lord said to Moses, 'See, I make thee a
God to Pharaoh.'" Cursing God and the king, with no distinction
made, is mentioned in I Kings xxi. 10 and Is. viii. 21.

[15] For their impressive authority, see Deut. xvii. 10, xviii. 5, xxi. 5.

would probably be equally heinous. It is significant that, whereas in M cursing parents is a capital offense, the comparable offense in D is disobedience to parents.

Two further indications can be found that the M material forms part of D's background thought. First, the expression in the leprosy law *niph.* ב שׁמר ("to take heed in") is the same form as that used in the M law about taking heed in obeying all that God has said (Ex. xxiii. 13). Another link may be the common use of the first person. Von Rad feels that the use of the first person in D, in reference to what God ("I") commands the priests, is alien to D's style and therefore an addition of some sort.[16] But D's eclectic method can often explain such divergences in style and indicate the source of the "addition," in this case the M law about heeding all that God ("I") says. The second indication lies in the fact that the laws in xxiv. 10–22 (that is, following the leprosy law) are all dependent on laws in the M double series, Ex. xxii. 20–30 *(21–31)* and Ex. xxiii. 9–19. That the leprosy law also involves D's reflections on two parallel laws from this series is thus the more likely.

The Neighbor's Pledge: xxiv. 10–13

(10) When thou makest thy neighbor a loan of any sort, thou shalt not go into his house to fetch his pledge. (11) Thou shalt stand outside, and the man to whom thou makest the loan shall bring the pledge out to thee. (12) And if he is a poor man, thou shalt not sleep in his pledge; (13) when the sun goes down, thou shalt restore to him the pledge that he may sleep in his cloak and bless thee; and it shall be righteousness to thee before the Lord thy God.

The dependence of the remaining laws in xxiv. 10–22 on the M double series (each of which begins with a law that concerns the sojourner and mentions the sojourn in Egypt) explains the explicit reference to the sojourner in vss. 14, 17, 19, 20, 21 and the slavery in Egypt in vss. 18, 22.

[16] *Deuteronomy* (Eng. ed., London, 1966), p. 151.

The law on the neighbor's pledge is a reworking of the similar law in Ex. xxii. 25, 26 (*26, 27*): "If ever thou takest thy neighbor's garment in pledge, thou shalt restore it to him before the sun goes down; for that is his only covering, it is his mantle for his body; in what else shall he sleep? And if he cries to me I will hear, for I am compassionate." The reworking involves a return to earlier material of D that is similar in substance to the M material. This practice of combining M material with similar D material, which is continued in the laws that follow the law on the neighbor's pledge, repeats the pattern of one of the laws in the Edomite series in xxiii— that on lending at interest (xxiii. 20, 21; *19, 20*), which is a reworking of the similar law in M (Ex. xxii 24, 25). In the case of xxiii. 20, 21 (*19, 20*), D partly accomplishes his reworking by returning to the law concerning the seventh year release of the money debt and loans to the needy (xv. 1–11). Now, in the law on the neighbor's pledge of xxiv. 10–13, he returns once more to the material in xv. 1–11. This material is not specifically concerned with the matter of a pledge (עבוט) but refers generally to lending (נשה).

Here, however, the matter of pledging is specifically taken up, and in his treatment D is influenced by M's law concerning pledges. D uses the term עבט in both xv and xxiv, rather than M's word, חבל. עבט has the technical and general meaning of a pledge or security. Initially, D refers to loans on pledge in general, but then he goes on to speak in particular of a garment as a pledge. This specific reference reflects the influence of M's law, which confines itself to the case of the garment handed over by a poor man to his creditor. D repeats M's condition that the creditor must return the poor man's pledge before sunset. However, whereas M holds out the threat of retribution if the pledge is not returned, D promises the poor man's blessing and divine approval if the garment is restored.

D's dependence on M is clear. The additions he makes are

typical. His concern with the debtor's dignity—shown in the stipulation that the creditor must remain outside—has already been noted (p. 182). He repeats M's positive command to restore the garment before sundown but places before it the related negative statement about not sleeping in the pledge, a prohibition not found in M but suggested by M's question, "In what else shall he sleep?"

The Hired Servant: xxiv. 14, 15

(14) Thou shalt not oppress a hired servant who is poor and needy, whether he is one of thy brethren or one of the sojourners who are in thy land within thy towns; (15) thou shalt give him his hire on the day he earns it, before the sun goes down, for he is poor, and sets his heart upon it; lest he cry against thee to the Lord, and it be sin in thee.

This law and the ones in xxiv. 16–22 that follow it represent a reworking of Ex. xxii. 20–23 (*21–24*):

Thou shalt not wrong a sojourner or oppress him, for you were sojourners in the land of Egypt. You shall not afflict any widow or orphan. If you do afflict them, and they cry out to me, I will surely hear their cry; and my wrath will burn, and I will kill you with the sword, and your wives shall become widows and your children fatherless.

The M law is primarily concerned with the oppression of the sojourner. In D the concern is with the oppression of the hired servant, whether he be a brother Israelite or a sojourner. The differences can be explained, but first a parallel may be noted. Each of the two series that comprise the M double series begins with a law against oppressing a sojourner; the D double series contain, in xxiii, a law against oppressing a fugitive slave and, in xxiv, a law against oppressing a hired servant. In other words, the two D laws are the equivalent of the two M laws.

The differences between the M and D laws result from D's eclectic interests. As well as reworking the M law on oppression D is also revising some of his own material, namely, the law concerning the release of slaves (xv. 12–18). This slave law mentions the hired servant only in passing: "For at half the cost of a hired servant he [the slave] has served thee." D expands upon this reference to the hired servant with a law specifically dealing with his needs. There is a connection, both in spirit and in language, with the material in xv which is being revised in this law on the hired servant (and in the preceding law on the neighbor's pledge). The common elements are a reference to the poor and needy and a statement about the cry of the oppressed to God indicating that an offense has been committed.

Individual Responsibility: xxiv. 16

The fathers shall not be put to death for the children, nor shall the children be put to death for the fathers; every man shall be put to death for his own sin.

No law appears quite so haphazardly placed as this one. With some measure of probability, however, its appearance at this point in D can be explained. Three factors should be considered.

First, D has just reworked the M law concerning the oppression of the sojourner (Ex. xxii. 20ff., 21ff.). This M law also warns against oppressing the widow and orphan. Should they be wronged, God will slay the wrongdoers, whose wives will become widows and whose children orphans. This consequence is stated unnecessarily; obviously if a man is put to death for wronging a widow or an orphan then his own wife is widowed and his children are orphaned. The M law is based upon a principle of individual responsibility but does not achieve the most desirable of results. The man who wrongs a widow or an orphan is put to death, and the result is another widow and more orphans. The lawgiver intends the punishment to be retaliatory—this must be the significance of the redundant statement; in fact, the death penalty makes the result illogical, for the injustice done to the widow and orphan redounds upon the wrongdoer's widow and children.[17] It is likely that D's reflection upon this M law suggests his concern with the problem of individual responsibility.

Second, given its context in the Egyptian series, the law on individual responsibility may owe something to D's continuing reflection on events involving the Egyptians. The slaughter of the Egyptian first-born in retaliation for the oppression of Israel (Ex. xi)—a case in which children were put to death for the sins of their fathers—may play a role in the background to this law. D has specified that, because Israel was once a sojourner in Egypt, Egyptian children of the third generation are to be permitted to enter the assembly of Yahweh. The generations excluded are those responsible for Israel's enslavement and oppression.[18] Their predecessors, however, the generations that received Israel as a sojourner

---

[17] The rhetorical and admonitory nature of the law has to be borne in mind.

[18] Although the question of how long Israel spent in Egypt bristles with problems (especially difficult, even for the authors of the LXX, is Ex. xii. 40, which has Israel's total stay extending to 430 years), D's estimate that 3 generations of Egyptians were involved in Israel's oppression makes good sense. Ex. i, ii can be read as suggesting that the first Egyptian generation to oppress Israel coincided with the generation to which the parents of Moses belonged. Ex. vi. 16ff., which give the line of descent—Levi, Kohath, Amram, Moses—readily supports this view. Levi and Kohath would both have belonged to the "good" time in Egypt (cf. Ex. i. 6). Allowing for the second and third Egyptian generations to oppress Israel brings one, roughly, to the exodus from Egypt. The fourth generation was born at the time of the final plague.

M. Noth thinks that the estimate of 400 years for Israel's stay in Egypt has all historical probability against it. He judges the calculation in Ex. vi. 13–30, which gives a period of about 100 years, as the more correct one. See *Exodus* (Eng. ed., London, 1962), pp. 99, 100.

The oppression in Egypt lasted for 400 years according to Gen. xv. 13–16, but as von Rad points out (*Genesis*, p. 182) these 400 years are said to equal 4 generations, which gives the odd equation of one generation = 100 years.

in Egypt, are well regarded; it was during their lifetime that Israel's assembly came into being (Gen. xlix). D seems to judge each Egyptian generation according to its merits.

From the standpoint of D's historical setting, the offspring of the Egyptian generation that are to be admitted into Israel's assembly coincide with the generation of Israelites that is about to enter the new land.[19] D has no reason to associate these Egyptians with the persecution of Israel and is therefore favorable to them; in others words, they do not stand condemned because of their fathers [20] any more than those Egyptian "fathers" who were well disposed toward Israel are condemned because of their "children" who oppressed Israel. Because D judges each Egyptian generation according to its merits, he would be opposed to the slaying of first-born children as a means of punishing their fathers. The brothers of these slain children were the offspring of the last generation of Egyptians who persecuted Israel (Ex. xiff.), and according to D's assembly law it is precisely the children of this generation who are to be admitted into Israel's assembly. Such historical reflection may provide the motivation for D's law on individual responsibility.

The third factor relating to the appearance of this law at this point in D also strengthens the argument that D is reflecting upon Egyptian history as he presents his law on individual responsibility. The law on the hired servant that precedes the law on individual responsibility is an expansion of the incidental concern with the hired servant in the slave law in xv. In terms of the probable train of thought that

---

[19] The Egyptian offspring were the children of that generation of Egyptians who were punished by the death of their first-born, who pursued the Israelites to the Red sea, and who were being destroyed by God "until this day" (xi. 4), that is, at the time just prior to Israel's entry into the new land.

[20] Compare how the children of that generation of Israelites who rebelled in the wilderness are not to be punished because of their fathers (Deut. i. 39).

leads D to his law on individual responsibility, it is significant that the slave law in xv recalls Israel's enslavement in
Egypt and that the law following it, on the sacrifice of animal
first-born, concerns a subject that is associated with the
slaughter of the Egyptian human and animal first-born (Ex.
xiii. 11–15). The D code has no law relating to human first-
born; the explanation may be that D simply avoids the subject because he disapproves of the slaying of the Egyptian
first-born [21] and because this event is so closely linked with
existing legislation on human first-born.

D's law on individual responsibility is proverbial in character—the mention of the death penalty is an expansive,
severe way of covering every offense, not just capital ones.
Comparable proverbial statements occur in Jer. xxxi. 29, 30
and Ezek. xviii. 1–4, both of which refer to fathers eating
sour grapes and the children's teeth being set on edge (*cf.*
Job xxi. 19).

Sojourners, Orphans, Widows: xxiv. 17–22

(17) Thou shalt not pervert the justice due to the sojourner or
to the fatherless, or take a widow's garment in pledge; (18) but
thou shalt remember that thou wast a slave in Egypt and the
Lord thy God redeemed thee from there; therefore I command
thee to do this.

(19) When thou reapest thine harvest in thy field, and hast
forgotten a sheaf in the field, thou shalt not go back to get it;
it shall be for the sojourner, the fatherless, and the widow;
that the Lord thy God may bless thee in all the work of thine
hands. (20) When thou beatest thine olive trees, thou shalt not
go over the boughs again; it shall be for the sojourner, the fatherless, and the widow. (21) When thou gatherest the grapes of thy
vineyard, thou shalt not glean it afterward; it shall be for the
sojourner, the fatherless, and the widow. (22) Thou shalt remember that thou wast a slave in the land of Egypt; therefore I
command thee to do this.

---

[21] Although D has many references to the defeat of the Egyptians
(e.g., vi. 22, xi. 3ff.), the slaying of the first-born is not mentioned.

D continues to rework the M law (Ex. xxii. 20–23; *21–24*) on the oppression of the sojourner, the widow, and the orphan in the final two laws in xxiv, both of which are explicitly concerned with these three categories of persons. So far in D's treatment (in xxiv. 14–16) of the M oppression law nothing has been said about the widow and the orphan. In xxiv. 17, 18, however, D directs that the justice owed both to them and to the sojourner must not be perverted. (Possibly D is influenced also by another M law, Ex. xxiii. 6, which is about perverting justice to the poor.) The law of xxiv. 17, 18 refers generally to justice for the sojourner and orphan and specifically to the injustice of taking a widow's garment in pledge. The detail about the widow may owe something to the fact that while both widows and orphans are in the background of the xxiv. 16 law on individual responsibility only the children are singled out. In his comprehensive way, D singles out the widows in xxiv. 17, 18.

In support of his law against oppressing the sojourner, the orphan, and the widow, D commands that the slavery in Egypt be remembered. The actual statement, "But thou shalt remember that thou wast a slave in Egypt and the Lord thy God redeemed thee from there; therefore, I command thee to do this," is virtually identical to that of xv. 15. It has been noted that D is partly concerned in xxiv. 10–15 with revising the material in xv.

The sojourner, the orphan, and the widow are again D's concern in the xxiv. 19–22 law on the gleanings from the cornfield, the olive-garden, and the vineyard. This law appears to be an eclectic one, formed from material already given in D and, probably, some M material. Gleanings for the poor are not the subject of any M law, but close in spirit is the release of the land's produce for the poor in Ex. xxiii. 10, 11. The fact that D reworks so many M laws at this point in xxiv suggests this additional M influence.

In terms of the writing up of the law, it is apparent that

D returns to the feast laws in xvi. 9–17. The feast laws are themselves developed from M laws; in the law on gleanings it seems clear that D is revising his own material. This material in xvi concerns the yield of the harvest, the threshing floor, and the wine press, and says that the sojourner, the orphan, and the widow should be included in the feasts that follow. The gleanings law, which is also about what happens after the harvesting of the crops, can be construed as D's expansion of, or variation on, the intent of the feast laws. The gleanings of the harvest, the olive trees, and the vineyard are to be left for the same classes of poor, the sojourner, the orphan, and the widow. It is also noteworthy that the motive clause is the same as in xvi. 12, "Thou shalt remember that thou wast a slave in Egypt."

Summary

The legal material in xxiv constitutes the Egyptian series of laws. The "Egyptian" element is loose and diversified, but, in contrast to the "Edomite" element in the laws of xxiii, it is explicitly mentioned in some of the laws. This explicit reference is presumably due to the fact that it is Moses—so one is to understand—who lays down the laws and who, therefore, speaks from firsthand experience of certain Egyptian events. The inspiration for the Egyptian theme in xxiv is the law of xxiii. 8b (7b) admitting the children of the third generation of Egyptians into Israel's assembly on the grounds that Israel once was a sojourner in Egypt. The history encompassed within the range of this assembly law explains the diversity of the Egyptian references, which are both implicit and explicit in the laws in xxiv. Thus, the assembly law's concern with Israel as a sojourner explains why the patriarchal traditions, which show only a loose connection with Egyptian matters, underlie the initial laws in xxiv. Moreover, the fact that the assembly law admits some Egyptians into Israel's assembly but refuses others inspires

D's continuing preoccupation with the theme of admittance into or exclusion from a place.

The Egyptian traditions underlying the laws are: (*i*) Abram's wife, Sarai, being taken by the Egyptian Pharoah and later restored to Abram (Gen. xii); (*ii*) Sarah's childlessness and the connection with the story of the Egyptian slave-girl, Hagar, and her son, Ishmael (Gen. xxi); (*iii*) the sale of Joseph by his brothers to the Egyptians through the agency of the Ishmaelites (Gen. xxxvii); (*iv*) Miriam's complaint, at the time of the exodus from Egypt, against Moses' foreign marriage (Num. xii); and (*v*) the slavery in Egypt (Exodus).

Just as some Edomite laws in xxiii are related to D's own material in xv, so some laws in xxiv are also related to this material in xv, as well as to material in xvi. Likewise, just as the Edomite laws are reworkings of some laws in the M double series (Ex. xxii. 20–30; *21–31* and Ex. xxiii. 9–19), so laws in xxiv also rework some of these laws from the M series. Finally, the substance of some of the laws in xxiv is influenced by more of D's own material, in particular by the law concerning an Israelite's marriage to a foreign captive maid (xxi. 10–14).

11. Final Laws: xxv. 1–xxvi. 11

The final laws, in xxv and xxvi, cover a strange assortment of subjects—corporal punishment, the muzzling of an ox, levirate marriage, a woman's immodest behavior, weights and measures, elimination of the Amalekites, the ceremony of first fruits—the arrangement of which appears to be quite haphazard. A study of these laws reveals, however, that there are connections between one law and the next. Although the selection of subjects seems random at the superficial level, these laws actually reflect a depth of background that plays an important role in their conception. Once again, D returns to laws he has already set down, as well as reworking M laws and being influenced by traditional narrative material.

In Chapters 9 and 10, the influence, formal and substantial, of the M double series on the D laws was noted. D's use of M is rarely systematic, and it is often tangential, in that D selects from M a matter of interest to himself and develops it in his own way. Certain laws in xxv afford striking examples of D's allusive, selective use of M. Since they are also the final examples, some general observations about D's relationship to the entire M code may be made.

The Deuteronomic Laws and the Mishpatim

Of the laws in Ex. xxi, D reworks only Ex. xxi. 2–17. Ex. xxi. 18–27 are not treated, but there is some indication that this section is touched upon in the laws of xxv. The connections are roughly as follows: Deut. xxv. 1–3, concerning moderation in the physical punishment of a guilty party in a dispute, are related to Ex. xxi. 18, 19, concerning men in dispute, and Ex. xxi. 20, 21, 26, 27, concerning the severe beating of slaves; Deut. xxv. 5–10, concerning levirate marriage and the special case of denial of progeny, and Deut. xxv. 11, 12, concerning a woman's shameful assault on a man engaged in a brawl, are related to Ex. xxi. 22–25, concerning a miscarriage caused by two men fighting. The connections are not coincidental but reflect elements selected by D for combination with other matters of interest.

D's casual method in xxv of revising the M material means that in one case a rule relating to a dispute between men and rules relating to slaves are considered together by D in one law dealing with moderation in punishment. This treatment of several M rules together is indicative of D's eclecticism and has a parallel in the way D treats a number of M laws in his law concerning the hanged man (see Chapter 7). In a second case in xxv, D develops one M law into two laws through a process of contrast. There are many instances throughout D in which the revision of a previously given law expands it into more than one law. And D also uses the device of contrast throughout his work. For example, in the laws concerning permission to eat flesh and permission to have a king, the use of contrast in relation to existing traditions is noteworthy (see Chapter 5). The law on the rebellious son prompts a contrasting law on the wicked daughter (see Chapter 8). The leprosy law involves a contrast with the captive maid law (see Chapter 10).

In considering the affinities between Deut. xxv. 1–3, 5–12 and Ex. xxi. 18–27 in greater detail, it must be kept in mind that D's use of M is selective and that the resulting D laws are artificial creations. This artificiality explains why D and M laws can be very different in nature even though D consciously creates affinities between them. For example, D's first law in xxv provides for the administration of justice, while some of the M rules that have an influence on it constitute a limitation on the arbitrary powers of a master over a slave.

Disputing Parties, Severe Beating of Slaves: Ex. xxi. 18, 19, 20, 21, 26, 27

(18) When men quarrel and one strikes the other with a stone or with his fist and the man does not die but keeps his bed, (19) then if the man rises again and walks abroad with his staff, he that struck him shall be clear; only he shall pay for the loss of his time, and shall have him thoroughly healed.

(20) When a man strikes his slave, male or female, with a rod and the slave dies under his hand, he shall be punished. (21) But if the slave survives a day or two, he is not to be punished; for the slave is his money.

(26) When a man strikes the eye of his slave, male or female, and destroys it, he shall let the slave go free for the eye's sake. (27) If he knocks out the tooth of his slave, male or female, he shall let the slave go free for the tooth's sake.

Moderation in Punishment: Deut. xxv. 1–3

(1) If there is a dispute between men,[1] then they shall come into court, and the judges shall decide between them, acquitting the innocent and condemning the guilty, (2) and if the guilty man deserves to be beaten, the judge shall cause him to lie down and be beaten in his presence with a number of stripes in proportion to his offense. (3) Forty stripes may be given him, but not more; lest, if one should go on to beat him with more stripes than these, thy brother be degraded in thy sight.

The initial part of the D law concerns a dispute between men. The dispute is brought to court, where judgment is given, and the guilty party is to be beaten. Von Rad points

---

[1] The RSV begins the apodosis at a different point in the law: "If there is a dispute between men, and they come into court, and the judges decide between them, acquitting the innocent and condemning the guilty, then if the guilty party deserves to be beaten, the judge. . . ."

out how this regulation approaches its main point, moderation in punishment, in a roundabout manner.[2] No reason
for this circuitous legal drafting is suggested by von Rad,
but an examination of D's methods in reworking certain M
laws provides one. D has in mind the example of the dispute
between men given in Ex. xxi. 18, 19, where a man strikes
another man and causes him injury but not death. The D
law represents a stage in legal development when disputing
parties are encouraged to bring their cases to court. D develops a trend, already present in M, toward court interference. In M the court eventually intervenes to deal with
the difficult problem of deciding when consequences should
no longer be imputed to an act.[3] The court's control in M
over the consequences of a physical quarrel is extended by D
to—such is D's intention—complete court control of any
dispute between parties. In M, self-help in a dispute brings
about certain consequences, and at that point there is court
interference. In D, the view is that self-help should be cur-
tailed, that parties should not resort to it, and that disputes
should be brought to court.

The main point at which D eventually arrives in this law
is that, with court control of a dispute, justice should be
tempered by moderation and the infliction of punishment by
humane considerations. This concern in D with moderation
in punishment, where there is a limit on the number of
stripes, provides a nexus with the M rules (Ex. xxi. 20, 21,

[2] *Deuteronomy* (Eng. ed., London, 1966), p. 154.
[3] The law decides that from a certain moment the assailant is free
against any later developments for the worse (Ex. xxi. 19) and lays
down that the injured party is to be paid for the loss of his working
time and to be thoroughly healed. The same problem of causation
exists in the following law (Ex. xxi. 20, 21), where a time limit is set
beyond which a master who has beaten his slave cannot be held responsible for the slave's death. A master would frequently beat his
slave, and a period of more than one or two days when he would be
punished if the slave dies would be onerous on the master. For a discussion of these laws and the problems they raise, see D. Daube,
"Direct and Indirect Causation in Biblical Law," *VT,* 11 (1961), 254ff.

26, 27) on the beating of slaves. These M rules are directed against the excessive punishment of slaves, and this trend toward leniency inspires the same concern in D's law. The death of a slave not long after a beating by his master is to be legally avenged (Ex. xxi. 20). A slave is to be set free if his master beats him so harshly that he loses an eye or a tooth (Ex. xxi. 26, 27). This concern with excessive punishment of a slave is reflected in D's restriction on the number of stripes the successful party in a dispute may impose on the other. In each case the helpless state of one party, the slave in M and the offender in D, is taken into account. The appearance of the law stipulating that a slave must be released if he loses a tooth, after that on a slave's release for the loss of an eye, is an indication that the M law represents an advance toward moderation in punishment. The loss of a tooth is hardly to be placed alongside the loss of an eye. It is probable that at an earlier stage of Israelite legal history a slave was released only if his eye was knocked out, and simply on the basis that he had a right to be freed because of what had been done to him. At the stage represented by the final compilation of the M laws, both because of a more humane outlook and because of human revulsion at the sight of such physical deformities as the loss of an eye, the slave was to be released if a tooth was knocked out—an occurrence that must have been frequent in beatings. The intent of the M legislation on the loss of a tooth is to lessen the possibility of a slave's eye being knocked out in a beating; for such a law might make the master more wary of beating his slaves about the head.

Miscarriage Owing to a Brawl: Ex. xxi. 22–25

(22) When men strive together, and hurt a woman with child, so that there is a miscarriage, and yet no harm follows, the one who hurt her shall be fined, according as the woman's husband shall lay upon him; and he shall pay as the judges determine. (23) If any harm follows, then thou shalt give life for life.

Refusal of Levirate and the Immodest Woman:
Deut. xxv. 5–12

(5) If brothers dwell together, and one of them dies and has
no son, the wife of the dead shall not be married outside the
family to a stranger; her husband's brother shall go into her, and
take her as his wife, and perform the duty of a husband's brother
to her. (6) And the first son whom she bears shall succeed to the
name of his brother who is dead, that his name may not be
blotted out of Israel. (7) And if the man does not wish to take
his brother's wife, then his brother's wife shall go up to the gate
to the elders, and say, "My husband's brother refuses to perpetuate his brother's name in Israel; he will not perform the duty
of a husband's brother to me." (8) Then the elders of his city
shall call him, and speak to him: and if he persists, saying, "I do
not wish to take her," (9) then his brother's wife shall go up to
him in the presence of the elders, and pull his sandal off his foot,
and spit in his face; and she shall answer and say, "So shall it be
done to the man who does not build up his brother's house." (10)
And the name of his house shall be called in Israel, The house
of him that had his sandal pulled off.

(11) When men strive together, and the wife of the one draws
near to rescue her husband from the hand of him who is beating
him, and puts out her hand and seizes him by the private parts,
(12) then thou shalt cut off her hand; thine eye shall have no
pity.

The M law on a miscarriage caused by two men fighting
contributes to the two D laws concerning the denial of
levirate and the immodest woman. The one feature common
to both the M law and the first D law is a concern with the
loss of anticipated progeny. In each case material consequences follow. In M, a woman loses her expected child
because of a fight between two men. The gist of the offense
is the deprivation of offspring suffered by the husband, and
in an earlier version of the law, before the interpolation of
the clause about the judges,[4] the husband was to exact dam-

[4] The statement in Ex. xxi. 22 that the criminal will pay as the
judges determine conflicts with the preceding part of the sentence,

ages from the culprit for the loss of the child. In D there is
first described the custom of the levirate marriage. If a man
dies childless it is the duty of his brother to raise a child to
him by his widow. The son so born succeeds to the dead
man's name and also to his share in the ancestral property.[5]
The main interest of the D law, however, lies in the special
situation where a brother refuses to raise a male heir to his
dead brother. The widow, anticipating a child because of
the levirate custom, is deprived of such a child by his re-
straint—which is economically motivated in that he, as the
surviving brother, will receive his dead brother's share in
the family estate. D is led to consider this special case of
denial of progeny by reflecting on an M example of loss of
progeny.[6]

The argument for a connection between the D and M
laws is supported by the intriguing parallel in the following
D law about a brawl with the physical fighting described in
the M law as causing the loss of progeny. In the D law, as in
the M, two men are involved in a fight (both laws have the
same opening) and a third person, a woman, becomes in-

---

which lets the fine be fixed by the husband of the woman who was
hurt. The interpolation would have been made in order to limit the
powers of the offended husband, and thereby to establish official supervision over the settlement of the affair. E. A. Speiser, "The Stem PLL
in Hebrew," *JBL*, 82 (1963), 301–306, rejects the common rendering of
בפללים, "as the judges determine." He argues for a meaning similar
to the LXX, "according to estimate." The law would then be similar
to the Hittite law No. 17 in which damages are assessed according to
the estimated age of the embryo. This interpretation also implies
official supervision over the settlement.

[5] See G. R. Driver and J. Miles, *The Assyrian Laws* (Oxford, 1935),
p. 243, and, for a full discussion, D. Daube, "Consortium in Roman
and Hebrew Law," *JR*, 62 (1950), 71ff.

[6] There is no evidence to suggest that the Genesis narrative concerning the failure of Judah's sons to fulfil the levir's duty is also in
D's mind. It is nonetheless interesting that such a tradition exists, and
the point may be that a levir's refusal was proverbial. There is a
general tendency in D to present matters of a proverbial character.

volved. But this time it is not a pregnant woman who is hurt in the affray. Rather, there is a contrasting situation; the wife of one of the contestants interferes by putting out her hand to help her husband, seizing the other by his testicles, his place of progeny. D is led to this example of a situation that must have occurred but rarely by his finely developed method of association. Elsewhere, as we have seen, he presents his material through the device of contrast.

In M, the law of talion is to apply if the woman is hurt in the fight. The issue of the penalty in D—loss of a hand for the offending woman—is more complicated. D is only concerned with the shamefulness of the woman's act and does not consider the question of any damage to the man.[7] Hence application of the law of talion does not arise. As he often does, D concentrates on only one aspect of a law because he is reaching beyond its legal aspects to a matter that preoccupies him, in this case shameful, abhorrent behavior.

Some final and more general observations about D's relationship to the entire M code may be made at this point. The most interesting fact, illustrative of D's relationship to M, is D's omission of the more technical section of the Mishpatim. D appears to rework or touch upon almost all the M laws except those in Ex. xxi. 28–xxii. 14 (*15*), a section concerned with animal assault, negligence, damage to property, theft, and deposit. No conclusive answer can be given to the question of why this section is not treated, but the reasons probably lie in the intention that underlies D's presentation of his laws. D's tendency is to ignore the narrow, legal, technical side of the M laws with which he deals, and to concentrate on the unenforceable aspects of a law and to point to matters in a law which overlap with religion, morality, and social conduct. The laws in xxv illustrate this tendency.

[7] Par. 8 of the Assyrian laws concerns damage to a man's testicles by a woman involved in an affray. See Driver and Miles, *The Assyrian Laws,* p. 385.

For example, D does not go into the question of compensation for the wronged party in a dispute; and having chosen an example of loss of progeny he works with it in an area beyond that of the law, to draw attention to the social and religious disgrace of a man's name being blotted out in the land.

It is not D's primary intention to draft rules for the needs of functioning law, and this is probably why he does not rework the more technical section of M. These M rules belong to the complex area of civil and private law and would, for D, constitute a different field of interest. To say this is not to imply that in D's time there existed any formal distinction between private and public or civil and criminal law.[8] It is a matter of D's intentions and interests. For example, the M law on seduction (Ex. xxii. 15, 16; *16, 17*) belongs to the private law section in M but is reworked by D because he has a strong interest in marital relations, adultery, and seduction, an interest that reflects the pervasive concern with sexual morality in wisdom circles. Some D laws are presented as new legislation—for example, those on adultery and seduction; some constitute an ideal social program of reform; some inculcate a moral, historical lesson; and some express a doctrinaire bias—for example, those concerned with notions of rest and inheritance. Their chief contrast to the M laws is that they operate in a broader area of law, morality, and social behavior.

Further Sources of the Laws in xxv

As well as selecting aspects of M laws for treatment in some of his laws in xxv, D also returns to earlier laws of his own, in particular to his laws dealing with mixtures of one kind or another (xxii. 5ff.). It will be recalled that D's

---

[8] On systematization in biblical and Near Eastern legal material and the distinctions implied, see V. Wagner, "Zur Systematik in dem Codex Ex. xxi. 2–xxii. 16," *ZAW*, 81 (1969), 176–82.

double series of laws in xxiii and xxiv are prompted by the
law admitting the Edomites and Egyptians into Israel's assembly (xxiii. 9, *8*). The section on mixtures precedes, and
leads up to, this topic of inclusion in Israel's assembly. In a
typically free way, D selects some matters of interest from
this section and expands them according to his interests.
Several links may be noted.

The subject of punishing a man by whipping (xxv. 1–3) is
suggested by the punishing of the man who brings an evil
name upon a virgin of Israel (xxii. 13ff.). The earlier law does
not specify that the punishment is to be by whipping, but
the verb יסר implies corporal punishment. It is the kind of
reference D likes to develop into a law.

Two factors suggest a possible correlation between the law
on the unmuzzled ox (xxv. 4) and the law dealing with the
ox and the ass (xxii. 10). First, xxv. 4 yields a satisfactory
interpretation only if, like xxii. 10, a figurative meaning is
intended. In other words, the "treading" ox is suggested by
the "plowing" ox. Second, it may be that in dealing with the
unmuzzled ox D is thinking in terms of a compatible mixture. That is, the ox and the corn that it treads is a natural
combination, and no obstacle, such as a muzzle, should interfere with the ox's enjoying the fruit of its labor.

The law concerning the duty of levirate (xxv. 5–10) has
some affinites with material in xxii. 13ff. Although the M law
on miscarriage (Ex. xxi. 22–25) suggests to D the topic of
denial of progeny, it does not otherwise contribute to the special nature of the D levirate law. Four points of similarity
and contrast with xxii. 13ff. may provide some illumination.
First, it is possible that D thinks of the levirate custom,
whereby a man takes his brother's wife, in terms of permitted sexual relations. As Driver points out,[9] in Lev. xviii.
16, xx. 21 a man is prohibited from marrying a brother's
wife (widow), but the exceptional circumstances specified in

[9] *Deuteronomy*, ICC (3d ed., Edinburgh, 1902), p. 285.

the D law make it permissible in this instance. If D is thinking along these lines, he may well be recalling the material in xxii that is directly concerned with sexual relations. Second, the law in xxii. 13ff. concerns a man who brings an evil name upon a virgin of Israel. The levirate law is also much concerned with the "name," in this instance with an Israelite's name being silenced in the land. The xxii. 13ff. law indicates how public dishonor is brought upon a house because of an offense. If a woman acts the harlot in her father's house, then that is the place where she is to be publicly punished. In the levirate law, stigma attaches to a man's house if he refuses to raise a child to his dead brother. Third, the formal structure of the two laws is similar: each has two parts. The law in xxii addresses itself first to the issue of a bad name brought upon a virgin of Israel and then to the harlotry of a daughter of Israel. The levirate law considers first the duty of a man to continue his dead brother's name in the land and then the special case of a brother refusing to fulfil this obligation. Finally, the levirate law may, like that in xxii, provide an example of D's fondness for drafting contrasting cases. In the law on the Israelite wife, a man goes into a woman and finds cause to bring her before the elders. In the levirate case, a man refuses to go into a woman and she is given cause to take him before the elders.

The law following the levirate law, that dealing with the woman who interferes in a fight, is partly derived from the M law on men fighting and causing a woman to miscarry. In M there is no offense by a woman; D's inclination to present a contrasting case accounts for his discussing the woman who interferes in a fight between two men by grasping the genitals of one of them. The one conceivable connection with the material in xxii is that, in a similarly contrasting fashion, D there presents the case of a woman's offense—the daughter's harlotry in her parents' house—as a counterpart to the preceding law on the rebellious son. D may be repeating the process in xxv, being encouraged to do so by his prior model of a "wicked" woman.[10]

The next law, on weights and measures (xxv. 13–16), is related to material in xxii in two respects. First, the law's direction against having two kinds of weights in one's bag or two kinds of measures in one's house recalls forcibly the laws on forbidden mixtures (two kinds of seed, two kinds of cloth) in xxii. Second, the double reference to payment (by weight) of shekels found only in D's material in xxii (vss. 19, 29) is expanded into the law on weights and measures.

The final law in xxv, concerning what Amalek did to the Israelites on the way from Egypt, is related to the law refusing the Ammonites and Moabites entry into Israel's assembly because of what they did to the Israelites on the way from Egypt (xxiii. 4–7; 3–6). This assembly law is from that section in D which follows the material on mixtures in xxii and precedes the law admitting the Edomites and Egyptians into the assembly. The Edomite/Egyptian law influences the section of D that precedes xxv. D's final law in xxv thus fits into the structural pattern of D's revision method.

The Unmuzzled Ox: xxv. 4

Thou shalt not muzzle an ox when it treads out the grain.

This is a puzzling prohibition. Part of the puzzle stems from the position of this law in the code; it comes after the law on moderation in punishment and before the law on the refusal of levirate. Commentators see a loose humanitarian nexus between it and the law on moderation in punishment, but the connection is too loose to be revealing. The ox is not being punished by muzzling, and the question of a degrading sight, as in the case of a man after a whipping, does not arise. To muzzle an ox in its threshing is to prevent the

---

[10] One is reminded of the stereotype of the wicked woman in Proverbs, e.g., Prov. v. 3ff., vii. 5ff.

ox from eating grain. To unmuzzle the ox is to leave it free to eat. This is the plain reading of the law, but one wonders why a lawgiver should show such a concern. Is he, like the sage in Prov. xii. 10, "A righteous man has regard for the life of his beast, but the mercy of the wicked is cruel," thinking of a generous attitude toward an animal, but at the same time primarily concerned with the human world? The pro- verbial nature of D's law (only four words in Hebrew) indi- cates such a possibility; and a link with the law on the refusal of levirate is suggested.

An ox should not be denied its due portion from the work of its treading. Likewise, an Israelite—who belongs to the house of Israel, which is symbolically represented by the ox (Gen. xlix. 6, cf. Deut. xxxiii. 17, see p. 160f.)—should not be denied his portion in the land. This denial is the chief concern of the levirate law. A man who dies childless is de- nied the continuation of his name in the land. This means that his house, his estate, his fields, his place in the land dis- appear. They are absorbed in the brother's estate. The sur- viving brother therefore gains without labor, whereas it should be that the one who labors gains, as in the proverbial example of the unmuzzled ox. The similar concern voiced in xx. 6 that the Israelite who plants (and tends) a vineyard should enjoy its fruits, and not go to war lest he die there, should be recalled. The brother's refusal to raise a male heir to his dead brother is motivated by his unwillingness to lose his acquired possessions. This is a dishonorable atti- tude, and the appropriate punishment is public opprobrium. The widow spits in his face before the elders and takes off his sandal. The disgrace (though how this act of removing the man's sandal symbolizes disgrace is difficult to discern) [11]

---

[11] It confuses the problem to suggest that there is an analogy with the custom described in Ruth iv. 7, where, to confirm the transfer of an immovable object, such as land, one party takes off (שָׁלַף, not חֲלִץ as in D) his sandal and hands it to the other. This symbolic action

is to be perpetuated in the name given to his house—"The house of him that had his sandal pulled off."

If the reference to the unmuzzled ox is designed to direct attention to the human world,[12] there is a similarity with the reference to the plowing ox, which symbolizes a member of the house of Israel, in xxii. 10. In both cases the prohibition has the same form. Moreover D's reversion to material in xxii for his laws in xxv has been noted. An ingenious connection between the two prohibitions may explain how D arrives at the subject of the treading ox that is not to be muzzled (חסם). The Hebrew חרש, "to plow," also means "to be silent." [13] Muzzling, as an allusion to the human world, may symbolize the concept of silencing a person,[14] a concept that is the concern of the levirate law, which speaks metaphorically of an Israelite's name being wiped out. In short, D's penchant for clever lines of association and his use of literal and nonliteral meanings suggest that the prohibition concerning the unmuzzled ox is placed before the levirate law to serve as an introduction.

Narrative Traditions

D often takes up a topic that forms only a minor element in a preceding law and expands it by relating it to a narra-

---

makes sense because probably at some early stage (*cf*. Deut. xi. 24) the way in which a man acquired land was by actually stepping on it. The custom in Ruth describes a legal form; the custom in D is a ceremony of disgrace.

[12] The proverbial flavor of D's law may be reflected in the story of Ruth. Compare, particularly in Ruth iii, the picture of Boaz at the threshing floor, Ruth at his feet, the details about the reestablishment of her husband's house, and the gift of grain that anticipates this.

[13] D's double use of חרש could be compared with the double meaning given to קרה in the law of the bird's nest (see Chapter 8). U. Cassuto, *Exodus* (Eng. ed., Jerusalem, 1967), p. 297, suggests a double use of עזב ("to forsake" and "to arrange") in the law of Ex. xxiii. 5.

[14] The noun form of חסם in Ps. xxxix. 2 (*1*) indicates a person silencing himself.

tive tradition. Such a process occurs in the law concerning weights and measures, where D takes up the references in xxii. 19, 29 to the payment (by weight) of shekels and expands them by relating them to the tradition in Ex. xvi about the divine provision of manna. The law that follows the weights and measures law concerns the Amalekites and explicitly recalls the historical incident relating to them. That history is recounted in Ex. xvii, that is, just after the manna tradition. These two traditions are thus, in a sense, sources of D laws.

Weights and Measures: xxv. 13–16

(13) Thou shalt not have in thy bag two kinds of weights, a large and a small. (14) Thou shalt not have in thine house two kinds of measures, a large and a small. (15) A full and just weight thou shalt have, a full and just measure thou shalt have; that thy days may be prolonged in the land which the Lord thy God gives thee. (16) For all who do such things, all who act dishonestly, are an abomination to the Lord thy God.

D's law underlines the necessity for correct weights and measures with the eloquent words, "a full and just weight thou shalt have, a full and just measure thou shalt have." A feature of the narrative in Ex. xvi is that God is represented as adhering to such a law in his exact provision of food for Israel. Each day the people are to gather one day's portion, except on the sixth day when they are to gather double the amount. The gathering is to be done in a remarkably exact way. Each man is to receive an omer, and the number of omers to be gathered is to be determined by the number of persons living in each man's tent (vs. 16). The exactness of the measures is stressed again in vs. 18: when the manna is gathered and quantified, the man who gathers much because he has a large household has nothing over, and he who gathers a smaller amount lacks nothing.

The didactic element in the story is strong, and two-fold.

There is, first, the notion that the purpose of the food distribution is to test the people to see whether they will obey the
law. Specifically, the sabbath command is the issue. It is,
therefore, noteworthy that a parallel has already been drawn
in the story between a historical event and a law—precisely
the kind of correlation that D so often constructs. Second,
an omer of manna is to be kept to remind and to instruct
future generations about—and it may be so paraphrased—
God's full and just treatment of the house of Israel at a certain point in its history. There is reference to the fullness
(מלא) of the omer that is to be kept (Ex. xvi. 32, 33), and D's
reference to the full (שלמה) weight and measure should be
compared with this.

It is likely that this narrative concerning the just and careful divine provision of manna is used as an example of the
way in which God himself dispensed just measures to the
Israelites on their journey from Egypt. Moreover, this model
provides a background for the presentation of D's law. Just
as the Ex. xvii narrative about Amalek (which follows the
manna story) prompts the D law on Amalek (which follows
the law on weights and measures), so the narrative about the
provision of manna influences D's law on weights and measures. The didactic character of D's law is clear, the more so
because similar laws occur in the wisdom literature. Prov. xi.
1, xvi. 11, xx. 23 show an identical concern, expressed in
similar langauge, about true weights and measures. Prov. xvi.
11 speaks about a just balance and scales being the Lord's
and all the weights in the bag as his work. D considers the
manna narrative to indicate precisely this, that God uses a
just balance and scales. The narrative itself shows signs of
being used for this didactic purpose. This purpose is seen in
the care with which the story relates how no person is to be
given more or less of the manna. Even clearer is the fact that
God actually uses "omers", a technical standard of quantity,[15]

[15] God's consummate technical competence is dwelt on by Job.

in distributing the manna. Moreover the didactic purpose of the story accounts for the notice at its end that an omer is the tenth part of an ephah. The term in the D law on weights and measures is the ephah.

It is probable that the Exodus story has undergone a priestly redaction.[16] If so, this does not preclude the possibility that D used an earlier version that was similar to the present form of the story. It is interesting that the equivalent priestly law on weights and measures (Lev. xix. 35, 36) cites Israel's exodus from Egypt as the reason why the law should be kept. B. Gemser thinks this to be an unexpected and unrelated connection.[17] However it appears less so in light of the correlation between D's law and the story of the exact distribution of the manna to the Israelites at the time of the exodus from Egypt. If this story reveals a priestly redaction, then the didactic aim detectable behind it of indicating that God himself gives true weights and measures could have been carried over into the Levitical law with its reminder of the journey from Egypt.

Amalek: xxv. 17–19

(17) Remember what Amalek did to thee on the way as you came out of Egypt, (18) how he attacked thee on the way, when thou wast faint and weary, and cut off at thy rear all who lagged behind thee; and he did not fear God. (19) Therefore when the Lord thy God has given thee rest from all thine enemies round about, in the land which the Lord thy God gives thee for an inheritance to possess, thou shalt blot out the remembrance of Amalek from under heaven; thou shalt not forget.

In creating the universe, for example, God determined the measurements of the earth and stretched out his line upon it (Job xxxviii. 4ff.).

[16] M. Noth, *Exodus* (Eng. ed., London, 1962), pp. 131–36, assigns most of the story to a P redactor of earlier traditions. Interestingly, he sees a "Deuteronomistic gloss" in vs. 28.

[17] "The Importance of the Motive Clause in Old Testament Law," *SVT*, 1 (1953), 61.

This law, calling for the extermination of the Amalekites, refers to an incident and an injunction to future generations that are reported in Ex. xvii. In Ex. xvii, future generations are called upon to blot out the memory of Amalek because of Amalek's attack on Israel. A discrepancy can be seen, however, between D's implied account of the incident and the existing account in Ex. xvii. Driver thinks that D's statement about Amalek cutting off at the rear all who lagged behind does not have its equivalent in, and therefore is not directly related to, the earlier account.[18] This assessment is wrong because Driver only considers the second part of the story in Ex. xvii (vss. 8–13) as relevant to D's law and omits consideration of the first part, which is essential, not just to seeing the bias of the D law, but also to understanding why Amalek's attack on Israel is regarded as dastardly.

In Ex. xvii it is not at all clear why Amalek's attack is considered as heinous as it is, nor why he deserved the curse he got. The story opens with Israel at camp in Rephidim with no water to drink. The people complained about this, and Moses traveled ahead with some of the elders to the rock at Horeb and there obtained water by striking the rock with the magic rod. It is important to note that Horeb is a good distance from Rephidim. In Num. xxxiii. 14, 15 (P), camping at Rephidim and camping at Sinai (which is Horeb in P) are two different stages on the journey from Egypt. In Ex. xvii Amalek attacks Israel at Rephidim, not at Horeb (vs. 8). In other words, the people were attacked when they were thirsty, before they found water at Horeb. Hence D rightly relates that Amalek attacked when Israel was faint and weary. The term עָיֵף, "faint," often refers to weariness from thirst—Is. xxix. 8, Job xxii. 7, Prov. xxv. 25. This is why Amalek's attack is considered dastardly. For D, reflecting wisdom thinking, Amalek's crime was that he attacked Israel when it was weary from thirst. The story relates how Israel prevailed over

[18] *Deuteronomy*, ICC, p. 287.

Amalek whenever Moses held high his rod and how Amalek prevailed whenever Moses' hand grew heavy and the rod was lowered. The situation seems to have been that by this time Moses had reached the rock at Horeb and the people were attempting to go in that direction. When the rod was held high the people were encouraged and fought well, but when the rod was lowered they could not see it and despaired. In any case, D apparently interprets all this activity to mean that Amalek cut off those worn out by thirst and exhaustion, probably those who could not see the beckoning rod.[19]

Amalek's crime, although more heinous, is of a kind with that of Ammon and Moab, whose failure was that they did not meet Israel with bread and water on the way from Egypt (xxiii. 4ff., 3ff.). Such unsympathetic regard for the weak, even if there is enmity, is regarded as a crime in wisdom literature, and is so seen in D. Eliphaz, for example, is aroused by the wickedness of failing to provide water for the weary (עָיֵף, Job xxii. 7). The nonprovision of bread to those in need is equally dastardly (Job xxxi. 16, 17, 31). If one's enemy is hungry and thirsty, bread and water should be given to him (Prov. xxv. 21). Clearly, to attack him, as Amalek does, is cowardly. How closely D reflects wisdom teaching in this law is seen in another remarkable respect. D claims that Amalek, a foreigner, who should have shown fear of Yahweh, did not. It is in wisdom circles that such an international idea exists that the fear of God should be in every man.[20]

---

[19] D's use of חשל in the *niph.* form to mean all the broken down, worn out Israelites may be intended as a contrasting word play on חלש in Ex. xvii. 13, where the reference is to the Amalekites prostrated by Joshua. If so, D's sensitivity to language further underlines the suggested play upon חרש behind the law of the muzzled ox in xxv. 4. BDB, p. 365, suggests that possibly חלש should be read in the law on Amalek, but the contrasting element in D should not be dismissed lightly.

[20] For further discussion of both this law and the preceding one on weights and measures, see C. M. Carmichael, "Deuteronomic Laws, Wisdom, and Historical Traditions," *JSS*, 12 (1967), 198–206.

Climactic Ceremony of First Fruits and the
Historical Credo: xxvi. 1–11

(1) When thou comest into the land which the Lord thy God
gives thee for an inheritance, and hast taken possession of it, and
live in it, (2) thou shalt take some of the first of all the fruit of
the ground, which thou harvest from thy land that the Lord thy
God gives thee, and thou shalt put it in a basket, and thou shalt
go to the place which the Lord thy God will choose, to make his
name to dwell there. (3) And thou shalt go to the priest who is
in office at that time, and say to him, "I declare this day to the
Lord thy God that I have come into the land which the Lord
swore to our fathers to give us." (4) Then the priest shall take
the basket from thine hand, and set it down before the altar of
the Lord thy God. (5) And thou shalt make response before the
Lord thy God . . . [see below].

The ancient agricultural ceremony of first fruits (Ex. xxiii.
19, xxxiv. 26) is put to a new symbolic use by D. The ceremony is now brought into historical association with the
initial entry into the new land. D's laws are intended for this
time of rest from enemies and inheritance of the new land
(i. 1–8, xii. 1, 10). The law on Amalek, which precedes the
law on the ceremony of first fruits, refers to this rest and inheritance. D relates the first fruits to the new situation and
introduces a special speech of historical commemoration,
which is to be made at the new ceremony.[21] Accordingly, he

---

[21] G. von Rad, *Das formgeschichtliche Problem des Hexateuch*
(Munich, 1958), pp. 11ff., assumes that the connection between the
ceremony of first fruits and the speech to be spoken at it was ancient,
since early Israelite belief would have readily related thanksgiving for
the harvest with thanksgiving for deliverance from bondage and the
gift of the land. A. Jirku, *Die älteste Geschichte Israels im Rahmen
lehrhafter Darstellungen* (Leipzig, 1917), p. 49, holds a contrary point
of view and rightly sees such a connection as a later theological development. In fact, the evidence indicates a Deuteronomic innovation.
Other feasts by D's time were only in the process of becoming historicized (see Deut. xvi for feasts with much historical commemoration,
with little, and with none). The first fruits were probably presented at
the feast of weeks (Deut. xvi) and it is noteworthy that D treats them

employs certain traditions in order to forge something that is new in one respect but archaic in another. Two of the traditions he brings together are the custom relating to first fruits and the tradition about Israel's first contact, through the spies, with the fruit of the new land. The incident of the spies obtaining the land's fruit anticipates the event with which D is concerned in xxvi.

It is important to note that the presentation of material in xxvi is historically directed. D adopts the perspective of Israel about to enter the land for the first time. If D is seeking to relate an ancient festival to this occasion, then the offering of the first fruits of the land is the obvious one. Moreover the event at Kadesh, when the spies brought back some of the fruit of the new land, is an obvious source for reflection. That tradition is found in Num. xiii and is related by D, both in substance and language,[22] in Deut. i. When the spies returned the intention was to conquer the land at once (the situation D depicts in xxvi). This intention was frustrated, however. Only after other events, in particular the long wandering in the wilderness, had taken place was Israel once more to find itself at Kadesh and again to anticipate entry into the new land (Num. xx).[23]

It is this second period at Kadesh that illuminates both the form and the content of the historical speech of commemoration attached to D's ceremony of first fruits. At this time Israel met Edom and Edom refused his brother per-

---

separately at the end of his code. The implication is that D intends an innovation in connection with their celebration. Y. Kaufmann, *The Religion of Israel* (Eng. ed., Chicago, 1960), p. 188, also argues that the ancient custom of bringing the first fruits is preserved in a new, special rite in D. For a full discussion of these points, see C. M. Carmichael, "A New View of the Origin of the Deuteronomic Credo," *VT*, 19 (1969), 273–89.

[22] See Driver, *Deuteronomy*, ICC, pp. 19ff.

[23] On the relationship between the two events at Kadesh, see *ibid.*, pp. 31–33, and G. B. Gray, *Numbers*, ICC (Edinburgh, 1903), pp. 256ff.

mission to traverse his territory on the way to the new land. D considers both events at Kadesh in writing up his new ceremony of first fruits; consequently, the existence of such a peculiar association as a speech of historical retrospect on handing over the first fruits of the harvest can be explained.

D is additionally attracted to the speech at Kadesh, as will be noted, because of its concern with both Edom and Egypt. This concern plays a major role in D's code; the influence of the law admitting Edom and Egypt into Israel's assembly (xxiii. 9, 8) on the material of xxiii and xxiv has already been analyzed. Moreover, the laws in xxv revert to the D material that precedes the Edomite/Egyptian law. In other words, the Edomite/Egyptian law is again ripe for D's retrospective attention, and it is significant that this law and the Kadesh speech encompass the same span of history, from Jacob's relations with Esau to Israel's deliverance from Egypt. D's renewed reflection on the Edomite/Egyptian law possibly leads him to work with the Kadesh traditions. It is, after all, an obvious, but complex question to enquire how D moves from the subject of Amalek (the last law in xxv) to the speech for the ceremony of first fruits.

The speech at Kadesh is a request from Moses, through his messengers, to the king of Edom (Num. xx. 14ff.). By dividing this speech into three parts it may be aligned with D's "credo" speech.

I

Num. xx. 14: "Thus says thy brother Israel, 'Thou knowest all the adversity that has befallen us.'" [*scil.* because Jacob-Israel met thee, Esau-Edom, after leaving Laban, the Aramean, Gen. xxxiii.].

Deut. xxvi. 5: "A wandering Aramean was my father" [Jacob-Israel].

II

Num. xx. 15, 16a: "And our fathers went down to Egypt, and we dwelt in Egypt a long time; and the Egyptians dealt harshly with us and our fathers; and when we cried to Yahweh, he heard our voice, and sent an angel and brought us forth out of Egypt."

Deut. xxvi. 5–9: "And he went down into Egypt and sojourned there, few in number; and there he became a nation, great, mighty and populous. And the Egyptians treated us harshly, and afflicted us, and laid upon us hard bondage. Then we cried to Yahweh, the God of our fathers, and Yahweh heard our voice, and saw our affliction, our toil, and our oppression; and Yahweh brought us out of Egypt with a mighty hand and an outstretched arm, with great terror, with signs and wonders; and he brought us into this place and gave us this land, a land flowing with milk and honey."

III

Num. xx. 16b: "And, behold, we are in Kadesh, a city on the edge of thy territory";

Deut. xxvi. 10: "And, behold, now I bring the first of the fruit of the ground which thou, O Yahweh, hast given me."

It is noteworthy that, apart from the similarity in form, there is a similar fluctuation between singular and plural in both speeches. In Num. xx the messengers are to address Edom as a brother, "Thus says *thy* brother Israel." In recounting the events in Egypt the first person plural is used for Israel's experiences. Israel is then characterized both as an individual representing the entire nation and as a community of individual Israelites. In D the speech begins with *"my* father" and then for the subsequent history of Israel the first person plural is used. At the point of handing over the first fruits the first person singular is used. There is in D a similar use of Israel both as an individual and as a community of persons. The correspondences in content between the two speeches may now be noted.[24]

The hardship which Israel claims Edom knew about, men-

[24] For a detailed discussion of the differences and similarities in language between both speeches, see C. M. Carmichael, "The Deuteronomic Credo," *VT*, 19 (1969), 284–87.

tioned in I above, refers to Jacob's hardship and difficulties
under Laban, the Aramean. Num. xx. 14 should not, therefore, be understood as a preliminary summary of the enslavement in Egypt, as the English versions and commentaries
take it. Four reasons suggest interpreting the verse in reference to Jacob and Laban. First, the time Israel spent in
Egypt was one of well-being and expansion followed by the
oppression. D (xxvi. 5, 6) is explicit about these two different
periods in Egypt, and it is probable that they are compre-
hended in the statements of Num. xx. 15, "And our fathers
went down to Egypt, and we dwelt in Egypt a long time; and
the Egyptians dealt harshly with us." If so, it is wrong to
understand the reference to the "adversity" as a summary of
the events in Egypt. Second, the similar speeches in Deut.
xxvi and Josh. xxiv contain a straight chronological sequence
of events with initial reference to the patriarchal period.
Such a sequence can also be read into Num. xx. 14ff.: the
hardship (under Laban), the fathers going down to Egypt,
the dwelling in Egypt a long time, the Egyptian oppression.
Third, Num. xx. 14 refers explicitly to the brotherly ties between Israel and Edom and alludes to an earlier occasion
when knowledge of some kind of adversity was imparted to
the brother, Edom. Gen. xxxiii tells of such a meeting between the two brothers immediately after Jacob's flight from
the hardship under Laban; nowhere is there an account, on
the other hand, of a meeting after the exodus when knowledge of the troubles in Egypt was given. Fourth, a comparison between Num. xx. 14 and Gen. xxxii. 4, 5 (3, 4) reveals
a striking parallel. In Num. xx, Moses sends messengers
to the king of Edom with the words, "Thus says thy brother
Israel." The message is initially, as suggested, a reminder to
Edom of Jacob's meeting with Esau. In Genesis, Jacob sends
messengers to Esau, his brother, with the words, "Thus says
thy servant Jacob." The text goes on to refer to Jacob's
residence with Laban. That this is a striking parallel is con-

firmed by the similarity in substance between the two stories. In both, Jacob-Israel sends messengers to find favor with the brother, Esau-Edom, and in each case the messengers are repulsed. In Gen. xxxii the messengers return to Jacob with news of Esau's hostile intent, and in Num. xx Edom refuses Israel's request to pass through its land and threatens the sword. The conclusion to the Genesis story is that Esau does receive his brother affectionately, but this favorable reception is unexpected.[25]

The correspondence between the two speeches in II, in regard to the events of the exodus, is self-evident.

The correspondence between the two versions in III, the connection between the Israelite's bringing of the first fruits (Deut. xxvi. 10) and Israel's message to Edom that Israel is now at Kadesh (Num. xx. 16), has already been indicated. The reference to Israel at Kadesh reminds D of the earlier event at Kadesh when Israel first handled, through the agency of the spies, the fruit of the new land. That event foreshadowed the one with which D is concerned, the first complete entry into the land and the full enjoyment of its fruit.

Support for this correlation between the speeches in D and Num. xx can be found through form criticism. D composes a speech recounting the past on the occasion of a ceremony of first fruits. What is not apparent, however, is why a cultic ceremony of first fruits should include such a speech of historical recapitulation. The relation between this form

[25] As has already been argued (Chapter 9), this unexpected conclusion may illuminate the problem of the relationship between the Edom account in Num. xx and the contrasting one in Deut. i, ii. D's favorable account may be a deliberate attempt to cast Edom's historical relationship with Israel in line with the earlier Genesis history.

Gray, *Numbers*, ICC, pp. 268, 269, notes the striking nature of the parallel in language and substance between the two stories. The significance of the parallel escapes him, however, because he understands Num. xx. 14 to refer to the oppression in Egypt.

of speech and the corresponding setting in life is not obvious. Von Rad's solution, that the logic of early Israelite belief led to such a link, obscures a real problem of form criticism.[26] This solution, quite apart from its speculative character, takes for granted that the practice of reciting past events in a confessional form originated with an ancient Israelite cultic festival of first fruits. Form criticism enquires about the social circumstances in which past events might be recalled, about the natural setting in life wherein a historical retrospect might be found. The presence of historical retrospect in a religious confession as part of a ceremony of first fruits is likely to be a later and sophisticated development.

The speech in Num. xx illuminates the problem in D. A traveling company of Israelites comes upon a company of their brothers, the Edomites; in such a context a retelling of past fortunes, a historical résumé, is entirely true to life. Indeed, how natural that the first thing alluded to should be the last meeting between the two, when the fathers of each nation met—in other words, when Jacob fled from Laban and was met with a brother's unpredictable welcome. In Num. xx, then, the form of a historical retrospect fits perfectly its setting in life. A basic insight of form criticism in regard to ancient literature is that literary forms are readily transplanted into other, less familiar, settings in life. The form of the historical retrospect in D is such a transplantation from the material in Num. xx. 14ff.

This background explains the D credo's puzzling reference to the Aramean father. The key words are: "Thou knowest all the adversity that has befallen us" (Num. xx. 14). Israel is speaking to the brother, Edom, and referring to an earlier meeting between Jacob and Esau after Jacob had fled from Laban, the Aramean. It has already been noted how deeply D is interested in Jacob's relations with Esau. In his law on the fugitive slave, for example, he is thinking of the fleeing

[26] See n. 21.

Jacob, a slave under Laban in Aram, and probably in this regard correctly categorized as an Aramean, who came to his new "master," Esau (see Chapter 9). We can now understand, too, why D links the ceremony of first fruits and a recollection of past events. The ceremony in D is given a historical significance to symbolize Israel's entry into the land. This correlation is an innovation inspired by D's reflection on earlier events at Kadesh associated with the conquest of the land.

Because D has given a new character to the old ceremony of first fruits he places it at the end of his code of laws, where, with its new meaning, it provides a fitting climax to the preceding laws. (There is, it is true, a final rule [xxvi. 12–15] on the speech to be spoken after the tithe of the third year has been distributed, but at this point the historical viewpoint has probably shifted and the lawgiver is thinking of the situation after the land has been inhabited for three years.)

Summary

D's material in xxv and xxvi, which at first glance seems to lack coherence, falls into place, however, when considered in terms of his usual method of presenting material. It has been observed before that D consistently works with three different elements in constructing his laws. For the material covered in this chapter, these are: (*i*) Aspects of earlier M laws (Ex. xxi. 18–27, xxiii. 19) are built into D's laws. (*ii*) Subjects suggested by D's preceding laws are developed in the laws in xxv. The laws to which D returns fall in the section (xxii. 5ff.) that immediately precedes the law admitting the Edomites and Egyptians into Israel's assembly (xxiii. 9, *8*). It is this Edomite/Egyptian law which inspires the double series of laws in xxiii and xxiv, that is, the material immediately preceding xxv. (*iii*) The concerns expressed in two successive narrative traditions in the book of Exodus are

taken up in two successive laws in xxv. The two traditions
are the exact provision of manna in the wilderness (Ex. xvi)
and the attack on Israel by Amalek on the way from Egypt
(Ex. xvii); and the two laws concern exact weights and measures and the extermination of the Amalekites. The two
Kadesh traditions relating to the Israelite spies and the
fruit of the new land (Num. xiii, Deut. i) and Israel's meeting with Edom (Num. xx) influence D's material in xxvi on
the new, historicized ceremony of first fruits.

12. Conclusion

The main concern of this study is to demonstrate how D arranges and compiles his laws. D's methods of arrangement have long presented a problem.[1] It is suggested here that the associative, eclectic process used by D in compiling his laws may be closely linked with the methods used by the scribes in setting down their proverbs. It is also suggested that a comparison can be made between D's way of arranging laws and his style of writing in his historical retrospect and speeches (i–xi). Thus D's arrangement of his laws, like his general writing style, is characterized by a repetitive use of previously given material and thematic associations. Although scholars have seen some evidence of D's general writing style in the law code itself, they have found the apparently haphazard arrangement of the laws inexplicable. This study reveals that the consistency of D's general style of writing can now be linked to a similar consistency of style in the arrangement of the laws.

Another, more novel, conclusion about the D laws concerns their origins. Scholars have concluded that many of the laws are very old, coming down to D through those channels of tradition, mainly cultic, which have for so long engaged the attention of scholars working in the general area of Old

[1] See p. 67 for other scholars' statements on the problem. H. M. Wiener, in his *Studies in Biblical Law* (London, 1904), pp. 110ff., did propose that a theory of association of ideas would throw light on the order of the laws. He was not able to work anything out, however, and concluded that the arrangement had a value now lost.

Testament studies.[2] The fact is that D creates the "ancient" aspect of his laws. Certainly he works with old materials (the M laws, narrative traditions, proverbial teaching), but in doing so he treats them freely; through this treatment and his eclectic method of constructing laws, D in a real sense creates the laws. Critical scholarship has underestimated the importance of the D fiction of purporting to be Mosaic legislation and consequently misunderstood the archaic character of the work. The archaic and the ancient are not synonymous. The archaic is an effect that can be created, as D creates it. The motivating factor for this form of presentation of the laws is D's attempt, made in the seventh century, to give them the mark of ancient, Mosaic authority. This attempt explains why the laws embody the concerns enshrined in the historical traditions known to D. By D's time these traditions, associated with Jacob-Israel and Moses, were already old, and D, by weaving them in with his own ideological concerns in any one or a number of laws, achieves the fiction of a book of laws by Moses.

The analysis of the manner and extent of D's work with narrative traditions is difficult to summarize. Scholars have thought that the few instances in which D explicitly cites such traditions amount to little more than additions to the laws. In fact, narrative traditions play an integral, usually implicit, part in the compilation of many laws. Evidence for the role of these traditions in the laws, apart from connections in language and substance, is cumulative in character. An important factor is D's subtle allusiveness. This feature characterizes the sophistication and depth of the work and explains many odd, even bizarre, aspects of the laws. Allusiveness involves hidden meanings, the implicit rather than the explicit, and a cultivated style of writing. The eloquence of a

---

[2] For a survey of and observations about cultic traditions in Israel and their influence on D in particular, see E. W. Nicholson, *Deuteronomy and Tradition* (Oxford, 1967), pp. 37ff., 119ff.

late Roman writer such as Augustine is an illuminating example. Peter Brown refers to Augustine's practice of veiling his meaning, his love of the implicit, of hidden meanings, of rare and difficult words, and of elaborate circumlocutions.[3] In explaining this predilection, Brown refers to Augustine's life among fellow connoisseurs who had been steeped too long in too few books; these men knew a narrow canon of acknowledged classics so well that to avoid loss of interest they charged them with a halo of "Wisdom" and made them quarries of deep and hidden meanings. D's preoccupation with the limited range of old (JE) traditions is roughly parallel. His extensive use of them is evidence that they must have constituted a body of knowledge and instruction.[4]

In evaluating the setting of D one must recognize the literary influence of Jacob's farewell speech in Gen. xlix. D's setting, one in which the aged Moses, surrounded by the children of Israel just before his death, speaks to them about their future in the new land, imitates the model of Jacob-Israel speaking to his sons just before his death about what would befall them in days to come (Gen. xlix. 1). In each case predictions about the future are based on an assessment of the past: in D, on the past traditions in regard to Israel's relations with other peoples or persons, both in Jacob's time and during the exodus; in Genesis, on the past conduct of Israel's sons.[5] Connections between sayings in Gen. xlix and laws in D have been noted in this study. Moreover Deut. xxxiii directly imitates the scene in Gen. xlix, with Moses taking Jacob's place.

The fact that the people of Israel are addressed throughout in D should not lead one to think that this convention

[3] *Augustine of Hippo* (Berkeley and Los Angeles, 1967), pp. 259, 260.
[4] See Chapter 1 for discussion of D's implicit knowledge of much of the earlier material.
[5] See C. M. Carmichael, "Some Sayings in Gen. 49," *JBL*, 88 (1969), 435–44.

reflects a real setting in the life of ancient Israel, such as
that of a religious assembly where people are addressed by
priests or leaders. The tendency of scholars to take D's setting
at face value is puzzling, since it represents an uncritical
evaluation of the convention that ignores such things as the
assumption of the addressee's literacy, the often unusual,
even recondite, nature of the laws, and the socio-economic
status of the addressee. Possibly this willingness to see the
"people" as the real addressee stems from apologetic motives.[6] If one attempts to penetrate D's convention, the
considerations that require most attention are the wisdom
elements and the instructional character of the work. The
wisdom influence on D is undeniable and stems, not from the
general wisdom influence and utilitarian morality of the
ancient Near East, but from a thorough combination of Israelite prophetic, revolutionary morality with traditional
proverbial teaching. That same combination also characterizes much in the book of Proverbs, differentiates it from
comparable wisdom material, and explains why there are
affinities between D and Proverbs. In evaluating the instructional character of D, the frequent indications that a teacher
is instructing his pupils is a factor of importance.[7] It is tempting to conclude that this background may be close to the
actual life setting of D.

The task of uncovering the facts of the writing of Deuteronomy is singularly difficult. Possibly the book is the work of
an author who was influenced by but not directly involved in
educational activity. To admit the tempering influence of

[6] On the damaging role of apologetics in biblical scholarship, see
M. Smith, "The Present State of Old Testament Studies," *JBL*, 88
(1969), 19–35.
[7] Evidence from another angle that the recipients of the D material
may have been young men is suggested by the address in xvi. 19, 20,
which implies that some of the addressees are to be future judges (see
Chapter 5). Many of the laws concern young men: the law on the
rebellious son (xxi. 18–21), the sex laws in xxii, xxi. 10–14, xxiv. 1–5,
and the military conscription laws in xx.

this possibility would guard against too narrow a concentration on an academic setting, a concentration that might
diminish the importance of the ideological, reforming aim of
the book indicated in the general but comprehensive treatment of the judiciary, the prophetic office, the priesthood, the
monarchy and the military.[8] The centralization of the cult,
while owing much to beliefs stemming from wisdom influence and relating to security in a place, perhaps reflects a
historical background in which there was a concentration of
functions in Jerusalem. Nonetheless, the highly developed
literary interests of the author also reveal an element of
distance from the active, political life of his time. One interesting indication of his literary intentions may be offered
by his endeavor to set the record right on Edom's hostile
relations to Israel (see Chapter 9). This attempt may indicate either that the book of Deuteronomy was meant to
supersede such compositions as already existed or, more
likely, that Deuteronomy was composed as a standard-setting
work that was to be added to these existing works. Critical
work on the book's literary character remains the primary
need. The influence on D of known, written traditions is so
great that establishing the connections between D and these
traditions must take priority over tracing more general affinities with ancient Near Eastern material.[9]

[8] Recent research indicates that the D author is acquainted with
diplomatic treaty forms and, by implication, affairs of court. See, for
example, M. Weinfeld, "Traces of Assyrian Treaty Formulae in Deuteronomy," *Biblica*, 46 (1965), 417-27, *Deuteronomy and the Deuteronomic School* (Oxford, 1972), pt. I.

[9] This statement is not intended to underestimate such affinities. For
example, I would suggest a comparison between the ideal, artificial
nature of the D laws and the hypothetical, paradigmatic character of
ancient Near Eastern law codes. On the latter, see J. J. Finkelstein,
"Ammiṣaduqa's Edict and the Babylonian 'Law Codes,'" *JCS*, 15
(1961), 103, and, "Sex Offenses in Sumerian Laws," *JAOS*, 86 (1966),
368. See also, S. Paul, *Studies in the Book of the Covenant in the
Light of Cuneiform and Biblical Law* (Leiden, 1970), pp. 23ff., especially p. 24, n. 1.

Appendix

The Gates (שְׁעָרִים) *and Cities* (עִירִים) *in Deuteronomy*

S. R. Driver points out (*Deuteronomy*, ICC, p. 144) that the use of "gates" is characteristic of D, occurs there some twenty-five times, and is found outside D only in Ex. xx. 10 (= Deut. v. 14), I Kings viii. 37 = II Chron. vi. 28. Sometimes in D the term "gates" is preferred to "city" or "cities," sometimes it is the other way round. The problem can be seen if we compare xiii. 13ff. (*12*ff.), concerning instigation to idolatry, with xvii. 2ff., on an actual case of idolatry. The latter reads, "If there is found . . . in one of thy gates," and the former, "If thou hearest in one of thy cities." Driver takes the two terms to be synonymous, and in a physical sense they must be. However, there is more to the matter. The solution is that the "gates" refer to the city seen from within, while the term "city" or "cities" is used when it is a question of the city seen from the outside.

D thinks of Israel as a place where there is a series of gates; within these gates justice is dispensed. Judges are appointed within all the gates (xvi. 18). The variations in the expressions "within thy gates," "in all of thy gates," and "in one of thy gates" indicate that D is thinking of a series of gates within Israel. The two idolatry laws show how D is in fact limited in his use of "gates"; when this term cannot be used "city" is likely to be found. The term "gates" is not used, for example, whenever a legal matter goes beyond the bounds of the "gates" to belong outside them and become a matter for all Israel. Thus, while the case of idolatry in xvii. 2ff. is an offense within the "gates," the case of instigation to idolatry in xiii. 13ff. (*12*ff.) is different. In xiii an individual in Israel hears a report of instigation to idolatry in one of the cities of Israel, that is, outside his own gates and hence in a city seen by him from the outside.

Other laws indicate D's specific use of the terms "gates" and "cities." The law on the cities of refuge (xix. 1ff.) illustrates how D must use the term "city" in speaking of the places of refuge. These places are cities seen from the outside because, by their very function, they deal with matters beyond the local concern of the individual gates. Similar to this law is xxi. 1ff., concerning the untraced murder in the open field; this is a matter that falls outside the range of the local gates and becomes a concern for the "cities." In xii. 29ff. and xviii. 9ff. the abominations of the nations originate outside Israel altogether, and it is said that they must not be practised in the land, no mention being made of either "gates" or "cities." The observer here views the land from a position outside it. The cities are not mentioned because they only come into focus when the observer looks at them from a particular position, not just from inside the land but from inside the gates looking out.

Index of Biblical Sources

References in parenthesis are to the RSV where its numbering differs from that of the Hebrew text.

Subject Index

Subject Index